# WORLD CHRISTIANITY

# Middle East

# WORLD CHRISTIANITY

## Middle East

Rev. Don M. McCurry, Editor

**MARC**

919 West Huntington Drive, Monrovia, California 91016
A Ministry of World Vision International

Library of Congress Number 79-87790

Copyright © 1979 by
MISSIONS ADVANCED RESEARCH AND
COMMUNICATION CENTER
A Ministry of World Vision International

ISBN 0-912552-27-1

Printed in the United States of America

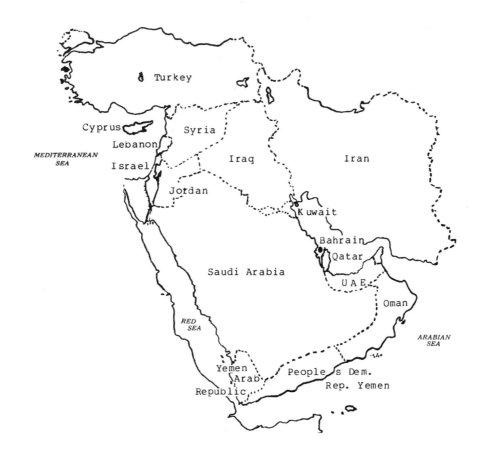

## CONTENTS         PAGE

# I
# INTRODUCTION

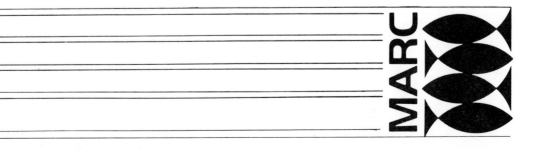

# FOREWORD

The Missions Advanced Research and Communication Center (MARC) was launched in 1966 at The Congress on World Evangelism held in Berlin, Germany. The phrase "That Every Man May Hear" became the theme for everything that was attempted in subsequent years. MARC was founded in response to the growing recognition that there were major segments of the world's people who were receiving no opportunity to hear the Good News that Jesus is Lord of all and Savior of all.

The early 1960s marked a turning point in world missions. Once again we came to realize that not only could people not hear without a preacher, but that the preacher could never reach them if they were unknown. There was much lost time to be made up in rediscovering both the immensity and complexity of the task of world evangelism, even as we discovered new ways to go about it. In direct response to this need MARC began producing country profiles on the status of Christianity in 1971. In preparation for the International Congress on World Evangelization held in Lausanne, Switzerland, in 1974, 53 Status of Christianity Profiles were completed. Since that time a number of other countries have been added, and older profiles have been revised. Meanwhile, a parallel effort was underway to describe the world in terms of unreached people groups, not just castes and tribes, and ethnic groups, but more specific groups found within the boundaries of occupation, income, geography, religion and age. As descriptions of unreached peoples have been compiled in the annual directory Unreached Peoples '79, they have also been made a part of the country profiles.

However, the production of such profiles on a one-by-one basis presented a problem both for the compilers and the users. Consequently, in the fall of 1978, a decision was made to issue country profiles in a format that would cover one particular area of the world. World Christianity: Middle East is the first of what is hoped will be an ongoing series.

Of necessity, some material in such a compilation is fresher than other. Any report such as this must be considered as "work in progress." We therefore welcome comments, corrections or additions that may be supplied by Christians throughout the world.

I wish to express a particular note of thanks to Don M. McCurry who has been the integrator for this particular issue. Mr. McCurry is the founder and director of The Samuel Zwemer Institute in Pasadena, California.

I also wish to express my thanks not only to the men and women who have contributed information for World Christianity but for those on our staff of MARC who have so painstakingly and carefully attempted to compile and analyze what has been handed to them.


Edward R. Dayton, Director
Missions Advanced Research and Communication Center

From the beginning of history, the Middle East has been the center for a majority of the significant events of history. Armies from three continents have criss-crossed the area from time immemorial. Today is no exception. There is hardly a country on the face of the earth that is not affected by what occurs here. Whether it is through interest in oil, the country of Israel or both, no one escapes the influences of Middle East events.

Christianity, as well as Judaism before it, and Islam after it, experienced their beginnings here. All of Old Testament prophecy found its focus in events around Jerusalem and the Messiah. Islam, which claims to have superseded Christianity, cannot tear itself away from concern with Jerusalem and its claims to the region.

From the Christian missions and the existing churches point of view, the memory of lost territories and lost people in an area where Jesus was owned as Lord for so long, is a painful one. Jesus has asked us to disciple the nations, every ethnic unit of people on the earth. This includes the Middle East.

The scope of this volume deals with 16 countries. Starting with the most populous, Turkey; and moving in a clockwise direction, the Middle East includes; Syria, Iraq, Iran, Kuwait, Bahrain, Qatar, United Arab Emirates, Oman, People's Democratic Republic of Yemen, Yemen Arab Republic, Saudi Arabia, Jordan, Israel, Lebanon and Cyprus.

The countries mentioned here are the ancient biblical lands spoken of in the Old and New Testaments. At certain points in history, some of them boasted of large Christian populations; notably, Turkey, Syria, Lebanon, Iraq, Jordan, Israel and Cyprus. Today, with the exception of Cyprus and Israel, Islam has replaced Christianity as the dominant religion. Lebanon, which used to be 50% Christian has continued to suffer a decrease through war and emigration. The maximum percentage of Christians in the remaining countries range from 10% in Jordan to 0% in Saudi Arabia (with the exception of foreign workers).

The total population of the area is approximately 123 million. Of this figure, no more than three million (3.25%) are Christians and most of these are members of ancient Eastern churches. These churches cast off the dominance of Rome and assert themselves as pre-dating Rome. Nevertheless, there is a small Roman Catholic presence in several of these countries. The Protestant presence totals no more than a few thousand for the entire area.

These churches of ancient traditions have lain dormant, but not dead, for centuries. Persecution and suppressive measures by Muslim governments have taken their toll. Protestant missions first entered the region in an effort to revive these churches. The unfortunate result of their early activities was that the revived minorities resulting from their activities were soon expelled from their parent churches for non-conformity to ancient, and sometimes unbiblical practices. The result was that the churches lost their creative and spiritually alive minorities. Those who were expelled formed the nuclei of the existing Protestant churches.

Missions have flooded into the area.  Before the recent civil war in Lebanon, Beirut boasted of over 80 different Bible correspondence schools being run by as many different missions.  Several different seminaries and Bible schools exist in the area.  Very few of them speak of students who are converts from Islam.

Recent events in Lebanon, contrary to popular misconceptions, have accelerated the pace of evangelism.  The dis-equilibrium, the displacement and disruption of "business as usual" routine have shaken old traditions and the teachings of Jesus Christi have become a topic that is easy to talk about Those missions which are serious about Muslim evangelization are finding a new receptivity and a larger number of Muslims than ever before are considering the claims of Jesus Christ and deciding to follow Him.

The following is a listing of the approximate Christian population within each country:  Lebanon-1,200,000;  Iraq-460,000; Cyprus-432,000;  Iran-350,000;  Jordan-270,000;  Israel-75,000.  In the other countries the Christians are virtually all foreigners who have come for work and business reasons.

These statistics do not tell the story.  Thousands of migrant workers have laced the entire region.  The dispersion of the Palestinians is the most prominent demographic phenomenon when looking at population figures for the oil countries and Lebanon.  This is especially true in the Arabian gulf states.  Westerners abound in most of these lands because of the advanced technological skills they bring with them.  An unexpected element of the population is the large number of Indians and Pakistanis working throughout the region.  Perhaps the biggest surprise of all has to do with the over 50,000 Koreans in the region. Many of the Indians, Koreans and Pakistanis are Christians.

An interesting phenomena concerning the heavy concentration of foreign workers in these countries is that the Christians among them have opened worship services for their own people.  Many non-Christians from the same countries are finding Christ under these new circumstances.  And curiously enough, Muslims are frequenting many of these meetings.  There is much room for hoping for a larger movement towards Christ as a result of this ferment and interpenetration.

In spite of all the items mentioned above, the heavy hand of Islam continues to dominate the region.  Only Israel and Cyprus have non-Muslim majorities.  Muslims perceive themselves as God's appointed vice-regents on earth.  They have a heavy sense of destiny and an irrepressible instinct for empire.  Whenever they have capability, they seek to expand the influence and control of Islam over others. Their ethos includes the idea that Islam has superseded both Judaism and Christianity.  Hence, they expect Christians to be converted to Islam and set about to try and make that happen.  There is no doubt that Christian missions are on a collision course with the plans of Muslim leaders.

Simultaneously with the Muslim resurgence, other trends are being evidenced.  Modernism and Marxism are making deep inroads into Islam. One of the seldom realized aspects of Islam is that it is "culturebound;" that is, it is an expression of the seventh century Arabic culture.  All orthodox Muslims are bound to the cultural practices mentioned in the Quran and the Traditions of Muhammed. These two foci of Islamic authority did not anticipate modern twentieth century technological society.  Disenchanted Muslims, aware of this, have turned increasingly to secular experiments or outright Marxism.

Turkey was the first to try to go secular. Orthodox Islam is attempting to re-assert itself there. Iran moved very rapidly towards secularism and experienced disastrous consequences. Iraq also appears to be headed towards secularism, if not Marxism.

Within Islam itself, Christian workers have found a surprising ally in the Quran. It is astounding to most Christians to discover that Jesus is mentioned in the Quran some 92 times. He is called the "Word of God," "the Spirit of God," and the "Messiah." His virgin birth is attested. He is described as performing miracles of healing the blind, the lepers, and raising the dead. He made a clay pigeon come alive and is described as the only righteous one and is alive in Heaven now.

Yet on the surface, the prospects for the expansion of Christianity are not very good. Islam forbids the conversion of its adherents to Christianity on the "pain of death." Where the Quran is the constitution of the country, as in Saudi Arabia, there is not one Muslim convert. In other countries where there is more of a tradition of tolerance, the wounds from ancient and modern ethnic struggles and wars, a case in point being Cyprus, are so deep that conversion is unthinkable. Christianity has fared no better under Marxism. And it is also heavily suppressed in Israel.

And yet there is a hunger for the things of Jesus Christ. The reception given to Christian radio, and the enrollment to Bible correspondence courses both indicate a receptivity to Christian teaching. This is evidenced more when it is divested of the ethnic influence of the evangelists. It is fair to say that many Muslims are attracted to the teachings of Jesus, but not to the churches of the existing Christians. Ethnic, linguistic, and cultural rivalries are the main hindrances.

Evangelism is possible. In fact, it is going on now in many of these lands and a small number of people are coming to Christ. New efforts in cross-cultural communication, and more serious attempts to plant truly indigenous or contextualized churches will have to be made before the gospel will grow in the Middle East.

It is highly unlikely that ancient churches will grow by the addition of converts from Islam. It is also doubtful that western style evangelical churches will have any significant growth from Muslim converts. What is most likely to happen is Muslims, discovering Jesus through their own Quran first, and then through the New Testament in their own languages either in written form or over the radio, will turn to him. As they come to believe, they will seek to work out their own form and structure for worship, fellowship, and ways of propagating the faith.

If this is to be the case, it is going to call for a new approach in Christian missions. A new appreciation for the elements of Islamic culture will have to be developed. The whole issue of how Christ relates to culture, any culture, and hence Muslim cultures will have to be studied. What may a Muslim retain and still say with real integrity after his coversion, that Jesus Christ is really Lord of his life. These and many more questions have to be seriously entertained by the existing churches and the missions as they enter this region.

From what we know of certain assemblies that are growing, comprised totally of Muslim converts, we know that the absence of western and ancient local church forms and people have been the main reasons that other Muslims feel free to attend the meetings where they eventually find Jesus Christ. The lessons for us are that we have to re-think our entire approach to the cause of Muslim evangelism.

The reading of these "Status of Christianity Country Profiles" should lead us to tears. The work of the Lord has suffered some tremendous reverses. The reasons can be laid at the feet of the Christians, both eastern and western. It is time for new approaches in Muslim evangelization. In the case of the Middle East, it will mean that additional efforts will have to be made with the Jews and with the secularists, especially Marxists.

Renewal movements in ancient churches will help alot, especially where love becomes the dominant note. Beyond that, out generation is waiting to see what new culturally congenial convert churches will emerge in Islamic settings and if Muslim converts will be permitted to work out the form and structure of their own fellowships without other Christians imposing theirs on them.

We hope as you read these "Status of Christianity Profiles" with all that they say about each country, that you will turn these papers into prayer sheets. We do trust that God wants us to trust Him for a turning to Christ in this region. We know that prayer is an indispensible prerequisite for this to happen. We also dare to ask that as you read these materials, you would consider going or helping others to go in an all out effort to reach this predominantly Muslim region for Jesus Christ.


Rev. Don M. McCurry

# II
# STATUS OF CHRISTIANITY
# COUNTRY PROFILES

Gospel communicated in a culturally acceptable form. As a result, Bahrain remains virtually unreached.

# BAHRAIN

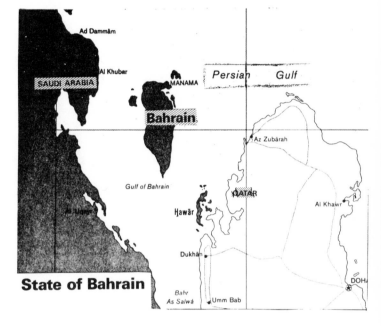

**State of Bahrain**

## SUMMARY

AREA - 372 square kilometers (231 square miles)

POPULATION - 277,000

RELIGION - 49% Sunni Muslim, 49% Shia Muslim, 2% Christian

Bahrain is a land of many minorities. Indigenous Bahrainis comprise 79% of the total population and the remaining 21% is comprised of people from over 45 nations of the world.

The Christian community (2%) is comprised mostly of immigrants. Bahrain, though conservatively Muslim, has proven to be very open to the Gospel in the past, yet presently there are few if any converts from Islam. Bahrain was one of the first countries in which Dr. Samuel Zwemer began his evangelistic ministry. In the early days of the Arabian Mission, they found Bahrain to be a stepping stone to the Arab world. Today, Bahrain remains open to the presence of the church and the government is supportive of the Christian community. In spite of the positive circumstances, very little is being done among Muslims in Bahrain. The one church working with Arabs is western in form and structure and many Bahrainis have not had the opportunity to hear the claims of the

*This program is jointly carried out by the Strategy Working Group of the Lausanne Committee for World Evangelization and MARC, a ministry of World Vision International. For further information on the program, please write: MARC, 919 West Huntington Drive, Monrovia, CA 91016 U.S.A.*

More than 98% of the total population are Muslim. Nearly 79% are Bahrainis with equal numbers of Sunni and Shia Muslim constituencies. Immigrant communities include large proportions of Pakistanis and Indians, in addition to Japanese, Yemenis, Iranian, Korean and Filipino immigrants who have joined thousands of Arabs from many different nations of the Middle East. Each of the people groups is unreached. Differences do exist among them with the presence of Christian witness in the Indian and Pakistani communities by members of various Christian fellowships. Arab Muslims, however, have virtually no Christian witness among them. Sunni Muslims in Bahrain are of the strict Wahabbi sect which advocates literal interpretation and application of the Quran. Shia Muslims tend to be more secularly oriented.

Bahrain was one of the first areas to express cordial sentiments towards Christians. The openness of the government has been demonstrated by the Amir (ruler) who contributed at least 25% of the funds and materials needed for the construction of the National Evangelical Church. The Amir attended the dedication service and public policy regarding Christians is positive. Persecution of Christians is not permissible. It is clearly stipulated, however, that Christian churches are not for Arabs and it is to be understood that Muslims are not to be converted to Christianity. The churches are for foreigners. At least a Christain testimony is visible and the Amir does attend public meetings such as the dedication of church buildings.

POPULATION COMPOSITION OF BAHRAIN
(SHADING INDICATES CHRISTIANS)

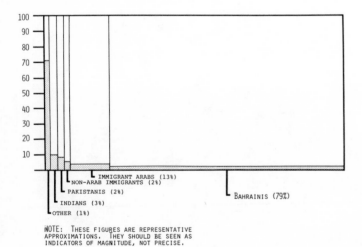

IMMIGRANT ARABS (13%)
NON-ARAB IMMIGRANTS (2%)
PAKISTANIS (2%)
INDIANS (3%)
OTHER (1%)
BAHRAINIS (79%)

NOTE: THESE FIGURES ARE REPRESENTATIVE APPROXIMATIONS. THEY SHOULD BE SEEN AS INDICATORS OF MAGNITUDE, NOT PRECISE.

# NATIONAL CHURCHES

## PROTESTANT CHURCHES

About 500 people, mainly British, actively participate in the Anglican church in Bahrain. A majority (80%) are located in Manama and the remainder in Awali and other towns. A small congregation of Indians belonging to the Church of South India uses the Anglican church building for services. Services are conducted in Indian languages by lay leaders.

The National Evangelical Church is large and centrally located in Manama. The English speaking congregation of 150 is self supporting. The Arab congregation also has about 150 members, 40% of whom are Bahraini citizens. Many of the Arabs immigrated to Bahrain and were already Christians. They too are self supporting. A large group of Indian and Pakistani Christians are Malayalam speaking Mar Thomites. Smaller groups of people hold services in Tamil, Urdu and Telegu at the National Evangelical facilities.

The Church Of God was organized in Bahrain in November 1977 with ten charter members. The thirty to forty expatriates who regularly attend are under the leadership and ministry of a pastor from the United States.

More than six other churches affiliated with various denominations are attended by a total of 300 people. Only one is specifically oriented for Christain Arabs and is western in form.

## CATHOLIC

Most of the 2,500 Roman Catholics are concentrated in Manama where they have a fairly large cathedral. Another 200 live in Awali, which is an oil town. All services are in English because that is the language understood by the Catholic consituency as a whole. The majority of the members are Indian immigrants, but they have no common Indian language. In addition to the Catholics of the Latin-rite background, there are also many Indian Chaldeans, who are members of the Syro-Malabar Church. Some Melkites, Maronites and Syrian Catholics from various Arab countries and Lebanon have settled in Bahrain. The Oriental-rite churches have no resident priest so all members attend the Latin-rite services together.

## ORTHODOX

The Oriental Orthodox Church has nearly 200 members most of whom are part of the Syrian Orthodox Church of Malabar.

## COOPERATIVE AGENCIES

The Ecumenical Fellowship, an inter-church association of clergy and laity, meets informally on arranged occassions.

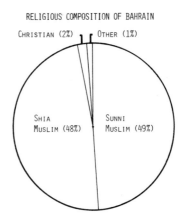

RELIGIOUS COMPOSITION OF BAHRAIN

CHRISTIAN (2%)  OTHER (1%)

SHIA MUSLIM (48%)  SUNNI MUSLIM (49%)

## PROTESTANT MISSIONS

Samuel Zwemer, founder of the Arabian Mission, entered Bahrain around 1890. He unexpectedly stayed and opened a store as a base for communications among the people. Essentially, he was a "tentmaker" living among the people and adopting many of their cultural patterns. In 1894 the Reformed Church of America (RCA) was able to fully support Dr. Zwemer. Clinics were opened to serve the people of Bahrain, Kuwait and Muscat, Oman. The patients were invited to Christian services and visiting families and friends were introduced to Christianity. In 1933 several small groups of Arabs gathered to study Scripture. By 1934 ten Muslim converts were baptized. Several orphans were cared for and trained in mission schools. A congregation of fifty-five men, women and children gathered for fellowship. Some came from distant towns for the once a month meetings. Weekly inspirational meetings and Sunday services for smaller groups maintained regular contact and guaranteed personal growth. Social pressure, however, prevented much expansion by conversion of Muslims but small groups of Christian Arabs have continued to meet since that time.

The American Mission hospital has been a center for Christian outreach through medical missions. The government commended their work by providing financial support as well as assistance in constructing the Evangelical Church of Bahrain. The pastor ministers to local residents and also travels to Saudi Arabia to minister to Christians in the oil company compounds.

MAP International is assisting the clinics in Bahrain by supplying drugs and medicines. They do not have any personnel working directly in Bahrain.

## CATHOLIC MISSIONS

Catholic workers in Bahrain are primarily committed to ministering to the expatriate population. Some social work is included in church activities. A very visible Catholic community is in existence among Indians. They do not have missions programs as such but do provide a testimony among their own communities.

## SOCIAL CONCERNS

The American Mission began a hospital, a girls' school and a boys' school. The Mason Hospital, now known as the American Missions Hospital, was dedicated in 1903 and was built on ground acquired by the mission because of a vision that came to an ancient ruler in which he was directed to sell a parcel of land to a missionary. The reputation of the Hospital was so widespread that for years it was the favorite hospital of Arabia. Because of the tremendous advancement of government health programs, the significance of the hospital has decreased. It is still operating and compatible with government plans. An orphanage was also started and well regarded by the government which later took it over. The schools have been combined into a co-educational system with an enrollment of 500 students. Many of the children rebelled against having been raised as Christians in an Islamic state.

## EVANGELISM

An important feature of the early evangelistic work in Bahrain was the touring of outlying villages at least twice a week. Both men and women often participated and were frequently accompanied by members of the medical staff. Similar tours were eventually permitted for other countries of Arabia. Tours are no longer carried on and evangelism is restricted.

## LITERATURE

A single Christian bookstore has a volume of US$ one-half million sales per year. Bibles and literature in many different languages are available.

## BROADCASTING

Several programs in Arabic and other languages are received by Christians in Bahrain. Radio is becoming a more popular medium and all citizens can turn to Christian programs aired from other countries particularly Liberia and Seychelles Islands.

NATION AND ITS PEOPLE

## POPULATION

The total population of Bahrain recorded in the 1971 census was 216,073. This increased to an estimated 277,600 in 1978. Manama, the capital and seat of government, contains nearly 50% of the nation's population. Muharraq has a predominantly Arab population which constitutes 20% of the total population. The rate of growth for Bahrain is 3.2% annually. The population density averages 460 per square kilometer (178 square mile) with a birth rate of 44 per 1,000. Approximately, 78% of the population lives in towns.

## COMPOSITION

Bahrain is often described as land of contrasts and this is particularly true of its inhabitants. In this small group of islands there are an estimated 277,000 people which have been drawn together from 45 nations. Arabs from the Persian Gulf region and South Arabia, including the Yemen Arab Republic and People's Democratic Republic of Yemen, comprise 9% of the population; Iranians, 4%; Asians, 5%; Europeans and Americans, 1% and the balance, indigenous Arabs.

## RELIGION

The majority of Bahraini immigrants and nationals are Muslims with equal numbers divided between the Sunni ans Shia sects.

## GEOGRAPHY AND CLIMATE

The state of Bahrain consists of a cluster of islands situated in the Arabian Gulf about 29 kilometers (18 miles) from the east coast of Saudi Arabia. The total area of the Bahrain group of islands is 670 square kilometers (258 square miles). The principal island, also called Bahrain, is 48 kilometers (30 miles) long and 16 kilometers (10 miles) wide. The Muharraq island lies to the northeast of Bahrain and is linked to it by a causeway with a freeway. The archipelago comprising the state of Bahrain consists of 33 islands. A causeway linking Bahrain to Saudi Arabia is scheduled for completion in 1981.

Most of the topography of Bahrain is low with a single central range of hills which reach a maximum height of 120 meters (400 feet). Apart from a narrow, fertile zone in the northern sector of Bahrain island, the country is rocky and barren. Limestone rocks are covered by a layer of sand which varies in depth and is often too poor and saline to support any vegetation apart from a few hardy desert species.

The climate is extremely hot and humid in the summer months with noon temperatures reaching 44 degrees centigrade (110 degrees Fahrenheit).

Three seasons in Bahrain include the cold season from December to March, when cold winds blow from the northwest; the temperate transitional months of April, May, October, and November; and the extremely hot and humid summer months with temperatures often hovering near 52 degrees centigrade (125 degrees Fahrenheit).

The prevailing wind is the "shamal,", a damp wind causing desert sandstorms with gusts of 64 kmp (40 mph). The "qaws" are also common. They are hot, dry blustery winds from the southwest. Rainfall in Bahrain averages just 7.5 centimeters (3 inches) per year with most of it recorded in February and March.

## HISTORY

Following centuries of independence, Bahrian was ruled by the Portugese (1521-1602) and then Iran (1602-1782). The Iranians were expelled in 1783 by the Ultub tribe from Arabia whose paramount family, the Al-Khalifas, became independent Sheikhs of Bahrain. The Sheikhs have ruled Bahrain ever since except for a short break in 1810.

European powers began to interest themselves in the Gulf region in the 19th century. In 1861, as a result of political claims set forth by Iran and Turkey, the Sheikh of Bahrain undertook to abstain from war, piracy and slavery in return for British protection. The Sheikh also chose not to mortgage or otherwise dispose of any of his territory to anyone other than the British. World War II and Middle East conflicts affected Bahrain's growth.

Extensive administrative and political reforms were finalized in 1970. A twelve member council of state became Bahrain's supreme authority. Only four of the original members were from the royal family. British advisors were reduced to the status of civil servants. Equal numbers of Sunni and Shia Muslims were included in all government affairs. Complete independence was proclaimed in 1971. The National Assembly has been dissolved but most Bahrainis have not questioned the complete rule by the Sheikh. The government is providing housing, employment and most other basic

commodities and the people are generally
satisfied.

ECONOMY

Before the 1930's, the economy of Bahrain
was based on the traditional activities of
agriculture (dates and alfalfa), cattle
rearing, fishing, pearl-diving and
boat-building.  Bahrain had some trade and
was an important entry port for goods from
Asia, India and the West.

The economy was transformed by the
discovery of oil in Bahrain and
neighboring areas in the 1930's and by the
rapid increase in production in post-war
years.  Activities related to the oil
industry are the main source of employment
and national income.  Some diversification
is planned so that the economy and society
won't fall apart when the oil runs out in
approximately 20 years.

## CHURCH STATISTICS FOR BAHRAIN

Note:  Statistics have been taken from different sources and are the most current data
available.  Definitions of "membership" vary among churches and may not always be
comparable.  Not all known churches have been included in this list.

| Church or Mission Name | Communicants (Full Members) | Community (Estimate) |
| --- | --- | --- |
| PROTESTANT | | |
| | | |
| Anglican | | 500 |
| Awali Inter-denominational | | 75 |
| Church of God | | 40 |
| Church of South India | | 75 |
| Indian Brethren | | 100 |
| Indian Pentecostal | | 75 |
| Mar Thomite | | 200 |
| St. Thomas Evangelicals | | 10 |
| | | |
| National Evangelical | | |
|     Arabic | | 150 |
|     English | | 180 |
|     Tamil | | 128 |
|     Telegue | | 35 |
|     Urdu | | 50 |
|   total | | 540 |
| | | |
| CATHOLIC | | |
| | | |
| Total | | 2,700 |
|     All under Latin-rite Capuchin priests; all services in English except when visiting priests meet separately with Melkites, Maronites Syrian and Indian Catholics. | | |
| | | |
| ORTHODOX | | |
| | | |
| Syrian Orthodox | | |
|     Church of Malabar | | 200 |

# SELECTED BIBLIOGRAPHY AND INFORMATION SOURCES

DOCUMENTS

General ,br,b 1

Area Handbook for the Peripheral States of the Arabian Peninsula, Washington D.C.:
    Stanford Research Institute, 1971

Fisher, W.B.,The Middle East and North Africa, London, England:  Europa Publications
    Limited,1978

Wallace, John,The Middle East Yearbook, London, England:  I.C.  Magazines Limited, 1978

Weekes, Richard,Muslim Peoples:  A World Ethnographic Survey, Westport:  Greenwood
    Press, 1978

Christian

Dayton, Edward R., editor,Mission Handbook, Monrovia:  MARC, 1976

Horner, Norman,Present Day Christianity in the Gulf States, New Jersey:  Occasional
    Bulletin,

## ACKNOWLEDGEMENTS

The information in this profile was taken from many resources which were the best
available to the editors at the time of preparation.  However, the accuracy of the
information cannot be guaranteed.  Views expressed or implied in this publication are
not necessarily those of World Vision.  The editors have tried to present the
ministries of various organizations in an objective manner, without undue bias or
emphasis.  Where we have failed, we apologize for erroneous impressions that may result
and request that comments and corrections be sent to MARC, 919 West Huntington Drive,
Monrovia, California 91016, USA.  We appreciate and acknowledge the comments and
contributions of various organizations and individuals in the preparation of this
publication.

# STATUS OF CHRISTIANITY COUNTRY PROFILE

# CYPRUS

SUMMARY

AREA - 9,251 square kilometers (3,572
    square miles)
POPULATION - 640,000 (mid-1976)
RELIGION - 78% Greek Orthodox, 18% Muslim,
    4% Catholic, Maronite, Protestant and
    Armenian Orthodox

As it has for centuries, Cyprus remains an illusive treasure. It is accessible, desirable, and indispensable as the eastern most island of the Mediterranean Sea. Many nations want to use Cyprus for their own purposes and in their own interests. Cyprus has an extensive history of conquest by world powers and remnants of several cultures still exist. During the Byzantine Empire, Cyprus developed a strong Hellinistic-Christian character. In 625 AD the Muslim religion was founded and for 300 years Arab Muslims fought Greek Christians for control of the island. From the year 965 to 1092 there was no peace. As the bloody battles of the Crusades set Christians against Muslims, the Cypriots were once again caught in the middle of opposing forces. In 1191, Richard I of England captured Cyprus and ended Byzantine rule. The island was given to the French who imposed a feudal dynasty. Cultures again clashed as Roman Catholics dominated the Orthodox Greeks who sought to maintain their own traditions and doctrines. By the sixteenth century fighting had resumed on Cyprus as Muslim Turkish forces took control for 300 years. In 1878 the British assumed control of Cyprus. Greek Orthodox and Turkish Muslim Cypriots were free to worship as they desired. Independence was granted to Cyprus in 1959. Cypriots elected a Greek president by majority vote and a Turkish vice-president was appointed.

The United Nations Peace-Keeping forces sought to prevent further conflict between the Greek and Turkish Cypriots. The Greek coup in 1974, which attempted to unite Cyprus with Greece, and the ensuing Turkish invasion prevented those hopes for peace. Since 1974 the island has been divided into two sectors. The government of the Republic of Cyprus controls the southern sector and most of the Greek Cypriots including the Armenians, Lebanese and other immigrants who identify themselves with the Greeks, live in the Republic. The "Turkish Federated State of Cyprus" controls the northern sector by military force. It is recognized officially only by Turkey. Two lifestyles, two governments and two ethnic groups remain separate with virtually no communication.

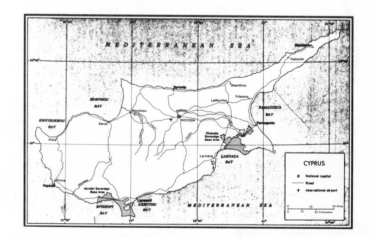

*This program is jointly carried out by the Strategy Working Group of the Lausanne Committee for World Evangelization and MARC, a ministry of World Vision International. For further information on the program, please write: MARC, 919 West Huntington Drive, Monrovia, CA 91016 U.S.A.*

## UNREACHED PEOPLES

Turkish Cypriots trace their ancestory to a group of 30,000 soldiers who were given land on Cyprus in 1571. Turkish immigration continued throughout the seventeenth century and the Muslim culture was established. Numerous colonial governments have suppressed the Turkish Cypriots as a minority group since the eighteenth century. As a result, they have consistently turned to Turkey for direct aid and military support. Turkish and Greek Cypriots lived in segregated sections of cities, towns and villages in all parts of the island until 1963. Intercommunal fighting occurred from 1963 to 1967 and threatened to throw Greece and Turkey into major wars on several occasions. Numerous conferences were held by representatives of Greece, Turkey, Great Britain, and the Cypriot communities in order to negotiate a peaceful settlement. A United Nations Peace-Keeping force was established for Cyprus and the troops from Turkey and Greece withdrew. Within one year over 22% of the Turkish Cypriots left mixed villages and cities across the southern sector. Refugees settled in poverty stricken rural towns and villages in the northern sector. Turkey sent troops back to the island in 1974 when a Greek military coup attempted to unite Cyprus with Greece. The Turkish troops occupied the entire northern sector, the ports of Famagusta, Varosha and Kyrenia were ridded of Greeks and settled by Turks and the city of Nicosia was divided. The Turks claimed that they were needed to protect the Turkish Cypriots and provide a safe area for all Muslims on Cyprus.

Political and religious convictions overlap considerably. Nominally, 100% of the Turkish Cypriots are Muslim and widespread emphasis on traditional ritual observances continues. Some secular trends have reduced the number of strict adherents to the Five Pillars which are all important to the Muslim faith. Properties donated by Muslims to the Religious Trust Council represent the islands largest official land holdings.

As a result of centuries of fighting and contemporary conflicts, the Turkish Cypriots express no interest in accepting any parts of Greek culture. Receptivity to Christianity is negligible and negative attitudes towards Christians and missionaries are accompanied by hostile actions. Turkish Cypriots have forbidden Christian services of any type in any of the occupied territory. More than 100 churches were either closed or transformed into mosques and community centers. At least 20 Greek Orthodox priests were arrested by the Turks; three died from maltreatment and over 200 priests and deacons fled with other refugees to southern Cyprus. The 9,000 Christians isolated within the Turkish sector meet only in small groups for Bible study and fellowship.

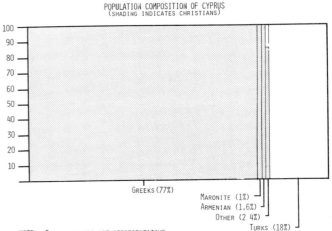

POPULATION COMPOSITION OF CYPRUS
(SHADING INDICATES CHRISTIANS)

GREEKS (77%)

MARONITE (1%)
ARMENIAN (1.6%)
OTHER (2.4%)
TURKS (18%)

NOTE: THESE FIGURES ARE REPRESENTATIVE APPROXIMATIONS. THEY SHOULD BE SEEN AS INDICATORS OF MAGNITUDE, NOT PRECISE.

Most Cypriots are Christians (82%) and maintain strong ties with churches. Many high ranking church officials are also elected or appointed to government positions and their religious convictions influence the policies which the Republic of Cyprus maintains. Turkish Cypriots or any other foreigners who suggest compromises in any affairs concerning Cyprus must wait for both politicians and church members to carefully analyze changes. For the Greek Cypriots, nationalism includes the teachings of the Greek Orthodox Church.

Christianity is indigenous to Cyprus and has widespread influence through a variety of church organizations. It is legally possible to change one's denominational affiliation but social pressure prohibits departure from the Orthodox Church. Few people have done so in centuries.

Barnabas, a native of Cyprus, returned to his home with the apostle Paul in 45 AD. The Roman Proconsul, Sergius, was converted to Christianity and Cyprus became the first area to be governed by a Christian. Traditions tell of the murder of Barnabas by a Jewish Cypriot mob. As the patron saint of the island, Barnabas is remembered for his bold missionary zeal.

## PROTESTANT CHURCHES

Cyprus was a crown colony and strategic military base for the British for over half a century. As a result, several Anglican churches were founded and served a community of 850 people by 1963 under the Bishopric of Jerusalem. The Church of God of Prophecy had three centers for worship with 104 members. The Reformed Presbyterian Church of North America worked among the Greek Cypriots. The nationals formed the Greek Evangelical Church and assumed full responsibility when expatriates were forced to leave. They formed a fully autonomous and indigenous church to serve the largest Protestant community in Cyprus after 1974. There are no Protestant Churches in the Turkish Federated State and the total number of Cypriot Protestants is approximately 150.

## CATHOLIC CHURCHES

Cyprus was conquered during the Crusades by Richard I and served as an important base for other holy war expeditions. Guy de Lusignan was appointed Lord of Cyprus in 1192 and established a feudal dynasty which lasted 300 years. Pope Alexander IV declared the Roman Catholic Church to be the official Church of Cyprus in 1260. Much proselytism and discrimination against Orthodox Christians ensued. During the feudal rule, the Maronite Catholics were given the task of policing the island. Thousands immigrated from Lebanon as mercenary police. Much of Cyprus was destroyed in 1571 by the Ottoman invasion. The Catholics had joined with the Venetians and lost control of the island to the Turks. The feudal rule was abolished and most Catholics fled the island or converted to Islam or Eastern Orthodoxy.

Presently, six parishes are active with 5000 members. Two monasteries of Franciscan brothers have been in existence since the thirteenth century. They operate several primary and secondary schools. Cyprus established diplomatic

relations with Vatican City in 1973.
Maronites remain under the jurisdiction of
the Bishop of the Maronite Rite in
Lebanon.

## ORTHODOX CHURCHES

Cyprus developed a strong
Hellinistic-Christian character during the
Byzantine Empire. Independent status was
granted to the Orthodox Church of Cyprus
in 488 A.D. Autocephalous privileges
included the election and consecration of
their own archbishop and bishops. These
rights continue today and serve as an
important factor in nationalism for the
Greek Cypriots. Over 107 saints of the
Greek Orthodox Church are associated with
the island. At least six of the 74
monasteries on Cyprus contain relics and
icons which have traditionally held
supernatural and curative powers. For
almost 1500 years the Greeks have
expressed fervor in maintaining Orthodox
traditions. When granted independence in
1960 the Cypriots proceeded to elect
Archbishop Makarious of the Greek Orthodox
Church as president of the Republic.
Official church statistics record 500,000
members which would be 97% of the
Christian population. The Armenian
Orthodox live in cities and are engaged in
industrial and commercial enterprises.
They support the 3,500 member Armenian
Orthodox Church.

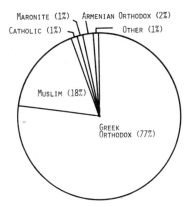

RELIGIOUS COMPOSITION OF CYPRUS

MARONITE (1%)   ARMENIAN ORTHODOX (2%)
CATHOLIC (1%)              OTHER (1%)

MUSLIM (18%)

GREEK
ORTHODOX (77%)

FOREIGN MISSIONS

## PROTESTANT MISSIONS

Christians have been living in Cyprus for
nearly twenty centuries. Greek Cypriots,
therefore, could not understand why Great
Britain would send missionaries to Cyprus
of all places. The Greek Cypriots
certainly did not need missionaries and
the Turkish Cypriots had been fighting
against Christians for centuries. Civil
wars between Muslim Turkish Cypriots and
Greek Orthodox Cypriots had historically
been religious wars. The Greeks were in
no position to help the missionaries and
knew how difficult it would be for the
foreigners to convert Muslim Turkish
Cypriots to Christianity. It was
culturally impossible for Turkish Cypriots
to become Greek Orthodox which they
assumed was inherent in converting to
Christianity.

The Reformed Presbyterian Church of North
America began work in Cyprus in 1887.
Major efforts included the establishment
of educational facilities and programs.
The American Academy was founded in
Larnaca and the American Academy for Girls
in Nicosia. Schools of evangelism were
also started in major cities. In 1974 the
Greek elders of the Reformed Churches
suggested that all work be put in the
hands of the Greeks and the Reformed
Presbyterian Foreign Mission Board
accepted their counsel. An evangelical
association of Greeks assumed full
responsibility for the Academy for Girls
and an alumni association continued the
operation of the Academy at Larnaca.
Seventh-Day Adventists operate a
physiotherapy clinic and offer various
correspondence courses. Foreign church
agencies, mostly from North America offer
financial support to maintain the Churches
of Christ, Missionary Churches, and the
Churches of God of Prophecy. The Armenian
Missionary Association, American Mission
To Greeks, and the Greek Evangelical
Churches are primarily supported and
operated by nationals yet maintain
contacts with sister organizations
throughout the world. Youth With A
Mission opened a Bible school in 1977
designed to train youth to reach the Arab
world. The United Church Board for World
Ministries offers aid for emergencies and
development.

## MAJOR CHRISTIAN ACTIVITIES

### BROADCASTING

Trans World Radio broadcasts one fifteen minute program each week via the Cyprus Broadcasting Corporation. Programs began in 1974 when most other missionary activities were terminated. A Trans World Radio relay station located on Cyprus broadcasts programs throughout the Middle East in Arabic, Armenian, English, Farsi, French, and Russian. Chaplains in the British armed forces produce Christian programs which are aired over the British Forces Broadcasting Stations. Radio Broadcasting Authority does not give out any statistics regarding religious broadcasting.

### LITERATURE

Bibles are available in Greek, Turkish, Armenian, and English. Literature is available through the Seventh-Day Adventists and American Mission To Greeks. Most religious books are available at the Logos Bookshop.

## NATION AND ITS PEOPLE

### POPULATION

The population of Cyprus fluctuates due to the many emigrants returning to Greece and immigrants arriving from Turkey and Lebanon. Total Cypriot population has leveled off at approximately 640,000 and the population growth rate (1%) remains one of the lowest in the world. Density is 73 people per square kilometer (190 per square mile).

### COMPOSITION

Many of the 200,000 Greek refugees, 39% of the Greek Cypriot population, now live in prefabricated government housing. The Greek Cypriots comprise 80% of the total population and live on 63% of the land. They inhabit the southern sector which contains less than 40% productive agricultural land. Approximately 100,000 Turkish Cypriots, 78% of the Turkish population, moved into homes and farms left behind by Greek Cypriot refugees.

### LITERACY

Newspapers are circulated only in the sectors in which they are published. Two separate educational systems provide free compulsory education for children six to fourteen years of age. Secondary schools and vocational institutes charge tuition. Literacy rates for both groups average nearly 82%.

### GEOGRAPHY AND CLIMATE

Cyprus is located just 64.36 kilometers (40 miles) south of the coast of Turkey and 152 kilometers (60 miles) west of Syria. Athens is more than 508 kilometers (200 miles) to the west. The temperate Mediterranean climate and fertile soil allows highly productive grape vineyards and citrus orchards to exist. Four distinct natural geographic regions add beauty and variety to the island. The Troodos Mountains occupy one-half of the island and rise to 1920 meters (6,400 feet). The Kyrenia Range stretches across the northern sector. A broad flat low Mesaorian Plain, with fertile soil readily available, lies between the mountain ranges. The circumference formed by the coastline totals 782 kilometers (486 miles), with widely varied landscape. The Troodos fall right into the sea, but sandy beaches extend into lowland farms in the northern sector. Rainfall averages 48 centimeters (19 inches) a year.

### HISTORY

Mycenean Greek traders introduced Greek culture and technology to the Cypriots as early as 1400 BC and a strong Hellinistic-Christian culture developed over a period of 700 years. It was maintained despite 2,700 years of almost uninterrupted control by foreign kings. Many of the ruling powers introduced their own cultural and religious systems and often suppressed the Greek Christians. Islam became dominant during the Ottoman empire. The extreme differences in cultures allowed the distinctions to remain since most Cypriots were not willing to adapt to the ways of foreigners. Clashes and conflicts in religious doctrines and political convictions were common. The history of Cyprus is a classic example of the failure of people to accept or at least tolerate other people with cultures different than their own. For a brief period of time during the early 1900's, Turkish and Greek Cypriots were significantly integrated. Ironically, at the time of independence, hundreds of century old reasons for division were revived. The people could not tolerate the differences of others once again.

The United Nations Peace-Keeping Force attempted to maintain a buffer zone and prevent open conflict. Division between the Cypriot communities remains the status quo as of 1979. Negotiations between the Greek and Turkish Cypriots have proceeded for years and recent plans include the removal of Greek and Turkish troops. Theoretically, 30,000 Greek Cypriots would be able to return to homes and farms in the northern sector. Whether Cypriots are willing to be integrated once again remains to be seen. Tensions, fears, and doubts threaten any compromises which are agreed upon. Most Cypriots have resolved to lead separate lives as long as separate cultures are maintained.

ECONOMY

Turkish Cypriots control 70% of the citrus orchards, 100% of the tobacco farms and 60% of the grain producing lands. Greek Cypriots have turned to industry and manufactured goods have replaced agricultural products as the leading components of export since 1975. By 1977 more clothing, shoes and plastics were produced by the Greeks than the entire nation had produced before 1973. Trade with western nations increased 44% and sales to Arab countries increased 210% by 1975. Unemployment reached 35% by late 1974 causing many refugees to camp in rural areas. Greeks have significantly lowered unemployment to under 12% through industrial development.

Tourism, once a million dollar enterprise, has never recovered from the wars and many of the hotels remain vacant. It is impossible for anyone to travel from one sector of the island to the other. Tourists must leave the island, register in another country, and then enter the other Cypriot sector if they desire.

The major exports of the island are minerals, fruits and nuts, wines, cereals, animal and dairy products. Increasing income is derived from the service facilities of companies formerly based in Lebanon.

CHURCH STATISTICS

Note: Statistics have been taken from different sources and are the most current data available. Definitions of "membership" vary among churches and may not always comparable. Not all churches have been included in this list.

| Church or Mission Name | Communicants (Full Members) | Community (Estimate) |
| --- | --- | --- |
| PROTESTANT | | |
| Anglican Church | | 50 |
| Church of God of Prophecy | | 60 |
| Greek Evangelical Church of Cyprus | | 150 |
| Seventh-Day Adventist | | 30 |
| Independant groups (Plymouth Brethren) | | 20 |
| CATHOLIC | | |
| Armenian | | 3,500 |
| Greek | | 200 |
| Latin-rite | | 1,000 |
| Maronite | | 5,000 |
| ORTHODOX | | |
| Archbishopric of Cyprus | | 86,000 |

# SELECTED BIBLIOGRAPHY AND INFORMATION SOURCES

The sources listed below are to help the reader find additional information on this country and Christian ministries there. This list does not try to be comprehensive or complete.

## DOCUMENTS

### GENERAL

Field, Michael, Middle East Annual Review, Essex, England: Middle East Review Co., Ltd., 1977.

Keefe, Eugene, Area Handbook For Cyprus, Washington D.C.: U.S. Government Printing Office, 19

Middle East And North Africa, London, England: Europa Publications, 1978

Minority Rights Group, Cyprus: Report No.30, London, England: Expedite Graphic Limited, 1978.

Wallace, John, Middle East Yearbook 1978, London, England: I.C. Magazines Limited, 1976

### CHRISTIAN

Coxill, H. Wakelin, World Christian Handbook, Nashville: Abingdon Press, 19

Dayton, Edward, Mission Handbook, Monrovia: MARC, 1976

Kane, J. Herbert, A Global View of Missions, Grand Rapids: Baker Book House, 1971

World Directory of Religious Radio and Television Broadcasting, Pasadena: Wm. Carey Library, 1973

### ORGANIZATIONS

AMG International, 801 Broad Ave., Ridgefield, New Jersey 07657

Orthodox Church of Cyprus, Archbishopric of Cyprus, P.O. Box 1130, Nicosia, Cyprus

Trans World Radio, P.O. Box 141, Monte Carlo, Monaco

Youth With A Mission, Katydata Postal Agency, Nicosia, Cyprus


# ACKNOWLEDGEMENTS

The information in this profile was taken from many sources which were the best available to the editors at the time of preparation. However, the accuracy of the information cannot be guaranteed. Views expressed or implied in this publication not necessarily those of World Vision. The editors have tried to present the ministries oganizations in an objective manner, without undue bias or emphasis. Where we have failed, we apologize for erroneous impressions that may result and request that comments be sent to MARC, 919 West Huntington Drive, Monrovia, California, USA, 91016. We appreciate and acknowledge the comments and contributions of various organizations and individuals in the preparation of this publication.

# STATUS OF CHRISTIANITY COUNTRY PROFILE

# IRAN

The monarch, Shah Mohammed Reza Pahlavi, has guided his people into the 20th century in a matter of decades. This enormous transition has not been without a price. The massive shift from an agrarian-herding society to an industrial one has created a rift between the old and the new, and has made many segments of Iranian society ripe for change.

Though officially a country which is Shiah Muslim, its people are first and foremost Persians. Christianity and other minority religions are tolerated. Conversion from Islam, though not officially illegal, is very costly. The approximately 1% of the population who profess Christianity are primarily "ethnic" or "born" Christians. Protestant and Catholic missions have made very few converts.

Iran is presently self-sufficient in food production, even exporting several billion dollars worth of food products yearly. Even so, some experts predict it will face food shortages within the next decade. Several factors set the stage for a volatile and complex future. These include: the rapidly growing population fanned by decreasing mortality rates and better medical and health care; political tensions with its traditional rival on the west, Iraq; tensions between its large relatively isolated ethnic groups, and the influx of Western military technology.

SUMMARY


AREA - 1,645,000 square kilometers
    (628,000 square miles)
POPULATION - 35 million (mid-1977)
RELIGION - 93% Shiah Muslim, 5% Sunni
    Muslim, 1% Christian, 1% (Bahais,
    Zoroastrians, Jews)

Iran is one of the OPEC (Oil Producing and Exporting Countries) nations which has been thrust into the 20th century by oil. The oil income has been used primarily to improve military hardware and secondarily to improve the quality of life of the people.

Industrialization has come quickly. Vast numbers of Iranians have been moving to the cities in search of a better life. Tens of thousands of foreign advisors operate the modern machinery of industry while training Iranians. Iranian high school graduates participate in a mandatory program aimed at increasing the literacy rate throughout the country. This program brings unity through emphasis on the national language. These shifts have brought social mobility, higher standard of living and inflation - the benefits and problems of industrial society.

*This program is jointly carried out by the Strategy Working Group of the Lausanne Committee for World Evangelization and MARC, a ministry of World Vision International. For further information on the program, please write: MARC, 919 West Huntington Drive, Monrovia, CA 91016 U.S.A.*

UNREACHED PEOPLES

The majority (93%) of the population of Iran's 32 million people claim to be Muslims of the Shiah sect. Christianity claims less than 1% of the population. There are some 27 ethnic groupings easily identifiable within Iran. Virtually none of these ethnic units has been penetrated with the gospel except to some extent those of Armenian descent, who consider themselves Christians by birth.

One of the biggest obstacles the small Iranian church must face is its own inability to adequately communicate to an influx of Muslim converts. Another challenge to the church is to find ways of reaching many of the seasonally nomadic tribes.

The tolerance towards Christianity is increasing. Some would say Iran is more open now than ever before to the Christian message.

In mid-1977 there were 45,000 foreigners employed in Iran. Some 8000 of these joined the Iranian labour market during the previous year. Most of these are employed by the government and industry.

The nine major dialects of Persian are composed of four tribally organized groups. The Kurds, who number approximately 1,000,000, are composed of forty tribal groups of semi-nomadic pastoralists, settled farmers in villages and towns, city dwellers, and Shiah Kurds in the Kermanshah region. They are primarily Sunni Muslims. The Baluchi, historically pastoralists, have 100,000 tribesmen who are still nomadic or semi-nomadic. Approximately 500,000 Baluchi have become settled farmers. The Lurs are composed of the Posht-Kuh Lurs, a nomadic group, and the Pish-Kuh Lurs, who are settled farmers. The Bakhtiari are divided into the Haft-Lang, nomadic sheepherders, and the Cahr-Lang who have settled.

Groups without tribal organization include the Gilani and Mazandarani, who are both farmers and fishermen, the Tajiks in Korasan, the Afghans, Tolish, Galeshi, Jamshidi, and Hazara.

Turkish is the second major linguistic family. The Azeri Turks in Azerbaijan are the largest Turkish-speaking ethnic group. The Qashqai, composed of fifteen major tribal groups, make up the second largest ethnic group. They are largely Shiah Muslims who migrate between summer and winter pastures. Other Turkish groups include: Turkoman, Qarepakhs, Qajars, Afshars, and Shahasavan. Other tribes are the Nafar, Boharlu, Iranlu, Teymurtash, Hondari, Karai, Kharansari, Phichagchi, and Karagozllu.

Other language groups include the Arabs, who are Sunni Muslims, and the Armenians and Assyrians, who consider themselves Christians by race. Nomadic tribal groups, settled farmers, fishermen and unskilled oil industry laborers make up the Arab group. Religiously, the Armenians are either Gregorian or Roman Catholic. The Assyrians are composed of Aramaics or Syriacs, Protestants and Roman Catholics.

The Bahais and Jews are other religious groups which overlap with some of the above language groups.

Some of these groups which seem particularly open to the gospel right now are: the Ahl-i-Hag, a sect of Islam having an incarnational view of salvation and showing an interest in Christianity; the Kurds and Turks of northwest Iran; villagers in Tehran; Shahvaks near Kermanshah; Gulf port peoples, and youth. Both the villagers in Tehran and the Shahvaks near Kermanshah are displaced peoples in new environments.

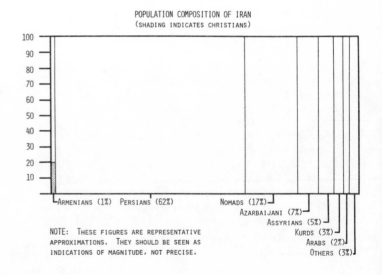

POPULATION COMPOSITION OF IRAN
(SHADING INDICATES CHRISTIANS)

ARMENIANS (1%)  PERSIANS (62%)  NOMADS (17%)
AZARBAIJANI (7%)
ASSYRIANS (5%)
KURDS (3%)
ARABS (2%)
OTHERS (3%)

NOTE: THESE FIGURES ARE REPRESENTATIVE APPROXIMATIONS. THEY SHOULD BE SEEN AS INDICATIONS OF MAGNITUDE, NOT PRECISE.

32

Less than 1% of the population of Iran is Christian. The Armenian Apostolic Church is the largest group comprising 75% of the Christian population. The Assyrian Church of the East and the Eastern Catholic Church make up another 20%. Smaller yet are the Protestant churches and the Greek and Russian Orthodox churches.

Although Christianity is a recognized minority religion, there are numerous restrictions on missionaries. Armenians and Assyrians identified as Christians rarely serve in high ministerial positions although they are represented in the Majlis. There appears to be a policy of advancing Muslims over Christians in government and university positions. Some government contracts through which some mission personnel have been employed include a restriction prohibiting "engaging in religious activity". Muslim converts are a very small percentage of Persian Christians. The impact of Iranian Christians on their Muslim neighbors is negligible, due primarily to voluntary segregation. Particualy for Armenians and Assyrians, Christianity is synonomous with ethnic-national identity. Nominality characterizes churches composed of "born" Christians. Many churches are based on Western patterns and fail to meet the needs of their congregations.

## Catholic Churches

The Catholic Church in Iran is divided into three branches: Chaldean, Armenian and Roman. The Chaldean Church is the largest, and has an estimated membership of between 15,000 and 20,000. The roots of this church go back to the work of Franciscan and Dominican friars in the 13th and 14th centuries.

In the beginning of the 17th century Shah Abbas of Persia took 35,000 Armenians to work on his capitol at Isfahan. These included several thousand Armenian Catholics. They formed the nucleus of the Armenian Catholic Church which has a present membership of about 3000. Roman Catholic work in recent years has made steady progress; the church presently numbers about 10,000 members, largely expatriate. The Armenian and Roman Catholic branches have shown faster growth than the Protestant church. The reasons for this are not clear apart from the growth of the expatriate community.

## Protestant Churches

The Protestant churches claim about 5500 communicant members. The two largest of these are the Evangelical Church with about 3000 members, and the Episcopal Church with about 1000 (plus 1000 expatriates). Both of these churches were established during the 19th century through the missionary efforts of the United Presbyterians and the Church Missionary Society respectively. There are six other denominations with smaller memberships, as well as six largely expatriate congregations. These were established in the 20th century.

Of the eight major denominations, two are shrinking at a rather high rate. The remainder are static. Two significant problems are a considerable amount of conflict among the ethnic units of the church, and a form of church government that is not suited to Iranian culture--a culture that demands authority figures.

The Evangelical Church of Iran is about 55% Assyrian, 21% Armenian, 15% Muslim convert, 6% Jewish convert, with the remainder being divided between Kurds, Zoroastrians and Bahais. The Episcopal Church is 50% expatriate, 30% Muslim convert, and 20% Jewish convert.

The Protestant Church is significantly involved in medical, literary and educational works. Cooperative agencies

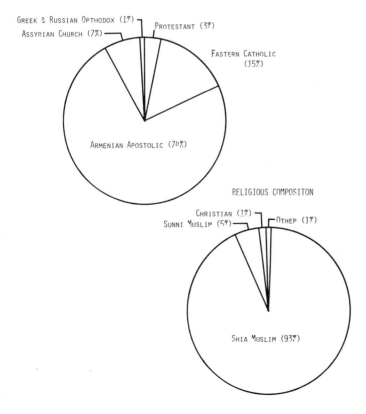

CHRISTIAN AFFILIATION OF IRAN

Greek & Russian Orthodox (1%)   Protestant (3%)
Assyrian Church (7%)
Eastern Catholic (15%)
Armenian Apostolic (74%)

RELIGIOUS COMPOSITON

Christian (1%)   Other (1%)
Sunni Muslim (5%)
Shia Muslim (93%)

bring together the Orthodox churches, Catholic churches and the larger Protestant denominations. Smaller denominations tend to be unaffiliated. Persian-speaking congregations are independent of Western missions, though fraternal relationships are maintained.

## Orthodox Churches

Since Christianity was established as the state religion of Armenia in AD 301, Armenian Christians have been present in northern Iran. The present Armenian church is by far the largest Christian community in Iran. Its size has been relatively static during the last five years with emmigration and deaths balancing the births.

The Assyrian Church of the East was established in Iran at the end of the first century AD. By the end of the second century there were 25 Bishoprics in the Persian empire. This church became the focal point of one of the great missionary movements which, during the eighth century, extended across Mongolia and China, and to the south in India and Sri Lanka. Since then, the church has experienced many reversals and now numbers about 13,500 in Iran. Large segments of it have been transfered to the Catholic and Protestant churches.

The Russian Orthodox Church was established in Iran in the 19th century. It maintains ties with other Russian Orthodox churches outside of Russia. Present membership is about 400, including a number of stateless refugees from Russia. The Greek-speaking community has, in the last 30 years, established an independent Orthodox church; membership is about 500.

## FOREIGN MISSIONS

## Roman Catholic Missions

Franciscans and Dominicans entered Iran in the late 13th century. A second wave of Roman Catholic missions commenced with the entry of the Augustinians in 1601. They were followed by the Carmelites in 1607, who became the most prominent society in Iran during this period. The Capuchins entered in 1628 and the Dominicans re-entered in 1670. The work of these missions was characterized by direct confrontation with Islam and by efforts to bring the ancient churches under the authority of Rome. Rather advanced ideas for the incorporation of local language

and culture were forwarded by some of the missionaries, such as Father John Thaddeus of the Carmelite mission. From 1750 to 1838, due to internal conflicts, virtually no work was carried on by Catholics in Persia.

In 1838 the Lazarist Fathers entered the country followed by Fouchald's Little Brothers and Sisters of Jesus in the early 1900's, the Dominicans in 1933, and the Salesians in 1937. At present personnel from six religious orders and communities staff schools, medical and social-service institutions and parishes throughout the country.

## Protestant Missions

The first 20 years of Protestant work in Iran was done entirely by itinerant missionaries passing through the area. The United Presbyterian Mission entered in 1834 and was the first to be established. Early missions used direct confrontation, Bible translation and literature as the touchstones of their work. Later, schools and hospitals were added to these approaches.

One of the most successful ministries of the Protestant missions was among the Jews, who were allowed to retain much of their own ritual on coverting to Christianity. Iran has proportionately one of the largest populations of Jewish converts in the world today.

The initial strategy of the early missions was to revive the ancient churches. Failing that, they endeavored to form new churches out of evangelical elements in them. Throughout the 19th and 20th centuries the trickle of conversions from Islam has continued, and along with the Jewish converts, they have been incorporated into the existing churches. With self-government, missionaries working in the Evangelical Church of Iran and the Episcopal Church came under the jurisdiction of the national Church. Since then, they have been involved primarily in church development rather than pioneer work or church planting. Even so, four missions in Iran have church planting as their primary focus. Most of the other agencies can be broadly categorized as service organizations.

## MAJOR CHRISTIAN ACTIVITIES

### Evangelism

Evangelistic work in Iran is carried on largely through mass media. Those who respond to the media are reached through village follow-up and Bible correspondence courses.

Studies indicate that friendship evangelism is one of the most effective methods. Muslim inquirers will commonly visit a Christian pastor in his home to ask questions and discuss religion. A regular meeting may be established and, after a long time, the seeker may respond to Christ's invitation.

### Broadcasting

The Episcopal Church and the Evangelical Church of Iran were jointly involved in the "Voice of the Gospel" broadcast out of Addis Ababa, until that station was closed by the Ethiopian government in March 1977. Two other Christian stations still broadcast to Iran: Far East Broadcasting Associates (FEBA) in the Seychelles and Trans-World Radio in Cyprus. The FEBA broadcasts in Persian, and is attempting to improve its effectiveness by obtaining a larger transmitter.

### Literature

Although there is a shortage of new literature in Persian, two agencies are producing new tracts. Scripture portions are widely available, and more than one-half million were distributed in 1976. Public schools encourage their students to purchase gospel portions, because the simple modern Persian is helpful to new literates.

### Bible Translation and Distribution

The only languages in which the Bible may be officially published or sold are Persian, Armenian, and Syrian. Translation into any other language is prohibited by law. Publication of written material in any language other than Persian is discouraged. This grows out of a nationalistic thrust to draw ethnic fragments into the Persian nation by separating them linguistically from their ethnic relatives in other countries.

The Iran Bible Society in Tehran has been a key source of Scripture in Persian. A new translation of the Persian New Testament has recently been completed.

### Education (Theological and Christian)

The Armenian National Anooshirenan School is the oldest school offering Christian education in Iran. About 200 pupils attend at the grade school level. Though there are Christian schools at every educational level, many are aimed at expatriates. Theological education by extension is available from the Iran Extension of the Near East School of Theology; 26 students were enrolled in 1973. The Evangelical Church of Iran and the United Presbyterian Church in the USA sponsor the Iran Extension, with several denominations participating in a smaller way.

Bible correspondence courses are offered by a few agencies. Their students are generally young people.

### Social Concern

Among the churches and missions in Iran, institutions of social concern such as hospitals, clinics, homes for the blind and educational institutions hold a primary place. Approximately 50% of the Western missionaries and the majority of non-congregational church budgets are invested in these institutions.

## NATION AND ITS PEOPLE

### Population

In 1977 the population of Iran was estimated at 35 million with a growth rate of 2.5% per year. Population density follows geography. Most of the people live near the mountainous regions, with increasing numbers on the axis from Tehran to Abadan.

The population is young with nearly half under the age of 16. The current life expectancy is 53 years, an increase from 41 years a decade ago. Although the infant mortality rate has decreased by half during this decade, it is still high with 110 deaths for every 1000 live births.

The population is becoming increasingly urban. In the period between 1967 and 1972, the urban population increased from 39% to 43%. City dwellers increased 24% and village dwellers increased 7%. Forced settlement of previously nomadic tribes accounts for some growth in both areas.

## Ethnic/Social Composition

The nation of Iran is composed of many different groups of people. The largest consists of those who speak Indo-European languages. Persians dominate government and industry, and are almost all Shiah Muslims. Zoroastrians are a very small minority.

Socially urban areas are composed of upper, middle and lower classes. The upper class comprises politicians and government administrators, military officers, professionals, technicians, industrialists and merchants, former large land owners, tribal chiefs and top Shiah clergy. Modernists and traditionalists make up the middle class. The lower class is composed of manual laborers, beggars and the unemployed. Market towns also have three social classes. Class differentiation is less obvious at the village level.

Most expatriates in Iran are concentrated in Tehran. Some follow geogaphical proximity with the few Russians and many Turks in the Northwest, and Arabs in the South. Several Europeans and Asians (mainly from India) also reside in Iran.

## Literacy and Language

Persian is the official language of Iran. Approximately 60% of the people speak it. Another 25% speak one of the Persian dialects. Gilaki is the most widely-spoken dialect, with 1,800,000 speakers, then follow Mazandari Tabri with 1,500,000; Kurdi with 2,000,000; Lori with 2,500,000, and Baluchi with 600,000 speakers.

Turkish and Turkoman are the major non-Iranian languages, with 5,000,000 and 200,000 speakers respectively.

Campaigns have been carried out to increase the literacy level in Iran. From 30% to 40% of the population is literate.

## Religion

Shiah Islam is the national religion of Iran. Adherents of Islam make up 95% of the population. From 88% to 93% of the total population belongs to the Shiah sect; the other large group of Muslims is the Sunni sect.

Historically Iran has been important in the heritage of several religious groups. The Zoroastrian religion, which began in Iran, has 36,000 followers today. Dating back to the Babylonian captivity, communities of Jews have lived in Iran for centuries. They presently number 85,000.

Christianity is officially listed as having 344,000 adherents, including all persons of Armenian and Assyrian backgrounds, (302,000) as well as people of other backgrounds. The Bahai faith started in Iran a century ago and now numbers more than 60,000 adherents.

## Geography and Climate

The area of Iran is 1,645,000 square kilometers (628,000 square miles). Iran lies between the Caspian Sea and the Persian Gulf, and has common frontiers with Iraq, Turkey, Afghanistan, and Pakistan.

There are four basic land regions: the mountains, the deserts, the Caspian Sea Coast, and the Kuzistan Plain.

## History

The Iranian calendar dates back more than 2500 years to the reign of Cyrus the Great; this was the beginning of the Persian Empire. With the advent of Cyrus of the Achaemenid dynasty, the Medes were overthrown. All of Asia Minor was conquered. A strong central government was built under Darius, and extended from India to Greece. Since then, Iran has undergone a number of invasions and conquests.

The beginning of the 20th century saw the constitutional revolution and the end of the Qajar dynasty. In the 20's an Army officer, Reza Khan Pahlavi, took control of the government and became king. The Pahlavi dynasty continues today with Reza Shah's son as ruling monarch.

## Government and Politics

Iran has a constitutional monarchy for its form of government. The constitutional revolution brought about the modern era of Iran's government. In 1906 the Majlis (Parliament) first met and the constitution was signed.

The Prime Minister heads the national government. Legislation is approved by the Majlis (lower house) and Senate (upper house). Governors generally administer the affairs of the fourteen provinces, and village government is conducted through "town" councils.

Iraq, which shares the western boundary of Iran, is a long standing enemy. The Shah has pledged to defend the Shiah minority there against the Sunni majority.

## Economy

Since World War II, Iran has made rather remarkable strides in its transition from a poor, underdeveloped agrarian society to an increasingly industrialized developing country.

Iran grows most of its own food and annually exports several billion dollars worth of agricultural products. Cotton, fruit, gum and casings, cumin, caraway seeds and licorice roots are the major agricultural exports. Animal exports include hides, wool, hair, mohair, and caviar. Lead, zinc, chromite, and iron are the major minerals mined.

The petroleum industry represents over one-fourth of the gross national product. Iran's importance as a major oil producing country has been an important factor in its rising economy.

The illegal use of children as laborers continues to be a problem in Iran. Inflation is likewise a serious problem. Although the gross national product has increased dramatically over the last decade, goods and services are not always available. Housing is a problem in the cities. In 1975 the per capita income rose from US$ 815 to US$ 1200, an increase of nearly 50%. On the basis of resources, Iran ranks as the 13th richest nation in the world.

## CHURCH MEMBERSHIP STATISTICS

Note: Statistics have been taken from different sources and are the most current data available. Definitions of "membership" vary among churches and may not always be comparable.

| Church or Mission Name | Communicants (full Members) |
|---|---|
| Armenian Apostolic Church | 154,900 |
| Armenian Catholic Church | 3,000 |
| Armenian Evangelical Spiritual Brethren | 55 |
| Assemblies of God | 130 |
| Assyrian Assembly of God | 450 |
| Assyrian Church of the East | 13,500 |
| Chaldean Catholic Church | 15,000 |
| Episcopal Church | 2,000 |
| Evangelical Church of Iran | 3,000 |
| Expatriate Churches | 605 |
| Greek Orthodox Church | 500 |
| International Mission Churches | 20 |
| Russian Orthodox Church | 400 |
| Seventh-day Adventist Church | 206 |
| Roman Catholic Church | 10,000 |

The sources listed below are to help the reader find additional information on this country and Christian ministries there.  This list does not try to be comprehensive or complete.

DOCUMENTS

General

Background Notes, Washington, D.C.:  Department of State, 1974
Gibb, H.A.R., et al, eds., Encyclopedia of Islam, New Edition, Vol. 1, London:  Luzac
    and Company, 1960
O'Ballance, Edgar, The Kurdish Revolt, 1961-1970, Hamdon:  The Shoe String Press, 1973
Wilber, Donald N., Iran, Past and Present, 6th Edition, Princeton:  Princeton
    University Press, 1967

Christian

A Century of Mission Work in Iran (Persia), 1834-1934, Beirut:  The American Press
A Handbook on the Christian Communities in Iran, Tehran:  Resource-Study Center, 1975
Dehqani-Tafti, H.B., Design of My World, London:  Lutterworth Press, 1968
Elder, John, Mission to Iran, Literature Committee of the Church Council of Iran
Horner, Norman A., A Handbook on the Christian Communities in Iran, 1970
----------,Rediscovering Christianity Where It Began, Lebanon:  Heidelberg Press, 1974
Miller, William M., Telling the Good News, Tehran, 1960
Waterfield, Robin E., Christians in Persia, London:  George Allen and Unwin LTD, 1973

ORGANIZATIONS

Bible Society in Iran, P.O. Box 1412, Tehran, Iran
Church Council of Iran, Box 1505, Tehran, Iran


ACKNOWLEDGEMENTS


The information in this profile was taken from many sources which were the best available to the editors at the time of preparation.  However, the accuracy of the information cannot be guaranteed.  Views expressed or implied in this publication are not necessarily those of World Vision.  The editors have tried to present the ministries of various organizations in an objective manner, without undue bias or emphasis.  Where we have failed, we apologize for erroneous impressions that may result and request that comments and corrections be sent to MARC, 919 West Huntington Drive, Monrovia, California, USA, 91016.  We appreciate and acknowledge the comments and contributions of various organizations and individuals in the preparation of this publication.

# STATUS OF CHRISTIANITY COUNTRY PROFILE

# IRAQ

For about a century-and-a-half, Protestant missionaries were active in Iraq. In 1969, Western expatriate missionaries were expelled from the country: some institutions were led by national Christians.

In 1974, schools were nationalized by the government, but Christian workers were allowed to fill staff positions. Roman Catholic missionaries have been present for centuries; they were also expelled in 1969. A few French and Italian missionaries remain.

Following several coups in the 1950's and 1960's, Hasan-al-Bakr became President and head of the Revolutionary Command Council which governs Iraq. The two political parties, one Arab socialist and the other Communist, joined in 1973. For about 20 years, the majority of aid, including military equipment, has been supplied by the Soviet Union.

Iraq is the fourth largest oil-producing nation in the Middle East. However, a large part of the country's economic base is still agriculture, which employs about 75% of the population.

The Christian Church survives in the midst of a strongly Muslim and Communist-influenced land. But the challenge for the ancient, established churches as well as for the young Protestant Christians is not only to survive, but to find creative ways of reaching out with the love of Christ in an unfriendly environment.

## SUMMARY

Christianity has been present in Iraq since the first century after Christ was on earth. Within Iraq's boundaries after the sixth century, near today's Baghdad, was the greatest Christian center outside the Roman Empire, with a missionary enterprise that extended into China. Later, Iraq succumbed to Muslim control as Mongol peoples invaded Persia (once a part of Iraq) and Mesopotamia. Today, the country is almost completely Muslim.

The majority of Christians in Iraq affiliate with the Catholic churches. Orthodox churches and the Assyrian Church of the East (historically known as "Nestorian") together comprise about one-fourth of the Christians. Less than 1% of the Christians are Protestant or Anglican.

About 77% of the Iraqis are Muslim Arabs of either the Shiah or Sunni sect. The remaining ethnic groups--Kurds, Turkomans, Lurs, Persians and Circassians --are strongly Muslim. Christians are found in most of the ethnic groups, but Armenians form the only strongly Christian people.

This program is jointly carried out by the Strategy Working Group of the Lausanne Committee for World Evangelization and MARC, a ministry of World Vision International. For further information on the program, please write: MARC, 919 West Huntington Drive, Monrovia, CA 91016 U.S.A.

The majority of the population of Iraq is Arab; 54% of the people are Arabs who follow the Shiah sect of Islam, and another 23% are Sunni Muslim Arabs. Kurds comprise 17% of Iraq's population; they are Sunni Muslim in belief. Smaller groups, all of which are either Shiah or Sunni Muslim, include Turkomans (2.5%), Lurs (1.5%), Persians (2%) and Circassians (0.1%). The few Christians in the country come from several ethnic groups. The only distinctly "Christian" group is Armenian, comprising less than 1% of the total country population. Most of the Christian churches in Iraq are composed of distinct ethnic groups. The Greek Orthodox Church (Antioch Patriarchate) is composed of Arabs and uses an Arabic liturgy. The Armenian Orthodox and Armenian Catholic churches have retained their own language and heritage as belonging to a distinctive people. Chaldean Catholics, as well, have retained their identity as Assyro-Chaldeans. Syriac is used in the Syrian Catholic and Syrian Orthodox churches. Christians of all ethnic groups and traditions comprise 4% of the country's population.

Less than 1% of Iraq is Jewish, mostly speaking Arabic and living in urban areas.

Christian converts are reported as early as 100 AD in Mesopotamia, now Iraq. Response was slow, as the new religion was viewed suspiciously by Rome's political enemies. Gradually, the Church in Mesopotamia and Persia took on a more eastern expression. The churches, both Assyrian and Non-Chalcedonian, that opposed Roman influence gained strength in Mesopotamia and Persia because they were not politically suspect.

Christianity gained strength, especially in the urban centers along the Tigris and Euphrates rivers, but the faith was not strong enough to withstand the Muslim invasions which came in the 13th century.

Since the 1200's, when Mongols took over the area, Iraq has been strongly Muslim. Christian churches have survived as small communities in an unfriendly environment. Although certain ministries are performed, overt evangelism efforts cannot be used.

Scriptures are distributed and radio broadcasts can be heard from neighboring countries, but on the whole, Christian witness must continue quietly.

NATIONAL CHURCHES

Iraq's population is about 4% Christian. Catholics of all rites comprise 3% of the people, and include Armenian Catholics, Chaldeans, Greek Catholics (Melkites), Latin-rite Catholics and Syrian Catholics. Other church traditions represented are Eastern (Byzantine) Orthodox, Oriental (Non-Chalcedonian) Orthodox, Assyrian, Anglican and Protestant.

PROTESTANT CHURCHES

Protestant mission efforts began in the 1840's with several societies attempting to establish permanent work in Iraq. A second wave of missionary effort began around the turn of the century. With the expulsion of western missionaries in 1969, Protestant and Anglican churches came under national leadership.

Church membership is small, and contains a high percentage of expatriates who reside in Iraq while working in secular careers.

Protestant, Anglican, nondenominational and independent churches together comprise less than 1% of the Christian population.

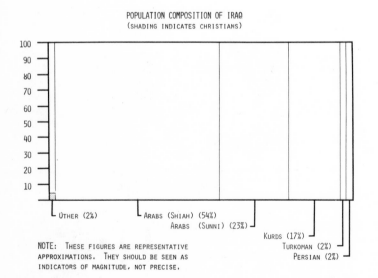

POPULATION COMPOSITION OF IRAQ
(SHADING INDICATES CHRISTIANS)

OTHER (2%)
ARABS (SHIAH) (54%)
ARABS (SUNNI) (23%)
KURDS (17%)
TURKOMAN (2%)
PERSIAN (2%)

NOTE: THESE FIGURES ARE REPRESENTATIVE APPROXIMATIONS. THEY SHOULD BE SEEN AS INDICATORS OF MAGNITUDE, NOT PRECISE.

Their churches include Seventh-day Adventists (150 members), Anglicans (500), Evangelical churches (1100) and other Protestant churches (100). The Evangelical group is composed mainly of churches from the Presbyterian and Reformed traditions, but the churches function independently from one another. There are three Arab Evangelical congregations, at Baghdad, Kirkuk and Busra; they are served by Egyptian pastors. Assyrian Evangelical congregations are also in Baghdad and Busra, but were without ordained pastors in 1974.

Church-operated schools were nationalized in 1974, but Christians continue to serve as staff. National churches quietly perform other social ministries, but these receive funding from outside organizations.

## CATHOLIC CHURCHES

During the first five centuries after Christ, Christianity spread throughout the Roman Empire, and began to move into surrounding countries as far away as India. But the success of Christianity in the Roman Empire may have hindered its acceptance in Persia, the hereditary enemy of Rome. Persia was officially Zorastrian in religion; this, combined with political rivalries, caused opposition to the Christian faith by governing officials. Christianity did, however, gain strongholds among the Syriac-using peoples of the Tigris-Euphrates Valley. In addition, it had the support of the influential and educated merchants and other professionals in the political and commercial cities of the region.

The eastern churches of today in Iraq are related to the Christian communities in the early centuries of the faith. One of the most important patriarchates was at Selucia-Ctesiphon, near today's Baghdad. The first split in the church in Persia was in 431 at the Ecumenical Council at Ephesus. The Roman Church at that point lost its authority in that area of the world, as the Assyrian Church, called later the Church of Persia, grew and became the most important Christian influence outside of the Roman realm. Over the centuries at various times, people left the Orthodox and Eastern churches to reunite with Rome; these formed Eastern-rite Catholic churches. They retained their eastern liturgies and practices rather than adopt the Latin rite. The five Eastern-rite Catholic Churches that were established between 1550 and 1824 are Chaldean Catholics, Greek Catholics (Melkites), Armenian Catholics Syrian Catholics. These five

are sometimes called "Uniates", indicating their union with Rome.

The first major setback for Christianity in the area now known as Iraq came in the seventh and eighth centuries, when Arab Muslims achieved political dominance in many countries, including Persia. For the next 500 years, Christianity and Islam remained in a stalemate, and Christians in Persia even succeeded in winning some of the Turks and Mongols of Central Asia. Then, in the 13th and 14th centuries, Mongol and Turkish invaders, converts to Islam, invaded Central and Western Asia. With the help of Muslim Arabs, they established Islam as the ruling power and dominant faith in Persia, Mesopotamia, and ultimately among the people throughout Central and Western Asia.

During the Mongol rule in Persia, the Roman Catholic Church sent missionaries, mainly Dominicans, into the area. Their main effort was directed toward bringing the eastern churches back into communion with Rome. By the fifteenth century, partly due to the decline of the Church in Western Europe during the Renaissance, Franciscan and Dominican Orders came to an end in that part of Asia.

The Roman, or Latin-rite, Catholic Church in Iraq today serves mainly expatriates, although a few Iraqis are members. About 75% of the Christian community, or 3% of the total population, is Catholic. Chaldeans, with 188,000, members form the largest group. They are followed by Syrian Catholics (27,000), Armenian Catholics (2700), Latin-rite Catholics (2500) and Greek Catholics, or Melkites (350).

The Catholic churches maintain a strong educational ministry, and some medical work administered by the Dominican orders. Redemptorist priests serve the Latin-rite parishes.

RELIGIOUS COMPOSITION

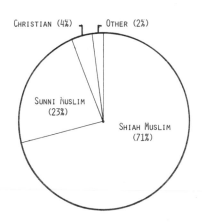

CHRISTIAN (4%)   OTHER (2%)

SUNNI MUSLIM (23%)

SHIAH MUSLIM (71%)

41

Iraq has three major Orthodox groups. The smallest in that country is Greek Orthodox, belonging to the Antioch Patriarchate and using an Arabic liturgy. The Greek Orthodox Church recognizes the authority of all seven ecumenical councils held between the fourth and eighth centuries AD. It also recognizes the Patriarch of Constantinople as "Ecumenical Patriarch", an honorary title. Membership in Iraq is 450.

The Oriental (Non-Chalcedonian) Orthodox Churches broke away from the Byzantine Orthodox group--of which Greek Orthodox is a part--in 451 at the Council of Chalcedon. They accept the authority of the first three ecumenical councils. Although this group comprises the Armenian, Coptic, Ethiopian and Syrian branches of Orthodoxy, only the Armenian Orthodox Church and the Syrian Orthodox Church are in Iraq. Together, they comprise just over 10% of the Christian community, or 0.4% of the total population of the country. Membership in the Armenian Orthodox Church totals 12,000; the Syrian Orthodox Church numbers 18,000.

The last major Eastern church in Iraq is the Assyrian Church of the East; its 42,000 members comprise about 14% of the Christian population, or 0.6% of the total country population. The church split from the Byzantine Orthodox Church at the third ecumenical council, held at Ephesus in 431. It came to be known as the Church of Persia, and grew considerably during the sixth century. Its center at Seleucia-Ctesiphon (modern Baghdad) became the most important Christian center outside of the Roman Empire. The church sent missionaries as far away as China and Japan between the sixth and thirteenth centuries but suffered considerably during the Mongol invasion. People in this church are often called "Nestorians", a term they dislike since Nestorius was not their spiritual founder. They do not consider themselves heretics, as the term has come to imply.

Until Islam sealed its dominance in the thirteenth century, Christian missionaries were active in Iraq (then Mesopotamia) and were also sent out by local churches. In the sixth century Persian Christian missionaries traveled as far as Japan and China with the Good News. By the end of the thirteenth century, mission activity had stopped as Muslim control tightened.

Modern Protestant missionary efforts began in the 1840's and continued until 1969, when most western expatriate missionaries were expelled. Foreign missions are now present primarily in the form of funds given to help support indigenous efforts.

## PROTESTANT MISSIONS

The first Protestant society to enter Iraq was the London Jewish Society in the 1820's. This work among the Jewish people continued for 15 years before closing. Attempts by the American Board of Commissioners and the Church Missionary Society lasted for a while, but both agencies were gone by World War I. Lutheran bodies entered Iraq in 1911 and 1942, working partly among the Kurds.

The most enduring effort began in 1924, when several churches of Reformed/Presbyterian tradition banded together to form the United Mission in Iraq. Missionaries from the union perservered through unresponsiveness, wars and occasional expulsions. Although direct evangelism was a part of their work, much of the effort focused on educational ministries. Western missions have not been allowed to return to Iraq since their expulsion in 1969.

## ROMAN CATHOLIC MISSIONS

Christian missionaries were present around the Tigris river as early as AD 100. By AD 225, twenty bishops existed in the Tigris-Euphrates Valley and on the borders of Persia.

The Christian groups were small and at times they suffered persecution from leaders of rival religions such as Zoroastrianism. After Constantine adopted Christianity, the new faith was suspect and considered by Persians to be a part of Roman political aggression.

Preaching of the gospel was done in the language of the indigenous population, either Greek or Syriac. This helped spread the faith, and it also provided a separation from Western Roman traditions in worship. Because of the political and cultural differences, by the fifth century the church in Persia and Mesopotamia was independent of Roman ecclesiastical structure, and Nestorian doctrine was taught.

Throughout the centuries, missionaries from the Roman Catholic Church and the Uniate Catholic Churches (churches that left Orthodoxy to reunite with the Roman church) have ministered throughout the area now known as Iraq. Many have been Franciscan Jesuits and Dominicans.

Western missionaries were expelled in 1969, but work continues through French Dominicans and Carmelites and through Italian-Redemptorist priests. Indigenous leadership is dominant.

## ORTHODOX MISSIONS

The variety of Orthodox churches have their origin in the Middle East; hence, Orthodox missionary activity would have originated locally. Ministries in the Orthodox churches today are under indigenous leadership.

## OTHER MISSIONS

The Assyrian Church of the East was formed as a result of a split from the Byzantine Orthodox group in 451. It grew rapidly during the sixth century and supported a foreign missionary effort that reached as far as China and Japan. Missionary activity declined after the Mongol invasion of the 13th century.

## MAJOR CHRISTIAN ACTIVITIES

## EVANGELISM

In Iraq, as in other Muslim nations, evangelism is carried out indirectly. Christians witness by performing medical and educational services, using whatever opportunities they can to explain and share the love of Jesus. A Muslim may be invited to a Christian's home on a regular basis, and eventually he may open his heart to Christ.

## BROADCASTING

There are no sending or receiving stations in Iraq; however, Christian broadcasts from other countries can be heard. Far East Broadcasting Associates (Seychelles), Radio ELWA (Liberia), Radio Voice of the Gospel (Lebanon and Cyprus) and Trans World Radio (Monaco) all beam gospel messages into Iraq. Most of the messages are in Arabic. The Roman Catholic Church also broadcasts to Iraq.

## LITERATURE

Although no specific literature ministries are reported, local churches may be providing newsletters and other literature to their members.

The Bible Society in Lebanon distributes Scriptures in five languages.

## BIBLE TRANSLATION AND DISTRIBUTION

Work in the United States continues on the translation of the Bible into Kurdish; Wycliffe Bible Translators are doing work, which includes several dialects. Translations of the Bible into modern versions are needed for the Arabic and Kurdish languages.

The Bible Society in Lebanon produces and distributes Scriptures, which are available in Arabic, Armenian modern, Syriac Modern, and Syriac Ancient. A limited number of Kurdish selections are also available. Distribution figures for 1976 were:

| | |
|---|---:|
| Bibles | 611 |
| New Testaments | 6,878 |
| Portions | 6,525 |
| Selections | 136,235 |
| | ------- |
| Total | 150,249 |
| Total 1975 | 8,684 |

## EDUCATION (THEOLOGICAL AND CHRISTIAN)

Until schools were nationalized in 1974, several schools were operated by missionaries and national church people. Carmelites, Dominicans and Jesuits served all the Catholic groups in schools ranging from primary to university levels. The Carmelites operate a 1500 student primary/intermediate school in Baghdad. The Armenian Orthodox still maintain primary schools in Baghdad, Mosul, Kirkuk, Busra and Suleimaniza and a large coeducational high school in Baghdad. Nationals that worked in schools prior to nationalization taking place have been allowed to remain on as staff people

Dominican Fathers continue to operate Pontifical Seminary in Mosul, which is considered the most advanced school of theological training for Chaldean and Syrian Catholic seminarians in the Middle East.

# NATION AND ITS PEOPLE

## POPULATION

Iraq's population of 11,124,000 is growing at a rate of 3.3% per year. About 65% of the people live in rural areas. There are three major urban population centers: Baghdad, the capital, with 2,800,000 people, Mosul with 857,000 and Basara with 854,000. Population density averages 18.5 per square kilometer (48 people per square mile).

About 75% of the people are engaged in agriculture. A few nomadic herdsmen exist, but the government is attempting to resettle them.

## COMPOSITION

Shiah Muslim Arabs are the largest ethnic group in Iraq, comprising 54% of the population. Sunni Muslim Arabs are the next largest group, comprising 23% of the population. The remaining population is divided among Muslims and five Christian groups. The Kurds (17%), Turkomans (2.5%), Lurs (1.5%) and Persians (2%) make up the remaining Muslims. The Christians are comprised mostly of ethnic minorities.

Occupationally, farmers and herders comprise 88% of the population of Iraq; these include sheep and camel herders. Arab-speaking Turkomen and Jews tend to live in urban areas, as do some of the Lurs. Other Lurs are village laborers. Persian Shiah Muslims and Circassian Sunni Muslims are middle-class merchants.

## LITERACY AND LANGUAGES

Between 20% and 40% of the population is literate.

Arabic and Kurdish are the two official languages of Iraq. While Arabic is the most widely used language, Kurdish and dialects of Turkish are spoken in the north, and Persian is used by tribesmen in the east. About 79% of the population speaks Arabic, 16% Kurdish, 3% Persian and 2% Turkish.

## RELIGION

Muslims comprise 90% of the population of Iraq, dividing into the Shiite and Sunni sects. Most of the Christians (4%) are descendents of the population which was not converted to Islam in the 7th or 14th century, and the Jewish community, which numbers between 2,000 and 7,000, is centered in Baghdad.

Along with Christianity, Judaism and Islam there exists a popular or folk religion. Rituals similar to those used elsewhere in the Middle East are practiced, and there is belief in supernatural spirits and magic.

## GEOGRAPHY AND CLIMATE

Iraq is located in the Middle East, bordered by Kuwait, Iran, Turkey, Jordan, Syria and Saudi Arabia. Much of the country is flat and slightly above sea level. The fertile area between the Tigris and Euphrates rivers varies from flat plains to dry rolling uplands. In the northeast portions of the country, mountains rise to over 12,000 feet.

Seasonal temperatures vary greatly with warm summer temperatures and severe winter frosts in the north. In the flood plains of the Tigris and Euphrates rivers summers are hot and humid. The remainder of the country has a relatively low humidity during the summer. Between November and March the central region of Iraq receives 10.1 to 30.4 centimeters (4-12 inches) of rainfall, its entire amount for the year.

## HISTORY

Iraq, formerly known as Mesopotamia, was occupied by many peoples before the time of Christ, including the Assyrians, Persians and Greeks. It was taken by the Ottoman Turks centuries later. In 1918 Great Britain was given a mandate over Iraq by the League of Nations. From 1921 to 1932, a national government ruled under British direction. In October of 1932 Iraq became a member of the League of Nations, admitted as an independent state.

Since that time Iraq has experienced a number of coups. A coup d'etat led by the army killed King Faisal and established a republic in 1958. Several regimes were overthrown until 1968, when the Ba'ath Party and the military succeeded in establishing a more stable government. Hasan al-Bakr became President and remains in office today.

## GOVERNMENT AND POLITICAL CONDITIONS

Iraq's Revolutionary Command Council (RCC) governs the country headed by the President, who is chief of state and supreme commander of the armed forces. This council appoints a Council of Ministers whose functions are both legislative and administrative. Two political parties exist in Iraq, the Ba'ath (Renaissance) Party, which controls the government, and the Iraqi Communist Party, which participates nominally. The Iraqi Communist Party joined with the

Ba'ath Party in 1973.

Each of the 16 provinces in Iraq have their own governor. There is no National Assembly, although the Constitution states that one is to be established.

The Iraqi Armed Forces were established after World War I and at that time received aid from Britain. Since 1958 they have been receiving aid from the Soviet Union, which also supplies their arms. An air force and navy also exist.

ECONOMY

Until the 1950's Iraq had few industries apart from oil. Most of the remaining work force was employed agriculturally. Today industry is expanding slowly into such areas as textiles, sugar refineries, flour mills, shoes and cigarette factories.

Iraq is the fourth largest oil producing nation in the Middle East. Made up of many western companies in the past, the Iraq Petroleum Company (IPC) nationalized the last western company in 1975, leaving no foreign interests in the country. Currently, the country is using its oil revenues to develop its natural resources and its agricultural and industrial base.

The national unit of currency is the Iraqi dinar; 1 dinar equals about US$ 3.44.

## CHURCH STATISTICS FOR IRAQ

Note: Statistics have been taken from different sources and are the most current data available. Definitions of "membership" may vary among churches and may not always be comparable. These figures may be high or low in some cases due to the difficulty of obtaining accurate statistics.

| Church or Mission Name | Communicants (Full Members) |
|---|---|
| **PROTESTANT** | |
| Anglican Church | 500 |
| Evangelical Church | 1,100 |
| Others | 100 |
| Seventh-day Adventist Church | 150 |
| **CATHOLIC** | |
| Armenian Catholic Church | 2,700 |
| Chaldean Catholic Church | 188,000 |
| Greek (Melkite) Catholic Church | 350 |
| Latin-rite Catholic Church | 2,500 |
| Syrian Catholic Church | 27,000 |
| **ORTHODOX** | |
| Armenian Orthodox Church | 12,000 |
| Greek Orthodox (Antioch) Church | 450 |
| Syrian Orthodox Church | 18,000 |
| **ASSYRIAN** | |
| Assyrian Church of the East | 42,000 |

# CHURCH STATISTICS FOR IRAQ

Note: Statistics have been taken from different sources and are the most current data available. Definitions of "membership" may vary among churches and may not always be comparable. These figures may be high or low in some cases due to the difficulty of obtaining accurate statistics.

| Church or Mission Name | Communicants (Full Members) |
| --- | --- |
| **PROTESTANT** | |
| Anglican Church | 500 |
| Evangelical Church | 1,100 |
| Others | 100 |
| Seventh-day Adventist Church | 150 |
| **CATHOLIC** | |
| Armenian Catholic Church | 2,700 |
| Chaldean Catholic Church | 188,000 |
| Greek (Melkite) Catholic Church | 350 |
| Latin-rite Catholic Church | 2,500 |
| Syrian Catholic Church | 27,000 |
| **ORTHODOX** | |
| Armenian Orthodox Church | 12,000 |
| Greek Orthodox (Antioch) Church | 450 |
| Syrian Orthodox Church | 18,000 |
| **ASSYRIAN** | |
| Assyrian Church of the East | 42,000 |

The sources listed below are to help the reader find additional information on this country and Christian ministries there. This list does not try to be comprehensive or complete.

## DOCUMENTS

### General

Background Notes, Washington DC: Department of State, 1974.
Gibb, H. A. R. et al, editors, Encyclopedia of Islam, New Edition, Vol. 1,
    London: Luzac and Company, 1960.
O'Ballance, Edgar, The Kurdish Revolt, 1951-1970, Hamdon: The Shoe String Press, 1973.

### Christian

Horner, Norman A., Rediscovering Christianity Where It Began, Beirut: Heidelberg Press,
    1974.
Kane, J. Herbert, A Global View of Missions, Grand Rapids: Baker Book House, 1971.
Latourette, Kenneth Scott, A History of the Expansion of Christianity, Grand
    Rapids: Zondervan, 1970.

## ORGANIZATIONS

Bible Society in Lebanon, Post Office Box 747, Beirut, Lebanon.


## ACKNOWLEDGEMENTS

The information in this profile was taken from many sources which were the best available to the editors at the time of preparation. However, the accuracy of the information cannot be guaranteed. Views expressed or implied in this publication are not necessarily those of World Vision. The editors have tried to present the ministries of various organizations in an objective manner, without undue bias or emphasis. Where we have failed, we apologize for erroneous impressions that may result and request that comments and corrections be sent to MARC, 919 West Huntington Drive, Monrovia, California, USA, 91016. We appreciate and acknowledge the comments and contributions of various organizations and individuals in the preparation of this publication.

# STATUS OF CHRISTIANITY COUNTRY PROFILE

# ISRAEL

## SUMMARY

AREA - 80,000 square kilometers (49,720
    square miles)
POPULATION - 3.5 million
RELIGION - 83% Jews, 13.4% Muslims, 1.4%
    Druzes; 2.2% Christian

Perpetual change characterizes the nation
of Israel. It is young, yet maintains
ancient traditions in its existence as a
Jewish homeland.

Israel, which means wrestler or contender
with God, finds itself in the midst of
international affairs. Boundaries with
Arab neighbors are constantly changing and
terrorist groups within Israel necessitate
tight security measures.

In May of 1948, 31.2% of the population in
Palestine were Jews and 68.8% were
non-Jews. By early 1964, only 11.4% of
the population were non-Jews and 88.6%
were Jews. Over one million Palestinian
Arabs left Israel. In 1978, 83% of the
population of Israel were Jewish.

Most Jews in Israel do not strictly adhere
to Judaism, but Jewish traditions
influence every aspect of life. The
people are returning to the promised land
with traditions and technology. Continued

industrial and agricultural advancements
strengthen Israel's position as a
developed nation.

The basic principles of Christianity are
derived from Judaism. Christianity
developed among the Jews nearly 2000 years
ago. The national government closely
regulates activities carried on by
missionaries. New laws forbid conversion
of religion in instances where material
benefits are received, yet there is
freedom to work among minority groups.

Arabs constitute 16% of the population.
The majority (84%) maintain Sunni Muslim
traditions. Several childrens' ministries
and evangelistic endeavors continue among
the Arabs.

Islam and Christianity are directly linked
to Judaism and share many of the same
traditions, theological principles and
concepts. Jerusalem remains an important
religious and cultural center for Jews,
Muslims and Christians. According to the
Jews, anyone who converts to Christianity
also becomes a Gentile. Since a Jew who
becomes a Gentile is not a part of the
Jewish culture, Christians can not be a
part either. Muslims equate conversion to
Christianity with rejection of Muslim
culture. Appreciation and acceptance of
established cultures must accompany any
attempts at cross-cultural interaction.

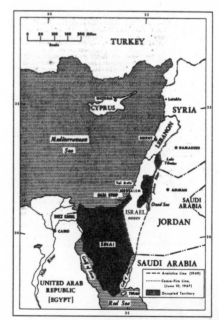

*This program is jointly carried out by the Strategy Working Group of the Lausanne Committee for World Evangelization and MARC, a ministry of World Vision International. For further information on the program, please write: MARC, 919 West Huntington Drive, Monrovia, CA 91016 U.S.A.*

# UNREACHED PEOPLES

Jewish traditions permeate every aspect of life for the Israeli Jew today. Even though 83% of the population are nominally Jewish, only 6% are Ultra Orthodox who practice strict adherence to the Old Testament and Talmad (Rabbinic tradition). Hasidism, one movement of Ultra Orthodox Jews, emerged in Poland in the 18th century. It teaches that God is in everything and encourages creativity in expression of honor to God. Most Ultra Orthodox Jews live in the city of Jerusalem.

The majority of Jews in Israel are secularly oriented. They emphasize the universal character and ethics of Judaism rather than adherence to the laws. This is the Modern Orthodox movement.

The Reform and Conservative movements have widespread followings in Europe and North America but have no status in Israel. A new movement known as Progressive Judaism is centered in the major urban areas and emphasizes only the social value of Judaism by the laying aside of all laws. Opposition from both Ultra and Modern Orthodox leaders has been widespread. Rabbis of the Progressive movement are not recognized as such and therefore can not perform traditional ceremonies. Recent surveys of socio-religious attitudes indicate that 109,500 Jews claim to be atheists.

Other groups include the Karaites and the Samaritans. The Karaites (.3%) are a small sect that reject Rabbinic traditions. They accept only the written law and follow it scrupulously. The indigenous Samaritans have lived in Palestine at Nabulus continuously since the 8th century BC and are an inbreeding people now numbering only 500. Samaritans are part of the Arab world culturally but have little to do with technology or development. They only accept the writings of Moses and Joshua as Law.

Ethnic designations related to location of birth exist alongside all the religious differences. "Askenazim" refers to Jews of European descent, including all who immigrate from such distant nations as the Soviet Union and United States. Refugees from Displaced Persons Camps in Germany, Austria, and Italy are in many cases natives of Poland, Romania, Bulgaria or Yugoslavia. A common inward longing to return to Israel has united Jews from all nations of the world. In 1948, Askenazim comprised 54% of the Jewish population but by 1970 the total had dropped to 29%.

Sephardim are Jews who are native to the Middle East (other than Israel) or North Africa. French speaking immigrants from Tunisia and Algeria joined neighbors from Morocco and Libya in the journey to Israel. Many Jews with Arabic cultural patterns left Iran, Yemen and Turkey. The Sephardim grew from 9.8% of the population in 1948 to 27% in 1970.

Sabras are Jews born in Israel. In 1948, 35.4% of the Jewish population was native to the land. That percentage has increased to 44% in 1977. Jews of Oriental descent comprise 26% of the Jewish population. Many Oriental immigrants were unskilled, illiterate and very poor when they entered Israel. Their average income is considerably lower than that of other Jews and their families are much larger. Measures have been taken to remedy the situation through education. Yet by 1978, over half (58%) of the children with Oriental backgrounds attended vocational schools rather than academic secondary schools. Only 15% of the university students come from this portion of the population.

Immigration is a factor which must be emphasized since it has been the basis for the creation and settlement of Israel. The ethnic and cultural backgrounds of Israels immigrants are extremely diverse. Although all left nations and people behind, they did not leave their cultures behind. Therefore, Israel has much diversity within its society. The Law of Return has given every Jew in any nation the right to enter Israel as a citizen with full rights. Over 1.5 million Jews have responded by returning to Israel. Jews seeking a homeland have gathered from more that 65 nations.

Arabs, once the majority in Israel, have become immigrants to other lands and now comprise 16% of the total population. Arab growth rate remains double that of Jews. Arabs are primarily Muslim within the four rites of Sunni Islam. Over half (56.7%) live in rural areas. Many continue ancient farming patterns.

The Druzes (1.4%) are a minority group among both Jews and Arabs. They have been reclusive, sedentary and homogeneous for over ten centuries. The 40,000 Druzes live in the 17 villages in or near Galilee, where their ancestors lived for centuries. Nine villages are entirely Druze and the remaining eight are mixed Druze and Arab Christian. They are followers of a mystical, esoteric and monotheistic faith stemming from Persian, Christian, Hindu and Muslim beliefs. They are officially recognized as an autonomous religious community.

The 2000 Circassians constitute the smallest people group in Israel. They were taken to the villages of Kafrakama and Rehaniya in Galilee by Sultan Abdel Hamid II in the 1800's. They are part of the Muslim Arab population.

Many Jews were at one time or another either prosyletized or persecuted by Christians. As a result, many dislike Christianity. There are disputes over many basic philosophical and doctrinal concepts. To the Jews, Christians appear to be pushing conversion and practicing polytheism since they worship a triune God. Another complicating factor is that most Christians are Arabs which makes Jews suspicious of them. In December of 1977, an amendment to the Israeli penal code was adopted. It is now an offense punishable by five years imprisionment to offer anyone material benefits to change religions. Conversion to another religion unders such terms is also punishable by three years imprisonment.

Biblical scholars and professors pursuing intellectual goals are allowed to study in Israel. Over 50 Christian archeological and Biblical institutions are allowed to continue operations with strict government supervision.

Christian tourists are welcomed and are free to visit the over 100 holy places. The Basilica of Annunciation in Nazareth remains the largest church in the Middle East.

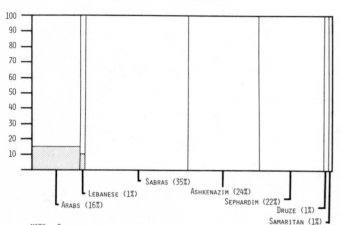

POPULATION COMPOSITION OF ISRAEL
(SHADING INDICATES CHRISTIANS)

Arabs (16%)
Lebanese (1%)
Sabras (35%)
Ashkenazim (24%)
Sephardim (22%)
Druze (1%)
Samaritan (1%)

NOTE: THESE FIGURES ARE REPRESENTATIVE APPROXIMATIONS. THEY SHOULD BE SEEN AS INDICATORS OF MAGNITUDE, NOT PRECISE.

# NATIONAL CHURCHES

## PROTESTANT CHURCHES

Protestants are one of the smallest groups among the Christian community. The 4000 members comprise 4.5% of the Christian population and only .1% of the total population. The Protestant movement began in 1820 with the establishment of an Anglican church. The 2100 member church reorganized in 1976 as the Episcopal Church in Jerusalem and the Middle East. Protestant churches are located in most of the major cities and some rural areas. Approximately 21% of all Protestant church services are conducted in Hebrew, 28% in English only and 51% in two or three languages including Arabic, Aramaic and other European languages. Many Protestants within Israel are Arabs and churches serve primarily the Arab communities.

The United Christian Council promotes the cooperation and communication among the major denominations. The Baptist Convention in Israel, Christian and Missionary Alliance, Church of Scotland, Church of the Nazarene, Lutheran Church, Seventh Day Adventist and Southern Baptist Churches interact in the Council.

## CATHOLIC CHURCHES

The Catholic community is the largest among Christians in Israel. The Melkite Church, also known as the Greek Catholic Church, has 40,000 members. It is organized separately but recognizes the authority of the Pope and maintains communication with Rome. Although a relatively small community, it is influential in political affairs. Many of the Catholics are Polish and Hungarian refugees. They wield a considerable amount of socio-political power and have custody of many holy sites. They operate several hospitals and cultural and charitable institutions. Members of the Maronite Church combine with the Melkites to form more than half of the Christian population. The Basilica of Annunciation in Nazareth is the largest church in the Middle East and serves as the center for Catholic community activities.

## ORTHODOX

Over 22,000 Greek Orthodox are part of the Arabic-speaking community and are led by an almost exclusively Greek-speaking heirarchy. Historically, the Greek Orthodox Patriarch has enjoyed a position of honor. He is highly regarded by the spiritual leaders of the Christian churches in Israel. Matters and issues he addresses are of highest priority. The Patriarchate of Jerusalem is the only autonomous Orthodox church in the country. Smaller groups of Armenian Orthodox, Syrian Orthodox, Russian Orthodox, Coptic Orthodox and Ethiopian Orthodox Church members are scattered throughout Israel. They are in communion with the ecumenical patriarch of Constantinople.

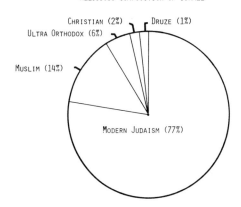

RELIGIOUS COMPOSITION OF ISRAEL

CHRISTIAN (2%)  DRUZE (1%)
ULTRA ORTHODOX (6%)
MUSLIM (14%)
MODERN JUDAISM (77%)

## PROTESTANT MISSIONS

The first missionary contingent to Israel was formed by the Anglican church in 1809. Since 1962 it has been called "The Churches Ministry Among the Jews." J. Nicolaysen, a Danish doctor, was the first individual missionary.

The largest group involved in missions is the Southern Baptist Convention. It began work with a single Syrian individual in 1911. The main center for their work is the Baptist Village in Petah Tiqua. Their facilities include a church, camp, conference center and a farm. They operate a school in Nazareth and a student center with an enrollment of 450 in Jerusalem. They also provide four bookstores, two library reading rooms and community centers in Jerusalem, Tel Aviv and Acre.

The Anglican and Scottish missions sent teams to every farming settlement, village and town in Galilee in 1938. Israeli residents are sent in teams to both southern and central Israel by the Pentecostals and The Voice of Healing. Small group Bible studies and churches in homes provide non-threatening opportunities for evangelism. Over 100 workers maintain assistance programs, educational and support ministries. There is some freedom in evangelism among Arabs where Child Evangelism reaches village families.

## CATHOLIC MISSIONS

The Roman Catholic's stated purpose in Israel is to lead lives of prayer for the Jews and to represent God's Church. They claim not to be involved in any direct evangelism. They support personnel working in five hospitals and several other institutions. There are 600 nuns as well as 200 monks and priests. Several hundred Jewish children attend the seven Roman Catholic schools. Youth rallies are held in the Hebrew language in Jerusalem and Jaffa by missionaries sent by the Roman Catholic Church.

## EVANGELISM

Very few evangelistic programs exist due to tight government regulations. Child Evangelism is able to work with the children of Nazareth and Galilee.

## BROADCASTING

Two radio broadcasts are currently being aired. One is the Voice of Israel, which began in 1950. Programs are done in Arabic once a month by different churches. This attracts few Jewish listeners. The only other broadcast is a daily program on the Voice of Hope which is aired over Radio Monte Carlo.

## LITERATURE

Only a few tracts and Hebrew New Testaments were available when the state of Israel was formed. In the 1950's the larger churches started publishing books in Hebrew. The first complete Hebrew Bible was published in 1950. The Baptists aquired a press in Tel Aviv which has printed several books and the only consistent Christian monthly magazine in both Hebrew and English. The Dolphin Press has published many pamphlets from its locaton at the Finnish School in Jerusalem. The United Christian Council has also published several books through its literature committee. Translations of the New Testament in Modern Hebrew have recently become available. Nine Bible shops sell Bibles, with a few of them selling Christian materials in Arab regions. Interest has increased as new translations are made available. Close to 40% of the Jewish population admit reading the New Testament.

## SOCIAL CONCERN

Hospital care has been a major source of contact with the people of Israel. Many remote areas are reached by medical missionaries. Arab communities are being influenced by several agencies including the Scots' Memorial Church and the Edinburgh Medical Missionary Society.

## NATION AND ITS PEOPLE

## POPULATION

More than 3.5 million people inhabit the land of Israel. Immigration continues to add nearly 20,000 Jews each year. About 88% of the Jews live in urban settings while 56.6% of the non-Jews live in rural settings. Peoples of occupied territories include approximately 460,000 people in Gaza, 680,000 in the West Bank region, 8,000 in the Golan Heights and 60,000 in Sinai. These figures vary as resettlement continues to occur. Presently, 3.5% of all Jews live in Kibbutzim, social and work oriented communes, and about 5% live on Moshavim, which are settlements of small cooperative farms. The Jewish population growth rate is near 2% and non-Jewish is 3.5%.

## COMPOSITION

Jews constitute 83% of the total population of Israel. Ethnic divisions among the Jews include the Askenazim (29%), which are Jews of European descent; Sephardim (27%), which are Jews of middle eastern or northern Africa descent; and the Sabras (44%), which are Jews born in Israel. Arabs comprise 16% of the population and tend to be of the Sunni Islam faith. They live in the rural areas, Jerusalem and occupied territories.

## LITERACY

The literacy rate (88%) is high among Jews between the ages of 14 and 48. The literacy rate (48%) is much lower among the non-Jewish. The national literacy rate is 70%.

A revised contemporary version of Hebrew is the first official language. Arabic is widely used among the Arab population and is also an official language. English is used in government publications and is being taught in most schools. Many ethnic groups still speak Yiddish, Ladino, Russian, Rumanian, Bulgarian, German and French.

## RELIGION

Israel, being a Jewish homeland, is greatly influenced by Jewish traditions. Although Judaism serves as a common bond, still many Jews are secularly oriented. The Muslim Arabs have many cultural differences. There is no single state religion.

## GEOGRAPHY AND CLIMATE

Israel lies between the harsh deserts of Asia and Africa and the Mediterranean Sea. Temperatures and rainfall vary according to proximity to the deserts or seas. Widespread irrigation supplements the rainy season which lasts from October to April. Amounts of rainfall vary from 75.7 centimeters (29.8 inches) in the central hill zone near Jerusalem to only 4.55 centimeters (1.8 inches) along the Dead Sea near Sodom.

## HISTORY

Israel has a society as ancient as any in existence and is still one of the youngest and most rapidly developing nations in the world. Jews which have been scattered throughout the world on numerous occasions are returning again to their homeland. The dry wilderness is being transformed into productive farm land and the people are rebuilding their land as their ancestors did in the past. The United Nations issued a resolution in 1947 which called for a creation of a Jewish state in Palestine. Israel became a Jewish state in 1948.

## GOVERNMENT

Israel is a parliamentary democracy. The Knesset is a 120 member legislative assembly that maintains highest authority. A president is chosen by the Knesset for a five year term. A prime minister, usually the leader of the majority party, is chosen by the president.

Twenty-four parties entered candidates in the national elections of 1977. The right-wing Likud party defeated the Labour party and the new Democratic Movement for Change party became the third largest. The Histadrut (General Federation of Labor) is the largest trade union to which almost everyone belongs, including housewives. The government of Israel spends proportionally more for defense than any other nation. This gives them a highly trained and well equipped military.

## ECONOMY

Agricultural products from the reclaimed lands are the leading exports. Diamonds, metal products, machinery, electronics and minerals are exported in large quantities to the European Economic Community, Asia and the United States. Imports exceed exports more than two to one which leaves a huge deficit.

The exchange rate of one Israeli pound (100 agorots) was US $.06 in 1978. The wars with neighboring Arab nations make it difficult to assess their per capita income. It had risen to US $1,225 in 1972 but has been declining since then while inflation rate has risen as high as 30%.

## CHURCH STATISTICS FOR ISRAEL

Note: Statistics have been taken from different sources and are the most current data available. Definitions of "membership" vary among churches and may not always be comparable. Not all known churches have been included in this list.

| Church or Mission Name | Communicants (Full Members) | Community (Estimate) |
|---|---|---|
| **PROTESTANT** | | |
| Bible Evangelistic Mission | 130 | 175 |
| British Society for Propagation of the Gospel Among the Jews | 20 | 50 |
| Children's Evangelical Fellowship | | |
| Christian and Missionary Alliance | | |
| Church of Scotland | | |
| Edinburgh Medical Missionary Society | | |
| Evangelical Episcopal Church | | |
| International Hebrew Church (Norwegian) | | |
| Church of the Nazarene | | |
| Mennonite Association in Israel | | |
| Mission of the Finnish Missionary | | 18 |
| Seventh Day Adventist Church | 183 | 721 |
| Zion Christian Mission | | |
| | | |
| **CATHOLIC** | | |
| Armenian Catholic Church | | 2,100 |
| Maronite Catholic Church | | 4,000 |
| Greek Catholic Church | | 24,000 |
| Roman Catholic Church | | 36,000 |
| | | |
| **ORTHODOX** | | |
| Coptic Orthodox Church | | 500 |
| Ethiopian Orthodox Church | 127 | 168 |
| Greek Orthodox Church | 250 | 350 |
| Syrian Orthodox Church | | 2,400 |

# SELECTED BIBLIOGRAPHY AND INFORMATION SOURCES

The sources listed below are to help the reader find additional information on this country and Christian ministries there. This list does not try to be comprehensive or complete.

## DOCUMENTS

### General

Area Handbook for Israel, Washington, DC: The American University, 1970.

Europa Year Book 1978, London, England: Europa Publications, 1978.

Middle East Yearbook 1978, London, England: I.C. Magazines Limited.

Minority Rights Group, Israel's Oriental Immigrants and Druzes, No. 24, London, Human Relations Area Files Press, 1971.

Minority Rights Group, The Palestinians, No. 24, London, Expedite Multiprint Ltd., 1972.

Sweet, Louise E., The Central Middle East, New Haven, Human Relations Area Files Press, 1971.

World Almanac 1978, New York, Newspaper Enterprise Association Inc., 1977.

### Christian

Dayton, Edward R., editor, Mission Handbook: North American Protestant Ministries Overseas, Monrovia, CA., 1976.

Foy, Felican A. O.F.M., editor, Catholic Almanac 1978, Huntington, IN: Our Sunday Visitor Inc., 1977.

Horner, Norman A., Rediscovering Christianity Where It Began, Beirut: Heidelberg Press, 1974.

## ACKNOWLEDGMENTS

The information in this profile was taken from many sources which were the best available to the editors at the time of preparation. However, the accuracy of the information cannot be guaranteed. Views expressed or implied in this publication are not necessarily those of World Vision. The editors have tried to present the ministries of various organizations in an objective manner, without undue bias or emphasis. Where we have failed, we apologize for erroneous impressions that may result and request that comments and corrections be sent to MARC, 919 West Huntington Drive, Monrovia, California, 91016. We appreciate and acknowledge the comments and contributions of various organizations and individuals in the preparation of this publication.

# STATUS OF CHRISTIANITY COUNTRY PROFILE

# JORDAN

### SUMMARY

AREA - 96,500 square kilometers (38,600 square miles)

POPULATION - 2.7 million (1975)

RELIGION - 80-93% Sunni Muslim, 10% Christian, small percentage Shiah Muslim

Jerusalem: Holy City for all. This ancient place is Arabic from the tip of the Dome of the Rock to its lowest foundations. Three world religions--Christianity, Islam, and Judaism--are centered here, but none is more at home than the Moslem.

The same can be said for the whole of Jordan. Although this country's historical roots lie deepest in Judaism and Christianity, most of its people today worship Allah.

The richest of its land, including the Jordanian sector of Jerusalem, has been occupied by Israel since 1967. However, it is a fairly tranquil place in comparison to the constant turmoil just outside its borders. Two factors contributing to the relative stability of the country are King Hussein's friendship with other Arab states and the United States and his strong interest in a permanent peace settlement with Israel.

The 10% of Jordan's people who are Christians face a challenging task in sharing the Good News of Jesus Christ with the rest of the population. Many Christians live in occupied Jordan, especially in the towns of Jerusalem, Bethlehem and Ramallah. There is an even greater need for Christian witness in the East Bank. The Christian community is primarily Eastern Orthodox. Sixty foreign missionaries work in the country. Most mission work is social ministry, which provides an opportunity for Christians to show concern for Jordan's people. With one Christian for every nine Muslims and one Protestant missionary per 45,033 persons, there is much to be done.

As both the cross and the crescent reach upward into the Jordanian sky, will this land of jets and camels, refugee camps and hotels, Bedouins and businessmen, and spires and minarets become God's strategic center for reaching people in other Middle Eastern nations?

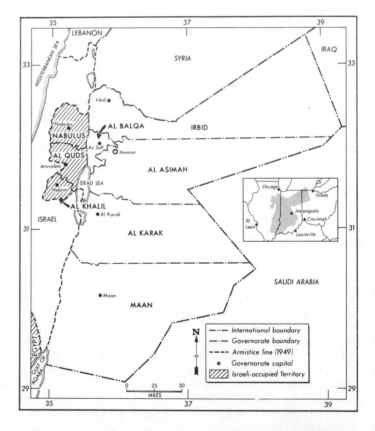

*This program is jointly carried out by the Strategy Working Group of the Lausanne Committee for World Evangelization and MARC, a ministry of World Vision International. For further information on the program, please write: MARC, 919 West Huntington Drive, Monrovia, CA 91016 U.S.A.*

# UNREACHED PEOPLES

The great majority of Jordan's population follows the Sunni Muslim religion. Over 93% are followers, and Sunni Islam is particularly strong among the rural people. Christianity is the next largest religion in Jordan, although Christians comprise only 10% of the people. Three other religions are followed by groups in the country. The Druzes follow a sect of Shiah Islam that is considered heretical by most Muslims. Samaritans represent an offshoot of Judiasm. The Bahai faith began as a breakoff from Shiah Islam during the 19th century; it has a few followers in Jordan.

Jordanian Arabs account for 25% of the population; they live primarily in the cities. Circassians, also city dwellers, comprise 1.2% of the total. Originally from near the Black Sea and Turkey, these nominal Muslims still hold to many of their pre-Islamic beliefs in gods and goddesses of nature. Another 2.8% of Jordan's people are unemployed Arabs, and 4.7% are military and government personnel. Urban social classes other than the unemployed Arabs and military and government personnel include landowners, professionals (38,000 in 1970), artisans and shop-keepers (44,000 in 1970), and migrants and industrial workers (22,000 in 1970).

The dedication of rural dwellers professing Sunni Islam is even greater than that of the urban population. Rural subsistence farmers comprise 6.7% of the population and can be considered 100% Sunni Muslim. Arabic is their major language, but the tribal peoples speak a rural version of Arabic. These nomadic and semi-nomadic Bedouins are also 100% Sunni Muslim. A large share of the army, especially leaders, is composed of people with tribal origins. Bedouins comprise less than 6% of the population and are decreasing as more enter the army and move to the cities. The king feels deep personal ties with the nomads and enjoys visiting with them. Some nomads were displaced by the creation of Israel.

Palestinians in Jordan, marginally unreached, are 80% Sunni Muslim, 2% Protestant, 6% Catholic and 12% Eastern Christian. Jordanian Palestinians living in cities account for 16% of the total population. Among Palestinian refugees, town dwellers comprise 24% of Jordan's people, while tent camp dwellers number about 16%. Most refugees in the East Bank dislike living there, see themselves as a separate people, and want to return home.

However, providing for the refugees' material needs has been more of a problem than assimilating them into society. Many refugees have undergone multiple shiftings and dislocations as a result of fighting in this part of the Middle East. All the Palestinian groups speak the Arabic language.

Unreached peoples who profess religions other than Sunni Islam include the Druzes, Samaritans and Bahais. The Druzes, originally related to the Ismaili branch of Shiah Islam, hold many secret beliefs. Samaritans, an ancient Jewish sect, worship on Mount Gerizim. There is a settlement of Bahais living in the north Jordan valley. None of these religious groups represents a large percentage of the population, but all need to hear the Good News of Jesus Christ.

Jordan's unreached peoples can be classified into four major linguistic groups: speakers of the Arabic, Kurdish and Aramaic languages and the Turkomen. The Samaritans speak Aramaic, a language also used by Jesus. Another language group, the Chechens who speak Armenian, cannot be considered unreached because most of them profess Christ as Savior.

POPULATION COMPOSITION OF JORDAN
(SHADING INDICATES CHRISTIANS)

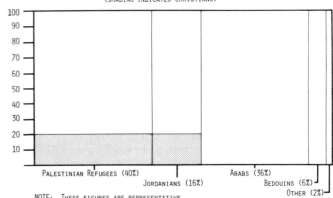

PALESTINIAN REFUGEES (40%)  JORDANIANS (16%)  ARABS (36%)  BEDOUINS (6%)  OTHER (2%)

NOTE: THESE FIGURES ARE REPRESENTATIVE APPROXIMATIONS. THEY SHOULD BE SEEN AS INDICATIONS OF MAGNITUDE, NOT PRECISE.

# CURRENT STATUS OF CHRISTIANITY

Christianity is a minority faith in this predominantly Muslim country. Including both East and West Banks, Christians account for about 10% of the total population. The Orthodox community numbers over 117,000, with Catholics about 67,000 and Protestants almost 7,000. Evangelical Christianity is growing gradually.

The primary ministries of national churches and foreign missions are social in nature--education, medicine, development, and relief.

## NATIONAL CHURCHES

### CATHOLIC

The Roman Catholic community, including West Bank, numbers 67,500, or about 3.5% of the population. Most orders serve in the West Bank area. The Greek (Melkite) Catholics and Latin-rite Catholics are the largest Catholic groups, but there are also Armenian, Maronite and Syrian Catholics in Jordan. Greek (Melkite) Catholics operate 20 schools, and Latin-rite Catholics conduct major education programs, including two seminaries.

### PROTESTANT AND ANGLICAN

The Protestant church community for all of Jordan numbers about 6,800 persons, or 0.35% of the total population. The Anglican and Arab Episcopal Church (East and West Banks) and Evangelical Lutheran Church of Jordan (West Bank) are the two largest. There are also congregations of Assemblies of God, Bible Presbyterians, Conservative Baptists, Southern Baptists, Nazarenes, Free Evangelicals, and Seventh-day Adventists. The Lutheran Church operates schools and supports a radio ministry. The Southern Baptists help a hospital and the Assemblies of God run a clinic. The Anglican and Arab Episcopal Church has been involved in primary and secondary education. Evangelical Christianity is experiencing gradual growth, but the national church needs more pastors from within itself, more and better pastoral training, and a deepened awareness among the laity of the missionary mandate.

### ORTHODOX

The Orthodox community, by far the largest Christian group in Jordan, numbers over 117,000 and equals 6.35% of the population. The Greek Orthodox Church alone has a community of 110,000 served by 14 bishops. There are over 3,000 persons in the Armenian Orthodox community, and about 3,400 in the Syrian Orthodox. The Coptic, Ethiopian and Russian Orthodox are considerably smaller in size. Church ministries include two Coptic primary schools and a Greek Orthodox seminary with 100 students. Unfortunately, location of the seminary in the West Bank causes problems to potential students from the East Bank area.

### COOPERATIVE AGENCIES

The Episcopal and Lutheran churches in Jordan belong to the Middle East Council of Churches headquartered in Beirut, Lebanon (currently inaccessible). There exists a great need for more cooperation among local churches and mission efforts, but the spirit of harmony that does exist encourages the progress of the Christian witness in Jordan.

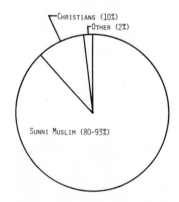

RELIGIOUS COMPOSITION OF JORDAN

Christians (10%)
Other (2%)
Sunni Muslim (80-93%)

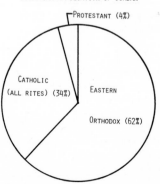

CHRISTIAN AFFILIATION OF JORDAN

Protestant (4%)
Catholic (all rites) (34%)
Eastern Orthodox (62%)

## FOREIGN MISSIONS

### CATHOLIC

As did much of Palestine and Mesopotamia during the early centuries of Christianity, Jordan tended to affiliate with eastern forms of Christian expression. Eastern Catholic communities did not appear until the 16th century, when some of the Orthodox Christians began to reunite with Rome. Eventually, "Uniate" churches were formed that recognized the authority of the Pope while retaining eastern liturgy. There are four Uniate Catholic churches in Jordan today. The largest is the Greek Catholic (Melkite) Church. Since these churches originated in the Middle East, they naturally have developed leadership from within their own countries. There is no resident expatriate leadership structure.

Latin-rite Catholics have been in the country for several centuries. Franciscan missionary efforts during the Crusades, along with the restoration of the Latin Patriarchate in Jerusalem in 1847, greatly helped to increase the number of Roman Catholics in the country. Presently, missionaries from this church are few in number. Two U.S. orders, the Franciscan Fathers and the Medical Mission Sisters, have a total of three missionaries in Jordan.

### PROTESTANT

Earliest efforts were by the Church Missionary Society; for over a century the Anglicans have ministered in Jordan. Their work was significantly cut back as a result of the war of 1948, but some institutions remain. The Christian and Missionary Alliance followed in the 1930's; their work has gradually been nationalized and they no longer support resident foreign missionaries in Jordan.

Twenty-one Protestant mission agencies from the United States, United Kingdom, and Australia, support a total of 60 missionaries in Jordan. Fifty missionaries come from the United States, and the Southern Baptist Convention has the largest number of reported personnel in Jordan. The Assemblies of God Division of Foreign Missions, the first North American agency in Jordan, began work there in 1908 and now supports six missionaries. Mennonite Central Committee reported six personnel in 1976. Christian Missions in Many Lands, of Australia, supports one missionary, and the Bible Lands Society and Church Missionary Society, both of the United Kingdom,

support a total of nine missionaries. There is one Protestant missionary per 45,033 persons in Jordan.

### ORTHODOX

Orthodoxy has been the dominant Christian tradition since the beginning of Christianity in the Middle East. Throughout the centuries the church has grown and split for various reasons, resulting in the presence of five Orthodox churches in Jordan. The Greek Orthodox Church is the largest, followed by the Syrian, Armenian, Coptic and Ethiopian Orthodox Churches. Except for those who serve the mostly expatriate Coptic and Ethiopian Orthodox communities, resident expatriate missionaries do not hold a place in the centuries-old Orthodox structure.

## MAJOR CHRISTIAN PROGRAMS AND ACTIVITIES

### EVANGELISM

Jordan is becoming a focal point for Christian witness to neighboring countries. As these efforts are strengthened and encouraged, the gospel can be taken into areas previously closed to Christian work.

### BROADCASTING

Although there are no Christian radio stations in Jordan, programming in Arabic can be heard over stations in Seychelles, Cyprus and Monaco. Far East Broadcasting Associates and Trans World Radio are the major agencies involved. This important ministry lacks publicity and needs more effective follow-up ministries to listeners.

### LITERATURE

Information on literature ministries is scarce. There appears to be a need for Christian written materials in Jordan.

The nearest Bible Society office is located in Beirut, Lebanon. The entire Bible is available in Arabic, and 46% of Arabic speakers are literate. Circulation of Scriptures by the United Bible Society in Jordan was as follows:

|             | 1976   | 1975   |
|-------------|--------|--------|
| Bibles      | 923    | 1,064  |
| Testaments  | 10,622 | 1,914  |
| Portions    | 21,829 | 10,893 |
| Selections  | 52,800 | 29,820 |
| Total       | 86,174 | 43,691 |

## EDUCATION

Theological. The Latin-rite Catholic Church supports two seminaries. One hundred students attend a Greek Orthodox seminary. East Bank students who would like to attend the Greek Orthodox school in the West Bank cannot reach the school; therefore, training is hindered.

Christian. The Lutheran Church and Anglican and Arab Episcopal Church in Jordan support schools. Twenty schools are affiliated with the Greek (Melkite) Catholics, two primary schools are connected with the Coptic Orthodox Church, and major education programs are supported by the Latin-rite Catholics. Several mission agencies also provide education and training.

## SOCIAL CONCERN

Social ministries provide a crucial opportunity for Christians to show concern for the people of Jordan. In fact, most mission and church activity falls into this category. For example, the United Church of Christ's Board for World Ministries has ongoing ministries of refugee relief, agricultural development, vocational training and medical services.

Additional agencies giving development assistance include Catholic Relief Services, Church World Service and Lutheran World Relief. Church World Service also does vocational and public health training. The blind receive help from Lutheran World Relief. Mennonite Central Committee operates schools and orphanages, and the Nazarenes and Franciscans also are engaged in childhood education. Almost 400 adults are enrolled in the Laubach Literacy training program. Medical ministries include five Lutheran World Relief clinics and one tuberculosis sanitorium each for the Southern Baptist Convention and World Presbyterian Mission.

## POPULATION

Jordan's 1975 population, including both the West Bank occupied by Israel and the East Bank, numbered 2.7 million. The same year 1.9 million people lived in the East Bank alone. Growth is occurring at 3-3.7% per year. Over 50% of the people live in villages averaging 400-800 persons, 44% live in urban areas, and less than 6% are nomadic or semi-nomadic. The capital city Amman, with over 750,000 residents, accounts for at least 30% of the East Bank population. The urban population is growing at twice the village rate, and nomadic groups are diminishing. Forty-eight percent of the total population is under 15 years of age, and 3% is over 64 years.

## COMPOSITION

Jordanian Arabs account for 25% for the population, Jordanian Palestinians 16%, nomadic Bedouins 2.9%, semi-nomadic Bedouins 2.6%, Circassians 1.2%, and Chechens (Armenian Christians) 0.5%. Palestinian refugees living in towns comprise 24%, and those in tent camps are another 16% of the people living in Jordan. About 2.8% of the total are unemployed Arabs, and another 4.7% are military and government people. Arab subsistence farmers in rural areas form another 6.7% of the population. The Bedouins are decreasing in numbers as many enter the army and move to the cities.

## LITERACY AND LANGUAGES

Between 55% and 62% of the people were literate in 1970, and this figure is climbing. Arabic is the official language, but there are also speakers of the Kurdish, Aramaic (Samaritans), Armenian (Chechens), and Turkish languages. English is also spoken in commerce and government.

## RELIGION

The predominant religion, Sunni Islam, embraces 80-93% of the population. A separate branch of Shiah Muslims has a small number of adherents. About 10% are Christians, if both East and West Banks are considered. Within the Christian community, Orthodox people number over 115,000, Catholics about 67,000, and Protestants almost 7,000. There is gradual growth among the evangelical Christian groups.

## GEOGRAPHY AND CLIMATE

Jordan's 96,500 square kilometer area (38,600 square miles) lies south of Syria, west of Iraq, west and north of Saudi Arabia and east of Israel. About 11% of the land is arable. The portion west of the Jordan River (West Bank), currently under Israeli military occupation, has about one-third of the population and receives 30-50 centimeters (12-20 inches) more rainfall than other areas. The hot Jordan River Valley is rich agriculturally. Dry desert and steppe lands characterize the sparsely populated East Bank, which receives less than 12.5 centimeters (five inches) of rain annually. The Mediterranean climate produces temperatures ranging from 12 degrees F (-11 degrees C) to over 100 degrees F (38 degrees C).

Although Jordan has no significant oil or coal deposits, it has other natural resources. Phosphate rock, copper, potash and soluble salts are the most economically feasible. Limestone for buildings and cement and materials usable for glass and ceramics are also available.

## HISTORY

The Jordan area was part of the Ottoman Empire from the 16th century until World War I, when the League of Nations awarded the regions now known as Israel and Jordan to the United Kingdom. The Transjordan area, east of the Jordan River, became the independent Hashemite Kingdom of Transjordan in 1946, while British administration of Palestine, west of the Jordan River, ended with the proclamation in 1948 of the State of Israel. After a period of armed conflict, the Transjordan was renamed the Hashemite Kingdom of Jordan to include portions of Arab Palestine west of the river. King Hussein began his reign in 1953. The Six-Day War in 1967 resulted in Israeli occupation of the entire Jordan West Bank, including the Jordanian sector of Jerusalem.

## GOVERNMENT AND POLITICAL CONDITIONS

Jordan is a constitutional monarchy, with King Hussein I as chief of state. Executive authority rests with the King and the Council of Ministers, which is led by the Prime Minister appointed by the King. Legislative power rests in the bicameral National Assembly; Senators are appointed and members of the House of Representatives are elected. Of the 60 seats in the House, 50 must go to Muslims and 10 to Christians. Traditionally 30 seats are from the West Bank and 30 from the East Bank, despite the Israeli occupation. Judges are appointed by the King to all three types of courts--civil, religious and special.

King Hussein leads a country remarkably tranquil for the Middle East and currently enjoys friendships with both the Arab powers and the United States.

## ECONOMY

About 75% of the population, excluding refugees, is engaged in agriculture, although much productive farm land was lost through Israel's occupation of the West Bank. Wheat, fruits, vegetables and olive oil are the principal crops. Major industries include phosphate extraction, cement manufacture, alcoholic beverages, tobacco, marble, and leather. Phosphates accounted for about 40% of total 1975 exports worth US$ 170 million (f.o.b.), while fruits, vegetables, and tomatoes accounted for another 20%. Imports for 1975 totalling US$ 610 million (c.i.f.) included transport equipment, machinery, metallic minerals, chemicals, textiles, food, and animals and animal products.

One Jordanian dinar in March 1977 was worth US$ 3.03. The 1974 per capita GNP was US$ 430.

# CHURCH MEMBERSHIP STATISTICS FOR JORDAN

Note: Statistics have been taken from different sources and are the most current data available. Definitions of "membership" vary among churches and may not always be comparable.

| Church or Mission Name | Communicants (Full Members) | Community (Estimate) |
|---|---|---|
| **PROTESTANT** | | |
| Anglican and Arab Episcopal Church | | 2,800 |
| Assemblies of God | | 250 |
| Bible Presbyterian Church | | 50 |
| Church of the Nazarene | | 250 |
| Conservative Baptist Church | | 200 |
| Evangelical Lutheran Church of Jordan | 850 | 1,250 |
| Free Evangelical Church | | 500 |
| Seventh-day Adventist Church | | 200 |
| Southern Baptist Church | 210 | 550-750 |
| | | |
| **CATHOLIC** | | |
| Armenian Catholic Church | | 900 |
| Greek (Melkite) Catholic Church | | 26,000 |
| Latin-rite Catholic Church | | 40,000 |
| Maronite Catholic Church | | 400 |
| Syrian Catholic Church | | 200 |
| | | |
| **ORTHODOX** | | |
| Armenian Orthodox Church | | 3,200 |
| Coptic Orthodox Church | | 500 |
| Ethiopian Orthodox Church | | 200 |
| Greek Orthodox Church | | 110,000 |
| Russian Orthodox Church | | negligible |
| Syrian Orthodox Church | | 3,400 |

# SELECTED BIBLIOGRAPHY AND INFORMATION SOURCES

The sources listed below are to help the reader find additional information on this country and Christian ministries there. This list does not try to be comprehensive or complete.

## DOCUMENTS

### General

Area Handbook for the Hashemite Kingdom of Jordan, Washington, DC: American University, 1974

Background Notes, Washington, DC: Department of State, 1974

Hamarneh, Michael, ed., Jordan, Washington, DC: Jordan Information Bureau, 1976

Pocket Guide to the Middle East, Washington, DC: Office of Information for the Armed Forces Department of Defense, 1969

The Middle East and North Africa 1976-1977, London: Europa Publications Limited, 1976

### Christian

Horner, Norman A., Rediscovering Christianity Where It Began, Beirut: Heidlberg Press, 1974

Kane, J. Herbert, A Global View of Christian Missions, Grand Rapids: Baker Book House, 1971

## ORGANIZATIONS

Bible Society of Lebanon, P.O. Box 747, Beirut, Lebanon
Middle East Council of Churches, Beirut, Lebanon

## ACKNOWLEDGMENTS

The information in this profile was taken from many sources which were the best available to the editors at the time of preparation. However, the accuracy of the information cannot be guaranteed. Views expressed or implied in this publication are not necessarily those of World Vision. The editors have tried to present the ministries of various organizations in an objective manner, without undue bias or emphasis. Where we have failed, we apologize for erroneous impressions that may result and request that comments and corrections be sent to MARC, 919 West Huntington Drive, Monrovia, California, USA, 91016. We appreciate and acknowledge the comments and contributions of various organizations and individuals in the preparation of this publication.

# STATUS OF CHRISTIANITY COUNTRY PROFILE

# KUWAIT

present in Kuwait since the turn of the century through the mission work of the Reformed Church of America (RCA). Christianity has lately grown to nearly 5% of the population, largely through the influx of expatriates. Mission work has left a legacy of good-will through schools and hospitals originally established by the RCA. Most of this work has been superseded by the government and it remains to be seen whether the present Christian community can effectively share their faith with the Muslim majority. At present there are no national Kuwaiti churches and no Kuwaiti Muslim converts.

SUMMARY

AREA -    17,656 square kilometers
                (6,800 square miles)
POPULATION - 1,129,000
RELIGION - 92% Sunni Muslim, 4% Christian,
     3% Shia Muslim 1% Other

Kuwait is unsurpassed in form as a contemporary nation state. Its 1,129,000 people are the product of the fastest increasing growth rate of any modern state. Originally a sparsely populated desert Sheikhdom, Kuwait now boasts the highest per capita GNP of any nation on the earth. A modern nation has been built on the strength of its public oil revenues. Public housing, education and health care are the hallmarks of modernization. In the midst of this change, the government of Kuwait continues to adhere to the strictures of Orthodox Islam. Muslim leaders in Kuwait have consciously sought to link modernization with the traditional framework laid down in the Quran as expressed by Muslim customs.

Less than 50% of the population of Kuwait are indigenous Kuwaiti. Until the discovery of oil in the 1930's, the population was under 100,000 and engaged in fishing, pearl diving and nomadic lifestyles. There have been Christians

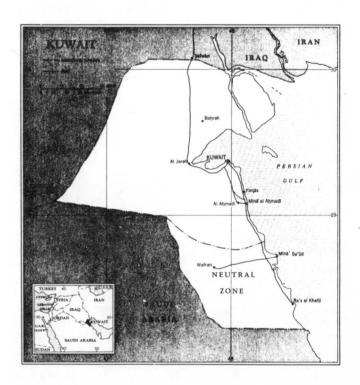

*This program is jointly carried out by the Strategy Working Group of the Lausanne Committee for World Evangelization and MARC, a ministry of World Vision International. For further information on the program, please write: MARC, 919 West Huntington Drive, Monrovia, CA 91016 U.S.A.*

Kuwaitis comprise 47% of Kuwait's population. Overall, 68% of the population are ethnic Arabs. Kurds (13%) comprise the next largest ethnic group which numbers about 145,000. Asians, particularly Indians, Pakistanis and Iranians comprise 11% of the population. A small group of Baluch, numbering about 5,000 people, are also found in Kuwait. Expatriate Europeans and Americans constitute the remaining 1.3% of the population. The largest expatriate Arab groups include the Egyptians, Iraqis and Syrians, each representing about 5% of the population.

About 18% of the population, or 80,000 people are non-Muslim. Most of these people are expatriate Arabs, along with Asians, Armenians and other expatriates. The practicing Christian community numbered 40,600 as of 1977, or about 4% of the population.

The major unreached peoples of Kuwait are Muslims, mostly of the Sunni sect of Islam. There is considerable variation among those Muslims and mission work among the Kuwaitis has been singularly unsuccessful. The Muslim Jordanians, Palestinians, Syrians and Iraqis have been resistant to Christianity, but some of the Muslim Kurds and Pakistanis show more openness to the Gospel. Among non-Muslims there are numerous Asians, nominal Christian Arabs and expatriates who represent potential for strong evangelism and church renewal ministries.

The number of Christians in Kuwait has been vastly increased in the last decade through immigration. Kuwait has little Christian history prior to the late 19th century. A high percentage of the present Christian community is nominal and about 5% are evangelical. Christian schools formerly established by the RCA have been completely superseded by the government's educational programs. Only one missionary continued in hospital work under the auspices of the government and one Christian bookstore has been established.

## NATIONAL CHURCHES

Nineteen church traditions are represented in Kuwait comprising a total Christian community of 40,600. The largest of these is the Catholic Church representing nearly half (48%) of the total Christian community. This is followed by the Orthodox Churches (40%) and the Protestant and Anglican churches (12%).

### CATHOLIC CHURCHES

Seven distinct traditions are represented among the 19,500 Catholics in Kuwait. The largest of these are the Latin-rite, half of whom are Indian. Melkite, Maronite and Chaldean Catholics are the next largest communities. Each has over 1,000 members. Smaller groups of Armenian, Syrian and Coptic Catholics are also represented. Catholics have produced a significant book entitled The Christians in Kuwait, (1970).

### PROTESTANT CHURCHES

Seven Protestant denominations have been organized in Kuwait. The largest of these is the Mar Thoma Church with 1,600 members (Indian). The Evangelical and Anglican Churches both have about 1,300 members. Indian Pentecostal, Church of South India, Indian Brethren and Seventh-Day Adventist churches comprise four smaller groups which total less than 500 people.

### ORTHODOX

Three Orthodox Church traditions are represented in Kuwait. The Oriental Orthodox is the largest and is sub-divided into Armenian, Coptic and Malabar Syrian. The total population is near 10,000, with Armenians accounting for nearly 6,600 members and the remainder is equally divided among the other groups. The

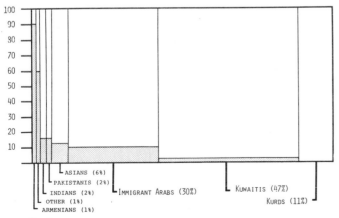

POPULATION COMPOSTION OF KUWAIT
(SHADING INDICATES CHRISTIANS)

ASIANS (6%)
PAKISTANIS (2%)
INDIANS (2%)
OTHER (1%)
ARMENIANS (1%)
IMMIGRANT ARABS (30%)
KUWAITIS (47%)
KURDS (11%)

NOTE: THESE FIGURES ARE REPRESENTATIVE APPROXIMATIONS. THEY SHOULD BE SEEN AS INDICATORS OF MAGNITUDE, NOT PRECISE.

Eastern Orthodox Church has 6,000 members and the Nestorian Church has 400 members.

## COOPERATIVE AGENCIES

Church buildings in Kuwait are shared extensively. The National Evangelical Church in Kuwait is used by seven different congregations and requires a precise hour-by-hour schedule. The Kuwait Church Council is an informal, though very active organization. It is the only ecumenical organization in the Middle East to which Roman Catholics officially belong.

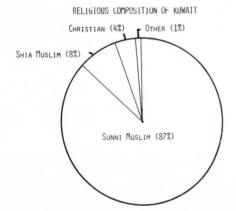

RELIGIOUS COMPOSITION OF KUWAIT

CHRISTIAN (4%)   OTHER (1%)
SHIA MUSLIM (8%)
SUNNI MUSLIM (87%)

Only one Protestant agency, the Reformed Church in America, is presently listed in Kuwait. No North American Catholic Missions personnel are listed in Kuwait at present.

## PROTESTANT MISSIONS

Protestant work began in Kuwait in 1910 when Sheikh Mubarak invited doctors from the Basrah hospital in Iraq to enter Kuwait in order to care for his family. Eventually a mission hospital was established under the auspices of the RCA. Four North American personnel managed the hospital with an Indian and Pakistani staff. The hospital was taken over by the government. Only one missionary continued working in the hospital after the church terminated its hospital work. Two other RCA missionaries have operated a bookshop which sells Bibles and other Christian literature. Over the years very few Muslim Kuwaitis have converted to Christianity. The few Christian Kuwaiti leaders of past generations have died and virtually no new conversions have been reported.

## CATHOLIC MISSIONS

The Catholic Church has had active members in Kuwait since 1950. There has never been any missionary work among the Muslim population. At present, the Catholic Church is the largest of all churches in Kuwait. It is ministering exclusively to the various Catholic expatriates.

## ORTHODOX

Congregations and priests have been established for the existing Orthodox community. Aside from ties to the other Christian traditions in Kuwait, no other work is being carried on outside immigrant communities.

MAJOR CHRISTIAN ACTIVITIES

## EVANGELISM

Open evangelism in Kuwait is simply impossible. An Arab Christian who attempted to go into a bazaar (market), several years ago, to distribute the Scriptures, was immediately arrested and deported the following day. Unexplored opportunities for evangelism exist among the Kurds and non-Arab Muslim groups.

## BROADCASTING

No Christian broadcasts are beamed specifically at Kuwait. There are several broadcasts to the Arabian Peninsula in Arabic which can be received in Kuwait.

## LITERATURE

One Christian bookstore makes Christian materials available as well as Bibles in several languages. It does a fair amount of business among all Christian groups. It is not known whether any materials are purchased by or for indigenous Arabs.


# NATION AND ITS PEOPLE


## POPULATION

Kuwait's present population of 1,129,000 had been growing at a rate of 6% per annum during the 1970's. That is the fastest growth rate of any of the independent states. Even that is down from the 10% average growth rate of the 1960's. Over 50% of the population is concentrated in six coastal town. The population of the towns is 88% immigrant while the population of the rural areas is 80% Kuwaiti.

## COMPOSITION

Arabs account for 68% of the total population and are predominantly (98%) Muslim. The majority of Muslims are of the Sunni sect. Kurds make up another 13% of the population, all of whom are Muslims. The majority of the Kurds are also Sunni though some may be of the Shia sect. Asians account for 11% of the population, including Iranians, Indians, and Pakistanis. The majority of the minority immigrant groups are also Muslims but many of them are of the Shia sect. Among the Indian and Pakistani populations there are significant groups of Christians and a few Hindus. A portion of the Kuwaiti Arab population belong to Bedouin tribes.

Socio-economic standing is quite high for all Kuwaitis. Some distinctions do exist between city dwellers, who are involved with rapid development, and rural town and country inhabitants. The Kurds, Baluchs, and tribal Bedouin are regarded as being at the bottom of the social scale. Laborers in the city doing menial tasks are also designated as lower class. The majority of Kuwait's population is taken care of by the government which provides housing, education and health care at minimal or no cost. At the top of the social scale are the ruling families, the Muslim holy men and the most highly educated, regardless of nationality.

## LANGUAGE AND LITERACY

Literacy in Kuwait is quite high with an average rate of 85% due to the growth of government schools in the past decade. Arabic is the official language although English and French are widely understood and used as second languages for trade and business purposes. A wide variety of ethnic and national languages are spoken by various expatriate populations and indigenous tribal groups.

## RELIGION

Of Kuwait's total population, 95% are Muslim, 93% of which are of the Sunni sect. Exceptions include Iranians and Kurds who are Shia muslims. Active Christians comprise 4% of the total population with another 1% coming from various religious backgrounds.

## GEOGRAPHY AND CLIMATE

The terrain of Kuwait is flat desert with an annual rainfall of 2.5 to 22.8 centimeters, (1-9 inches). It is located in the north-east corner of the Arabian Peninsula at the head of the Persian Gulf. The flat topography is basically unbroken except by two low-lying ranges of foothills and a few small oases. Temperatures range between 2 degrees centigrade in January, (37 degrees F.) and 47 degrees centigrade in June, (115 degrees F.).

## HISTORY

Little mention is made of Kuwait in history until the mid-18th century when a number of Bedouin tribes migrated to the area in order to escape severe drought conditions of central Arabia. One of these tribes, the Al-Sabah established themselves as the rulers of Kuwait and set up the dynasty which continues even today.

Kuwait became a British Protectorate in 1899 which allowed it to successfully challenge Ottoman suzerainity. As late as 1910 the population numbered only 35,000 and consisted of town merchants, fishermen and Bedouin tribesmen. Negotiations for the rights of British engineers to search for oil began in 1920 with agreements finalized in 1934. The Burgan oil-field was discovered in 1938 and high quantity production reached in 1946. At that time,

Kuwait began to develop from a tiny Sheikdom to become the highly developed state which it is at present.

## POLITICAL AND GOVERNMENT CONDITIONS

Kuwait is a constitutional monarchy under the control of Amir Jabbar Al-Sabah. Legislative power is vested in the National Assembly with 50 elected members. Administration is under the control of the Council of Ministers. It is significantly influenced by Saudi Arabia in its political policies. The basis of all law is the Quran.

## ECONOMY

The basis for the entire economy of Kuwait is oil, which accounts for 95% of all export revenue. An ambitious development program has been pursued which involves overseas investments, water desalinization plants, widespread housing development plans and other revenue diversification. Kuwait offers large interest free loans and non-refundable grants to other more slowly developing nations. Cutbacks in oil production to insure the development of a lasting economic foundation are now occurring. New projects in hydroponics, animal husbandry and atomic power are under way. The per capita GNP is over US$ 11,000 and the Kuwait dinar is equivalent to US$ 3.60 in 1979.

## CHURCH STATISTICS FOR KUWAIT

Note: Statistics have been taken from different sources and are the most current data available. Definitions of "membership" vary among churches and may not always be comparable. Not all known churches have been included in this list.

| Church or Mission Name | Communicants (Full Members) | Community (Estimate) |
|---|---|---|
| PROTESTANT | | |
| Anglican | | 1,350 |
| Church of South India | | 100 |
| Evangelical | | 1,300 |
| Indian Brethren | | 100 |
| Indian Pentecostal | | 200 |
| Mar Thomite | | 1,600 |
| Seventh-day Adventist | | 50 |
| CATHOLIC | | |
| Latin-rite | | 13,000 |
| Armenian | | 350 |
| Chaldean | | 1,200 |
| Coptic | | 50 |
| Maronite | | 1,800 |
| Melkite | | 2,900 |
| Syrian | | 200 |
| Orthodox | | |
| Eastern Orthodox | | 6,000 |
| Oriental including | | 10,000 |
| Armenian | | 6,600 |
| Coptic | | 1,300 |
| Syrian | | 2,100 |
| Nestorian | | 400 |

SELECTED BIBLIOGRAPHY AND INFORMATION SOURCES

The sources listed below are to help the reader find additional information on this country and Christian ministries there.  This list does not try to be comprehensive or complete.

DOCUMENTS

General

Area Handbook for the Peripheral States of the Arabian Peninsula, Washington D.C.: Stanford Research Institute, 1971

Fisher, W.B.,The Middle East and North Africa, London, England:  Europa Publications Limited,1978

Wallace, John,The Middle East Yearbook, London, England:  I.C.  Magazines Limited, 1978

Weekes, Richard,Muslim Peoples:  A World Ethnographic Survey, Westport:  Greenwood Press, 1978

Christian

Dayton, Edward,Mission Handbook, Monrovia: MARC, 1976

Horner, Norman,Present Day Christianity in the Gulf States, New Jersey:  Occasional Bulletin,

ACKNOWLEDGEMENTS

The information in this profile was taken from many resources which were the best available to the editors at the time of preparation.  However, the accuracy of the information cannot be guaranteed.  Views expressed or implied in this publication are not necessarily those of World Vision.  The editors have tried to present the ministries of various organizations in an objective manner, without undue bias or emphasis.  Where we have failed, we apologize for erroneous impressions that may result and request that comments and corrections be sent to MARC, 919 West Huntington Drive, Monrovia, California, USA, 91016.  We appreciate and acknowledge the comments and contributions of various organizations and individuals in the preparation of this publication.

# STATUS OF CHRISTIANITY COUNTRY PROFILE

# LEBANON

banking and educational center to a city of rubble and turmoil. Reconstruction has been hindered by disagreements among developers and government officials. The once prosperous economy has been reduced to subsistence levels. The ramifications of the loss of many professionals and skilled workers through emigration are presently widespread and will have long-range affects on the economy and society within Lebanon and the entire Middle East.

Mission agencies have been very busy in relief and development projects among thousands of refugees and war victims. Several church related organizations have made available millions of dollars for relief. Self-help projects are motivating Lebanese to rebuild even when it is difficult and costly.

## SUMMARY

AREA - 10,400 square kilometers (3,900 square miles)
POPULATION - 2,400,000
RELIGION - Sunni Muslim 36%, Shia Muslim 24%, Maronites 15%, Greek Orthodox 8%, Druze 5%, Armenian Orthodox 4%, Greek Melkite 4%, Other Christian 4%

The Lebanese civil war has resulted in radical social, economic and political changes. Thousands of Christians emigrated as thousands of Muslims immigrated. The Christians no longer dominate the majority in political or economic terms. Changes are rapidly occuring as the Muslims takes control and rearrange the government policies and values. Civil wars in Lebanon have been primarily social revolutions rather than religious conflicts. Some groups of Christians, specifically the Maronites, interjected religious differences as a basis for resisting Muslim rule.

Lebanon was a leader for the rest of the world in demonstrating the compatability of Christians with Muslims and Arabs with non-Arabs. The good will dissolved as the Muslim majority assumed more direct control. Chaos reduced Beirut from the position of being the leading Middle East

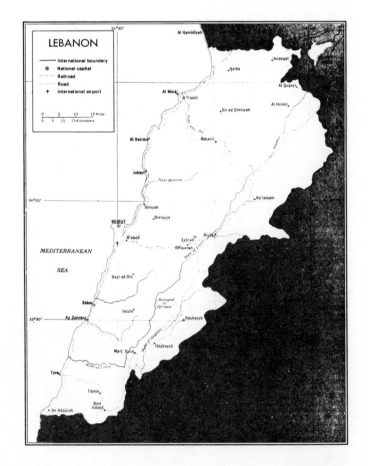

*This program is jointly carried out by the Strategy Working Group of the Lausanne Committee for World Evangelization and MARC, a ministry of World Vision International. For further information on the program, please write: MARC, 919 West Huntington Drive, Monrovia, CA 91016 U.S.A.*

Several distinct people groups within Lebanon remain unreached. The Druzes (6%) are members of a well organized community. They are a religious sect which is a schism of a schism of Islam. Their ancestors were part of the Ismaili tribes in Arabia which had broken away from traditional Muslim teachings in order to pursue mythical occult teachings. The Druzes broke from the Ismailis in the tenth century and moved with their clans to Egypt. They cannot be classified as Muslim since they reject Mohammad as 'The Prophet' and do not accept the Quran. They have been known to agree with whatever authority might be in power but simultaneously maintain their own secret beliefs. Only a few educated holy men know and discuss the secret teachings. Old social structures and cultural patterns are dissolving as the children go away to schools throughout Lebanon. For years they exerted political pressure for policies to preserve the rights of minorities. They shared the slopes of Mount Lebanon with Maronite Christians and thus were caught in the middle of fighting factions. They are not supportive of Maronite Christian resistance movements but have still been attacked by forces with whom they are in agreeement. Many of the Druze homes, farms and fields have been destroyed.

Syrian immigrants have streamed in to Lebanon since 1950 and now form 27% of the total population. Most of them are agriculturalists or industrial laborers. As Sunni Muslims they have strong ties with Damascus and other Arab nations. The Syrian Deterent Force was sent to Lebanon to stop civil war but became directly involved in conflict when it began shelling Maronite sections of Beirut. In the process they also destroyed many Greek and Armenian sectors of the city. Talk concerning the partition of Lebanon has been widespread.

Shia Muslims (24%) are a minority group within the population. For centuries they have been coastal town dwellers and rural farmers in southern Lebanon. Many are poor farm workers, uneducated and usually not involved in radical uprisings.

Christianity has been present in some form or other in Lebanon continuously since the first century A.D.. Lebanon is unusual as an Arab country in that such a high percentage of the population are Christian. Protestants, however, make up only a tiny minority (1%) of the total Christian population. Of the remaining 39%, the largest single group is the Maronite Catholic Church, which comprises 43% of the total Christian population.

The Lebanese constitution calls for complete freedom of religion. Christian missionaries have been faced with restrictions, particularly in recent years. Problems encountered are usually the result of a social tensions when a person desires to change religion. There has been considerable antagonism between Catholic and Protestant groups with regard to evangelistic endeavors.

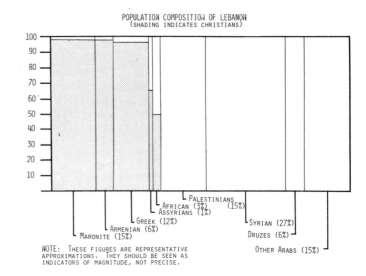

POPULATION COMPOSITION OF LEBANON
(SHADING INDICATES CHRISTIANS)

NOTE: THESE FIGURES ARE REPRESENTATIVE APPROXIMATIONS. THEY SHOULD BE SEEN AS INDICATORS OF MAGNITUDE, NOT PRECISE.

## NATIONAL CHURCHES

The Christian community in Lebanon is proportionally the largest of all the Middle East countries. The Protestants number around 23,000, or approximately 1% of the total population, whereas the Catholics (all rites) make up about 21%.

## PROTESTANT CHURCHES

The largest denomination found in Lebanon is the National Evangelical Union. It was at one time associated with the United Presbyterian Church which began its work in the middle of the nineteenth century. The National Evangelical Union has received aid from the foreign mission board in the U.S. which has been of tremendous help in the face of destruction and damage of church property. A total of 26 Synod churches throughout Lebanon are ministered to by 15 ordained pastors. Education and rural church ministry have been the outstanding areas of work. One seminary, one college, and five elementary/secondary schools are staffed and maintained by the denomination.

The Baptist missions have produced some of the fastest growing and most active national churches. Work began in 1890 by a young Lebanese man who had been converted while in the U.S. and then returned to his home with definite commitment to Baptist missions. Other missionaries did not begin work in Lebanon until 1948 when two Southern Baptists from Palestine settled in Beirut. Outreach to the Arab world is now centered in Lebanon. Baptist missionaries are involved in international ministries of literature publication, broadcasting and leadership training. Several national pastors were forced to emigrate and missionaries forced to leave but 12 Baptist churches continued serving the Lebanese. Project proposals include broadcasts in Arabic to every Arab nation. Membership dropped significantly (84%) in the middle of the civil wars.

The Middle East Council of Churches which serves the entire Arab world, is centered in Beirut. The MECC has been the agent of ecumenicity in the Middle East since its formation and has been active in many areas of ministry such as refugee aid, education, medicine and literature.

## CATHOLIC CHURCHES

Maronites are by far the largest Christian community. Their church, founded by St. Maron in the 5th century, is truly Lebanese in its constituency. Congregations now found in other countries are composed almost entirely of Lebanese emigrants. Although they use the Arabic language in their liturgy, they have been in full communion with Rome as an entire church since the 12th century and must be classified as an integral part of Roman Catholicism. Like the Uniate churches (a designation which the Maronites properly disclaim for themselves), they are administered through a patriarch who for them is second in ecclesiastical authority only to the Pope of Rome. The Maronite Patriarch was at one time a very influential figure in political affairs. With the suppression of the Maronite forces by the Muslims, the church has lost its influence.

## ORTHODOX CHURCHES

Eastern Orthodoxy has an ancient and venerable history in the Middle East through the auspices of the Greek Orthodox Church. The old Cathedral of St. George, in the middle of Beirut, symbolizes the antiquity of their ministry in the Middle East. Both lay workers and clergy of the Greek Orthodox Church of Lebanon have been prominent in the worldwide Orthodox Youth Movement. Their involvement in the World Council of Churches and the Middle East Council of Churches affirms their concern for a continuing influence in the world. Lebanon's Greek Orthodox populace employ Byzantine liturgy in Arabic, a liturgy and practice which has given rise to the description of these people as "Eastern Christians" because of a pervasive emphasis on the resurrection.

The term "Oriental Orthodox" refers to a smaller but still considerable number of Christians grouped in four large congregations, specifically; the Coptic Orthodox of Egypt, the Armenian Orthodox, the Syrian Orthodox, and the Ethiopian Orthodox. Oriental Orthodoxy is represented in Lebanon primarily by the Armenian and Syrian Churches. One Egyptian monk organized a Coptic Orthodox congregation among Egyptian immigrants to Lebanon.

The Armenian Catholicesate of Cilicia located at Antelias, is one of the two major Armenian centers in the world. The Armenian Catholicos Patriarch, who resides in Beirut, presides over a community which extends far beyond Lebanon and embodies one of the oldest continuing traditions. Armenians still find the cultural and religious focus of their lives in the church.

The Syrian Orthodox are more numerous in Syria and Iraq, but their number in Lebanon has grown through immigration. Their church has been in existence since the very earliest Christian centuries. It is open to involvement in the ecumenical movement and is a member of the Middle East Council of Churches.

Throughout Christian history minority groups have separated from the Orthodox churches for a variety of reasons, but all for the purpose of uniting with and submitting to the rule of the Pope. Four of these Uniate Catholic Churches are prominent in Lebanon. The Greek Melkite, Syrian, Chaldean (Assyrian) and Armenian Churches have active congregations in several parts of Lebanon though most were centered in Beirut before the destruction of many Christian sectors. They have kept most of their ancient customs and and have retained familiar liturgies in their own languages.

The Assyrian Church of the East, popularly called the Nestorian Church, claims a membership of 7,000. The struggle of the Nestorian Church to maintain and revitalize its witness in the modern world is motivated by a long history of heroism and missionary zeal throughout the Near East.

## COOPERATIVE AGENCIES

The Christian scene presents a bewildering variety of churches. Problems of disunity are baffling in Lebanon with Christian groups fighting against other Christian groups and against Muslims in civil war. Wide differences still continue in languages, customs, theological emphases, educational levels among clergy and even ecclesiastical calendars. An interconfessional group of clergy, "Groupe Occumenique de Pastorale, " met periodically for fellowship and mutual planning. The Middle East Council of Churches, the United Bible Societies, the Orthodox Youth Movement, the Near East School of Theology, the Association for Theological Education in the Near East, the Newman Club, the University Christian Center, the Clarist Sisters` Monastery of Unity, the YMCA, the YWCA and the National Evangelical Union are all active organizations in Lebanon.

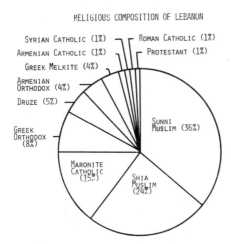

RELIGIOUS COMPOSITION OF LEBANON

Syrian Catholic (1%)
Armenian Catholic (1%)
Greek Melkite (4%)
Armenian Orthodox (4%)
Druze (5%)
Greek Orthodox (8%)
Maronite Catholic (15%)
Roman Catholic (1%)
Protestant (1%)
Sunni Muslim (36%)
Shia Muslim (24%)

## PROTESTANT MISSIONS

In 1968, there were 45 Protestant missions working in Lebanon with a total missionary force of 300, and church membership nearly 27,000. The largest number of missionaries were affiliated with the General Conference of Seventh-Day Adventists. The Lebanon Evangelical Mission was also substantially represented along with the Southern Baptist Mission and the United Presbyterian Church in the USA. A very large percentage of the missionary force in Lebanon was located in the capital city of Beirut. Most foreigners evacuated from Beirut and many from Lebanon in June of 1976 following the assassination of the U.S. ambassador. Only those with dual citizenship remained. Missionaries were forced to turn all work over to nationals or totally abandon the work.

The activity in which missions were involved with the most was education. The first Protestant missionaries established the Syrian Protestant College which became the well known American University of Beirut. Primary and secondary schools were an important part of the overall mission strategies. The Seventh-Day Adventists were almost exclusively involved in the field of education.

The Christian and Missionary Alliance (CMA) has been actively involved in relief and development work with self-help programs for the citizens of Lebanon. They found that many individuals had basically given up hope of ever rebuilding homes and livelihoods. When motivation was stimulated by matching fund self-help programs the people responded positively and started rebuilding communities. CMA has become the major agency through which funds are distributed. They have short term management personnel working closely with national church members and offer solutions to physical, mental, emotional and spiritual problems for the Lebanese.

## CATHOLIC MISSIONS

The earliest Catholic missionaries were Roman Catholics who entered Lebanon at the time of the Crusades. However, there was little missionary activity after that until 1823, when representatives of the American Board of Commissioners for Foreign Missions began work in Beirut. Later in 1870 they turned their evangelistic, educational and medical work over to the American Presbyterian Mission which took on the translation of the Bible into Arabic as their first task. The Catholic Relief Services developed a four million dollar program in which 12,000 tons of food and reconstruction materials were distributed following the civil wars.

## MAJOR CHRISTIAN ACTIVITIES

### EVANGELISM

Direct evangelistic efforts are limited in spite of the number of mission agencies, national churches and Christian organizations involved in ministry in Lebanon. Several groups have historically been involved in student evangelism including Campus Crusade, Navigators, Inter-Varsity and Youth for Christ. With major disruptions of educational institutions have come restrictions and limitations on student work.

### LITERATURE

The great majority of books being published in Lebanon are translations from English books. A very effective exception to this rule is the literature work sponsored by the Evangelical Carmel Mission, a German mission agency based in Beirut. Books, phamphlets, tracts, and magazines geared especially to the Muslim mind are published regularly. The civil wars have disrupted the service but it is being continued since it has proven to be very acceptable and effective. The Arabic Literature Mission and Christian Arabic Literature League are growing groups concerned with the publication and distribution of Christian Arabic literature. A number of other smaller groups are also involved extensively in the preparation of literature for Lebanon and the entire Arab world. Operation Mobilization has been involved in many different aspects of the literature production and distribution process. Several Christian bookstores in Beirut have supplied the city with Christian literature in Arabic, Armenian, English, and Farsi. Several were destroyed in war and others have been recovering slowly from economic and social upheavals.

A number of independent and denominational groups are active in correspondence courses. For years headquarters have been in Beirut. Some have moved out and others are attempting to rebuild within the city. They are able to reach a wide spectrum of people in most Middle Eastern countries and several North African nations.

## BIBLE TRANSLATION

The Bible Society in Lebanon handles almost the sole responsiblity for translation and distribution of the Scriptures. As far back as 1961, the Bible Society distributed 49,070 Bibles, Testaments and Scripture portions. The entire Bible was translated into Arabic by the American Presbyterians when they first began work in Lebanon in 1870. Although some minor revisions were made after that, no major revisions took place until the 1970s, when a new simplified Arabic version was published.

Translations in Syriac (Aramaic), as well as some dialects of Persian and Kurdish are available for members of minority groups within Lebanon and in surrounding territories. Armenian Bibles are available to Beirut businessmen, refugees and emigrating masses.

Distribution is mainly through direct channels within the Bible Society and by colporteurs within the country.

### EDUCATION

Much of the Protestant work was directed toward educational ministry. Twenty-three schools and four seminaries were operated by North American Protestant missions personnel. Most are now in the hands of national workers. The United Presbyterians related to and supported one seminary, one college, and five elementary/secondary schools. The Lebanon Evangelical Mission also contributed significantly to the educational field by sponsoring seven schools including a Bible Institute and a school for the blind. Most of 41 schools run by Protestants included religious teaching and evangelistic outreach. Theological Education by Extension enables national workers, pastors and teachers to be trained in the Scriptures.

Roman Catholics maintained nine seminaries in Lebanon, as well as the University of St. Joseph in Beirut, the only Pontifical university in the Middle East. They were also very involved in parochial elementary and secondary schools which once accounted for 20% of the total Lebanese school population.

### SOCIAL CONCERN

Several Christian Humanitarian organizations including World Vision are involved in aiding refugees, orphans and war victims. The Christian and Missionary Alliance Church is the major agency and organization through which materials, supplies, and funds for medical relief, and reconstruction are distributed. Many church related organizations are participating in massive relief projects for the people of Lebanon.

## NATION AND ITS PEOPLE

### POPULATION

The total population of Lebanon has dropped from 3.1 million in 1974 to approximately 2.4 million in 1979. The growth rate (3%) has remained relatively high. relating specifically to births and deaths. The number of people leaving the country is extremely high. They have found homes in Cyprus, western nations and even Israel. Density has understandably fluctuated with migration and is presently as high as 836 per square kilometer (334 per square mile) in some agricultural regions. Over 43% of the population in 1978 was under 14 and only 3% were over 65. Over 60,000 people, mostly nonmilitant citizens, were killed in the civil war in 1975-1976 and thousands more have died in shelling attacks since then.

Lebanon has for centuries hosted a multi-ethnic populace. Immigrants and emigrants have come and gone in huge numbers. Several distinct people groups with large populations resided in Lebanon shortly before the civil wars. Over 370,000 Palestinians including 70,000 refugees, comprised 15% of the total Lebanese population. Egyptians enjoyed positions of affluence as educators, film producers and entertainers. Nearly 75,000 Egyptians accounted for 3% of the population. African businessmen and civil workers (3%) totaled 75,000. Since relations with France had remained cordial since the colonial era, 30,000 French men and women were comfortable in residing in Lebanon. Assyrians constituted another 1%. Properly called Nestorian Christians, they were descendants of refugees from Iraq and Syria. Nearly 6% of the Lebanese population were Druze inhabitants of the rugged highlands of Mount Lebanon and over 180,000 Armenians had settled in Lebanon. Beirut became known as the Metropolis of Armenians in the Near East. Nearly 90% of their homes and shops were destroyed in shelling attacks and demolition projects. Many moved south or emigrated to other countries. Just a few of the 60 Armenian schools, 20 churches and hundreds of businesses have been rebuilt. Though they sought a neutral stance they were attacked from all sides. They have survived untold persecution across the centuries and the latest civil wars have forced many to once again flee from their homes.

Maronites, who comprised nearly 50% of the population before the civil wars, suffered heavy losses in battle although they were not directly involved in fighting. Radical factions of Maronites, however, kept the entire Maronite population under siege. Syrians and other Muslim groups now form a majority within Lebanon.

Over 25% of the inhabitants of Lebanon are refugees. Palestinians had journeyed to a land which they had hoped would provide security, employment and food. Their dreams were shattered along with the prosperous livelihoods of 400,000 Armenians, Assyrians and other Lebanese who became refugees in their own country. Many fled to southern Lebanon where they were offered protection by Israel if they were found acceptable. Those who had any association with groups or individuals whom the Israelis disliked, were sent back north or had the homes in which they were staying blown up.

### LITERACY AND LANGUAGE

Arabic is the only official language and both classical and modern forms are used. A few different dialects are used by Druzes and other Arab minorities but all understand and primarily use Arabic. Nearly 40% of the population speak French and government publications are published occasionally in French and Arabic. English is increasingly used for trade, travel and educational purposes. Other languages used by minority groups include Armenian Kurdish, Assyrian and for liturgical purposes, Syriac, Greek and Latin.

### RELIGION

Christianity has been present continuously in Lebanon since the first century. It was not until after the Arab conquest of Lebanon that Islam became a major religious factor in the nation. Of the Christian population approximately 43% are Maronite, 8% Greek Catholic and 1% Protestant. The Muslim majority is divided into the two sects of Sunni and Shia. There are also a number of adherents of the Druze religion.

### GEOGRAPHY AND CLIMATE

Lebanon is a tiny country situated on the eastern edge of the Mediterranean Sea and is bordered by Syria, Jordan, and Israel. It has an area of 10,400 square kilometers (4,015 square miles). A wealth of topographical and climatic variations are found in the nation in spite of its size. Moving eastward, a narrow coastal plain at the Mediterranean Sea abruptly changes into a beautiful, high mountain range famous for abundant springs and peaks as high as 3,500 meters (10,000 feet). Further east, a deep valley (the Bekaa) is a main agricultural center.

The climate varies from moderate temperatures on the coast to heavy snow falls in the mountains. Summers are very hot and winters cold in the Bekaa Valley. Rainfall varies from 38 centimeters (15 inches) per year in the Bekaa Valley to 100 centimeters (40 inches) per year on the coast. Most rainfall occurs only between the months of October and April.

## HISTORY

The Lebanese are descendants of the ancient Phoenicians, who were noted for their accomplishments in trade and exploration in early years of the history of mankind. They boast of a longstanding heritage and of having the oldest port in the world, Byblos, within their country. The cities of Tyre and Sidon are also very well known particularly because of their importance in Biblical records. The cedars of Lebanon were taken to ports throughout the world and used in temples and palaces. Following the earthly life of Christ, Lebanon was mainly Christian in religion until the ninth century, when an Arab tribe settled in central Lebanon bringing with it the Arabic language and the Islam religion.

At about 1840, the country came under the domination of the Ottoman Empire. In the 1860's, social and economic discontent led to a rebellion of the Lebanese making it condusive for the French to intervene. The French remained in Lebanon until 1946. In 1920, the French created the State of the Greater Lebanon, and in 1926 helped the Lebanese establish a constitution. It did not prove successful and was suspended after five years. Independence was granted to Lenanon in 1941 although France kept a hand in government affairs until 1946. Civil war disrupted Lebanon in 1975 through 1978. National industries were shut down, ports closed and many Maronite and Armenian sectors of Beirut were completely flattened. Palestians joined leftist Muslims who were joined by Syrians in combatting the Christian resistance forces.

## ECONOMY

Despite the fact that only 22% of the 40% cultivatable land area of Lebanon is cultivated, agriculture is the major economic activity. A wide range of crops includes wheat, oranges, grapes, olives, peaches, apples and other nuts and fruits. A majority of these crops are exported with over 63% going to Arab nations. Beirut, for years a free market, was one of the largest and most active ports in the Middle East until civil wars destroyed the city and economy. Little mineral wealth is found in Lebanon itself, but its geographic location and port facilities make it important to the oil industry. Before the wars, tourism stood as the second largest source of income for Lebanon. This has decreased considerably since many of the hotels in Beirut were damaged or destroyed.

# CHURCH STATISTICS FOR LEBANON

Note: Statistics have been taken from different sources and are the most current data available. Definitions of "membership" vary among churches and may not always be comparable.

| Church or Mission Name | Communicants (Full Members) | Community (Estimate) |
|---|---|---|
| **PROTESTANT** | | |
| Arab Episcopal | 1,200 | |
| Armenian Evangelical | 5,000 | |
| Armenian Brethren | 250 | |
| Baptist | 2,000 | |
| Christian and Missionary Alliance | 250 | |
| Church of God | 300 | |
| National Evangelical Church | 3,500 | |
| National Evangelical Synod | 9,000 | |
| Seventh-day Adventist | 750 | |
| **ROMAN CATHOLIC** | | |
| Armenian | 100,000 | |
| Assyrian | 5,000 | |
| Greek Melkite | 100,000 | |
| Maronite | 400,000 | |
| Roman | 28,000 | |
| Syrian | 14,000 | |
| **ORTHODOX** | | |
| Armenian | 28,000 | |
| Coptic | 4,000 | |
| Greek | 200,000 | |
| Syrian | 14,000 | |

SELECTED BIBLIOGRAPHY AND INFORMATION SOURCES

The sources listed below are to help the reader find additional information on this country and Christian ministries there. This list does not try to be comprehensive or complete.

## DOCUMENTS

### General

Europa Publication, ed., Middle East and North Africa, 1971-72, London: Europa Publications, 1971.

Lang, David Marshall, The Armenians, London: Minority Rights Group, 1977.

Rycroft, W. Stanley, and Clemmer, Myrtle M., Factual Study of the Middle East, New York: United Presbyterian Church in the USA, 1962.

### Christian

Horner, Norman A., Statistical Survey of Christian Communities in Cyprus, Egypt, Ethiopia, Iran, Iraq, Jordan, Lebanon, Sudan, Syria, Turkey, Beirut: United Presbyterian Church, USA, 1972.

Kane, J. Herbert, A Global View of Christian Missions, Grand Rapids: Baker Book House, 1971.

## ACKNOWLEDGMENTS

The information in this profile was taken from many sources which were the best available to the editors at the time of preparation. However, the accuracy of the information cannot be guaranteed. Views expressed or implied in this publication are not necessarily those of World Vision. The editors have tried to present the ministries of various organizations in an objective manner, without undue bias or emphasis. Where we have failed, we apologize for erroneous impressions that may result and request that comments and corrections be sent to MARC, 919 West Huntinton Drive, Monrovia, California, USA 91016. We appreciate and acknowledge the comments and contributions of various organizations and individuals in the preparation of this publication.

# STATUS OF CHRISTIANITY COUNTRY PROFILE

# OMAN

Oman remained isolated and unobtrusive until 1970 when the sultan's son realized that, in comparison with other Gulf States, Oman was the most underdeveloped. He led a bloodless coup and established a progressive regime which continues to rule. Since that coup, Oman has launched into many programs for national development.

By 1978, only 20 Omani citizens were Christians and even some of those were immigrants from other Gulf States. The small Arabic speaking fellowship faces an immense task of evangelism among the unevangelized of Oman.

## SUMMARY

AREA - 300,000 square kilometers (120,000 square miles)
POPULATION - 800,000 (mid-1977 estimate)
RELIGION - 99% Muslim, 1% Christian and other

Until 1970, Oman remained one of the most backward and underdeveloped of the various states on the Arabian Peninsula. Partly for that reason, it has one of the smallest expatriate communities and thus a smaller percentage of Christians. The history of Christianity within Oman, however, is significant. The Portugese fortified Muscat in the 16th century. Later, missionaries from the Reformed Church in America (RCA), led by Dr. Samuel Zwemer and Dr. James Cantine, established their first contacts in the Arabian Peninsula while in Oman.

Early history of Oman is recorded in Sumerian tablets of the third millenium B.C. After conversion to Islam, Oman figured heavily in the maritime history of the Muslim world. Her influence extended to East Africa and India. The ebb and flow of Oman's history depended largely on the power of the Ottoman sultanate.

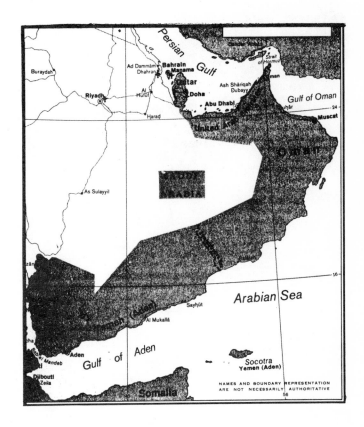

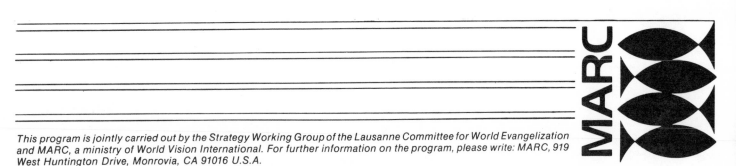

*This program is jointly carried out by the Strategy Working Group of the Lausanne Committee for World Evangelization and MARC, a ministry of World Vision International. For further information on the program, please write: MARC, 919 West Huntington Drive, Monrovia, CA 91016 U.S.A.*

Several varieties of Muslims comprise the vast majority of the population of Oman which is entirely unreached.  There are approximately 700,000 Arabs, a vast majority of whom have little knowledge whatsoever of the Gospel.  The indigenous Arabs are of the Ihmadi sect of Sunni Islam.  The total number of Arab Muslim converts is incredibly small and most people who have had any contact with the Gospel have expressed resistance to it.  The largest group of immigrant Arabs in Oman is the Iranians.  They are predominantly of the Shiite sect of Islam and number 50,000.  The Baluch, a people group from Iran and Pakistan, have a religious position which is unclear but seems to have elements of the Sunni sect of Islam.  About 25,000 Baluch have settled along the coast of the Persian Gulf but not all within the borders of Oman.  Nearly 12,000 Indians and 10,000 Pakistanis also reside in Oman.  Many of them are also Muslims but not all of them. A significant Christian minority exists among them and an Urdu speaking congregation has been established within the community.  Though the Pakistanis and Indians are unreached they at least have a Christian witness among them.

Christianity has had exposure in Oman in different periods throughout history.  The first was during the early centuries of the church.  Little is known about this period other than brief comments made by itinerant Christian disciples.  In the 16th century the Portugese, who were Catholics, established themselves in Oman. They were expelled just 100 years later. A few Christains stayed but most were forced to leave.  Initial contacts made by leaders of the RCA in 1890 resulted in the establishment of a missions station by 1900.  Oman was found to be one of the most open and receptive fields of work established by RCA missionaries.  As many as three dozen Omani Muslims converted to Christianity.  A few individuals from the original group of converts remain scattered throughout the country.  Others have joined with other Arabic-speaking Christians to form a small fellowship of 20.  Outside of the small Arabic group, Christianity is an expatriate phenomenon.

## NATIONAL CHURCHES

A large part of the Christian community in Oman is concentrated in the two cities of Muscat and Matrah.  A few small expatriate groups and perhaps six Omani Muslim converts are scattered over the remainder of the country.  About .25% of Oman's population is Christian.

## PROTESTANT

Protestant work in Oman dates back to 1890 when first contact was made by the Reformed Church of America (RCA).  Five Protestant denominations are present in Oman.  The services held in the English language draw nearly 500 people together, mainly expatriates.  A significant Urdu speaking congregation of 100 has been established among Pakistani Christians. Three small Indian denominations number a total of 200 members.  Finally, there is a small Arabic-speaking church with 20 Omani citizens as members, some of whom are Muslim converts.  Prior to the construction of the large multi-purpose church in Matrah, the RCA mission maintained the only church in Oman.  The government requires that the RCA church in Muscat be a multi-purpose facility. Presently, it us used by six different congregations of various Protestant, Catholic and Orthodox denominations. Several pastors minister to the various

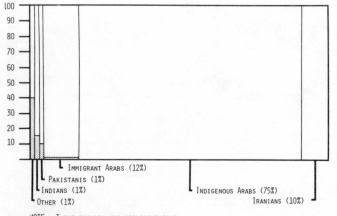

POPULATION COMPOSITION OF OMAN
(SHADING INDICATES CHRISTIANS)

IMMIGRANT ARABS (12%)
PAKISTANIS (1%)
INDIANS (1%)
OTHER (1%)
INDIGENOUS ARABS (75%)
IRANIANS (10%)

NOTE: THESE FIGURES ARE REPRESENTATIVE APPROXIMATIONS.  THEY SHOULD BE SEEN AS INDICATORS OF MAGNITUDE, NOT PRECISE.

Protestant congregations.

## CATHOLIC

Catholic clergymen began work in Oman in 1971 as the result of the needs of the expatriate communities. Worship services are Latin-rite and entirely in English. One Capuchin priest from Bahrain ministers to 700 church members in various locations throughout Oman. In 1976 the ruler of the country provided land for the construction of churches. Protestant and Catholic churches were built on the same sites.

## ORTHODOX

A small Syrian Orthodox church with 125 members meets in the RCA facilities in Muscat. This is a very recent work which focuses primarily on Malabar Indian expatriates.

## COOPERATIVE AGENCIES

No official church councils exist in Oman. Due to the small size of the Christian population, however, close cooperation continues particularly in the use of church buildings and related facilities.

## PROTESTANT MISSIONS

The first land on the Arabian Peninsula which Samuel Zwemer and James Cantine came in contact with was Oman. These pioneers of the Reformed Church of America began mission work in the Gulf in 1890. By 1900, the work was established on a permanent basis. A two-fold approach was pursued. Workers spent half of their time in itineration, travelling from village to village doing medical work as well as preaching and distributing Scripture. One of the major problems encountered was illiteracy. Nearly 98% of the Omanis could not read or write. The other half of their time was spent in establishing medical and educational programs and institutions. Clinics and later hospitals and schools were started in Muscat and Matrah. These became base camps for itinerant "touring" which extended as far as Saudi Arabia. Special trips by medical personnel were arranged for the royal family in Riyadh and Taif. As a result, rulers did not limit the work of missionaries in Oman. A school for slave boys was started in the early 1900`s but, with the termination of slavery, it was discontinued in 1926. Other educational programs established have continued. A girls school is in operation with 130 pupils.

The response to the Gospel was greater in Oman than anywhere else in Arabia. Small groups of converts gathered in Muscat, Matrah and in several of the villages. Oman remained outside the fast-paced development of most other Arabian Gulf states.

Some theorists attribute the openness of the Omanis to the Gospel, to the simple lifestyles of the people, who were less influenced by Great Britain than were citizens of any other Gulf State. The churches established for the new converts to Christianity were, however, structured according to western patterns.

The rapid developments which followed the overthrow of archaic rule in 1971, caused the RCA to significantly alter its ministries. The mission hospital was sold to the government of Oman. Four missionaries and several Christian Indian staff members continue to work at the hospital. A similar arrangement exists for two smaller medical clinics. The girls school is now co-educational and is also run by the government but with the same RCA principle. The only Christian bookstore is under the direction of the

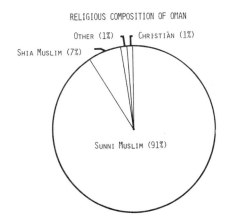

RELIGIOUS COMPOSITION OF OMAN

Other (1%)    Christian (1%)
Shia Muslim (7%)
Sunni Muslim (91%)

Reformed Church of Denmark. It is quite popular and exceeds US $1 million in general sales per year. Bibles and Christian publications are available in several languages.

## CATHOLIC MISSIONS

Saint Francis Xavier passed through the island of Socotra and Muscat during the 16th century on his way to China. He found that a monastery had been established during the Portugese occupation of Muscat and Matrah. When Oman's power declined during the early 18th century, the Portugese were thrust out. With expulsion, all traces of the Catholic community vanished. Modern work by Catholics dates from 1971. Apparently, no missionary emphasis is associated with it since they are there to serve expatriates.

## ORTHODOX

No records of any Orthodox missions work in Oman are available.

## EVANGELISM

In times past, Omanis have been fairly open to the preaching of the Gospel. With the discovery of oil in 1964 and growing development, open evangelism has become more difficult. Government regulations and social pressures which reduce receptivity are continuing to increase. Among Iranians, Baluchs, Pakistanis and Indians very little of the potential for evangelism has been explored. Friendship evangelism is a viable possibility.

## BROADCASTING

Broadcasts of the Gospel in Arabic and other languages can be received in Oman, although no programs are specifically beamed at the Omani people.

## LITERATURE

The Christian bookstore operated by the Reformed Church of Denmark is quite popular. One of the major problems which has just recently begun to recede is the high rate of illiteracy. Even by 1978, 80% of the men and 90% of the women in Oman were illiterate. Scripture distribution has not been widespread though several translations in various languages are available. Literature programs for major non-Arab Muslim communities in Oman are being expanded.

## CHRISTIAN EDUCATION

The mission school in Oman is operated by the goverment but the principal and several teachers are with the RCA. Recently, Muslim leaders charged the school with incompetency in quality of Arabic instruction. Its future is uncertain.

## SOCIAL CONCERN

One hospital and two clinics now operated by the Oman government, continue to be staffed largely by the RCA. The general atmosphere continues to be that of a mission hospital. How long that will continue is questionable.

## NATION AND ITS PEOPLE

### POPULATION

No census has ever been taken in Oman. Population in the 1950's was estimated at 500,000. By 1970 the population had reached 650,000 and in 1978 it approached 800,000. Rate of growth is 3.5% per year. Oman is still 85% rural but is changing rapidly as farmers and herdsmen are attracted to the cities by lucrative jobs.

### COMPOSITION

Arabs account for 86% of the population, or about 700,000 people. More than 99% of the Omani Arabs are Sunni Muslims. The largest immigrant group are the Iranians who number 50,000. They are predominantly Shia Muslims. Baluchs, who are Sunni Muslims, number 23,000. A large number (20,000) of Yemenis and other expatriate Arabs have been attracted by job opportunities. There are also 12,000 Indians and 10,000 Pakistanis in Oman. Most are Muslims of the Sunni sect but there are significant Christian and Hindu minority groups among them. About 5,000 Europeans and Americans reside in the country.

Socio-economically, most of the Omanis are quite poor. Baluchs and rural farmers are at the bottom of the social scale followed closely by laborers in the cities and Bedoiun nomads. Indians, Pakistanis, the educated and Iranians form what may be considered a middle class. At the top of the social scale are Muslim clergy and the ruling families.

### LANGUAGE AND LITERACY

Arabic is the national language in Oman. English is also frequently used by many different minority and majority groups as a common "lingua franca." Minority languages include Farsi, Urdu and Hindi. Many immigrants are literate whereas many Omanis are illiterate. Government policies are irradicating the problem of low literacy.(Approximately 10-20% in 1976)

### RELIGION

Oman is predominantly Muslim with 92% of the total population adhering to Sunni doctrines and 7% following Shia teachings. Christians and those of other religions account for 1% of the population. Most are expatriates.

### GEOGRAPHY AND CLIMATE

The Sultanate of Oman occupies the southeastern corner of the Arabian Peninsula. It borders the United Arab Emirates and Saudi Arabia on the north and the People's Democratic Republic of Yemen on the west. The tip of the Musendam Peninsula at the strait of Hormuz is also a part of Oman. The inland Hajar mountain range parallels the coast and runs the entire length of the country from Muscat to Ras Al-Had in South Yemen (PDRY). It rises to 3,000 meters (9,842 ft.) at its highest point. Two passes break these mountain highlands. Along the ranges where "wadis" (washes, riverbeds) meet, there are a number of inland oases. The southwestern region of Dhofar occupies about 33% of the country and contains woodlands and seasonal grasslands. In this area considerable agricultural and pastoral work is carried on. Rainfall is sporadic and various amounts fall in different areas in different years. As little as 10 centimeters (4 inches) of rain is the average for Muscat each year. Higher elevations may receive as much as 30 centimeters (12 inches) in years when monsoons occur.

### HISTORY

Oman is mentioned in the Sumerian tablets, and in records written by Roman geographers. Falaj irrigation was introduced by Persians during the second century A.D. Oman was one of the first areas converted to Islam during the seventh century. Though often subject to invasion, Oman has remained largely independent since that time. Oman's greatest period of prominence was in the tenth century when Sohar became the largest and most important city in the Arab world. Omani mariners established themselves in Zanzibar and the coast of East Africa. Later, they travelled as far as China. It was an Omani navigator who guided Vasco de Gama from Malindi to Calcutta in India.

Oman's power waned in the 16th century and some of the coastal regions were conquered by the Portugese. By 1730, however, Portugese power declined and sultanate power restored. Not until the mid 1800's was Zanzibar separated from Omani control. When Oman lost control of Zanzibar in 1850, slave trade was restricted and Omani power deteriorated. By 1960 Oman was considered one of the most underdeveloped Arabian sultanates. Oil was found in quantities suitable for commercial development in 1964 following 20 years of exploration. Development was hindered by rebellion in Dhofar which was supported by Marxists in South Yemen (PDRY), and the medieval outlook and policies of Sultan Said. His regime was overthrown by his son, Quboos bin Said, in 1971 and a progressive development program was established. Final victory over rebels was declared in 1975 though minor uprisings by Omanis who are supported by South Yemen have sporadically occurred. Balanced growth is being sought to prevent the shock and problems of economic and development booms.

## GOVERNMENT AND POLITICAL CONDITIONS

Oman is a monarchy ruled by a sultan. National administration is in the hands of the Council of Ministers and the National Development Council. There are 11 administrative regions in Oman. The judicial system is based upon Shariat law from the Quran. Oman is increasingly influenced by Saudi Arabia and conservative Islamic trends continue. The armed forces are small but quite modern with training and equipment supplied by Great Britain and other major powers.

## ECONOMY

Nearly 75% of Oman`s population is involved in agriculture. Primary crops include dates, limes, onions, alfalfa, and vegetables. There are also considerable livestock herds of goats, cattle and sheep. Some social and economic pressures have resulted from the attraction of lucrative jobs in cities, oil fields and refineries. The government, however, is emphasizing agriculture as a major element of balanced development.

A Korean firm has concessions for fishing Omanis waters and is involved in training a modern Omani fishing fleet. Total yearly catch for 1978 was 70,000 tons. Oman has extensive mineral resources. Oil has been commercially produced since 1964 and provides the largest revenues. Considerable copper reserves have been discovered in Sohar as well as coal, asbestos and manganese.

The Omani rial is worth US $2.89. Gross National Product for 1976 was just under US $2 billion. Per capita income is over US $2,000.

CHURCH STATISTICS FOR OMAN

Note: Statistics have been taken from different sources and are the most current data available. Definitions of "membership" vary among churches and may not always be comparable. Not all known churhes have been included in this list.

| Church or Mission Name | Communicants (Full Members) | Community (Estimate) |
|---|---|---|
| PROTESTANT | | |
| Anglican | | 500 |
| Urdu | | 100 |
| Arabic | | 20 |
| Mar Thomite | | 150 |
| Indian Pentecostal | | 30 |
| Indian Brethren | | 30 |
| CATHOLIC | | |
| Latin-rite | | 700 |
| ORTHODOX | | |
| Syrian Orthodox | | 125 |

# SELECTED BIBLIOGRAPHY AND INFORMATION SOURCES

The sources listed below are to help the reader find additional information on this country and Christian ministries there.  This list does not try to be comprehensive or complete.

DOCUMENTS

General

Area Handbook for the Peripheral States of the Arabian Peninsula, Washington D.C.: Stanford Research Institute, 1971

Fisher, W.B., The Middle East and North Africa, London, England:  Europa Publications Limited, 1978

Wallace, John, The Middle East Yearbook, London, England:  I.C.  Magazines Limited, 1973

Weekes, Richard, Muslim Peoples:  A World Ethnographic Survey, Westport:  Greenwood Press, 1978

Christian

Dayton, Edward R., editor, Mission Handbook, Monrovia: MARC, 1976.

Horner, Norman, Present Day Christianity in the Gulf States, New Jersey:  Occasional Bulletin, 1977

## ACKNOWLEDGEMENTS

The information in this profile was taken from many resources which were the best available to the editors at the time of preparation.  However, the accuracy of the information cannot be guaranteed.  Views expressed or implied in this publication are not necessarily those of World Vision.  The editors have tried to present the ministries of various organizations in an objective manner, without undue bias or emphasis.  Where we have failed, we apologize for erroneous impressions that may result and request that comments and corrections be sent to MARC, 919 West Huntington Drive, Monrovia, California, USA, 91016.  We appreciate and acknowledge the comments and contributions of various organizations and individuals in the preparation of this publication.

# STATUS OF CHRISTIANITY COUNTRY PROFILE

# PEOPLE'S DEMOCRATIC REPUBLIC OF YEMEN

## SUMMARY

AREA - 388,100 square kilometers (149,269 square miles)
POPULATION - 1,800,000
RELIGION - 50% Sunni Muslim, 49% Shia Muslim, 1% Other

Contrast and diversity best describes and characterizes the people, nation and land of the People's Democratic Republic of Yemen (PDRY). It is demonstrated in the differences between the Arabs living in Aden and the more numerous tribesmen in the rural areas. The Adenese are contemporary cosmopolitans who emphasize industrial development, educational advancement and political centralization. The tribesmen are cultivators with ancient cultures and lifestyles who emphasize Islamic law (Sharia), kinship ties and subsistence farming. Contrast is also expressed by the presence of communist leaders in an Islamic State. If either ideology were strictly adhered to they could not coexist. Nomadic Bedouins have roamed Arabia for centuries. The government is attempting to rapidly change their culture by destroying it. Both dust storms and monsoons damage crops because of the floods and droughts which occur within the same year.

Christian missions accompanied British colonialism. Both had significant affects on the lives of the people and most assumed that the two were directly associated. Hospitals, clinics and stations established by the missionaries were welcomed since there were very few medical facilities operating and the people needed them. The Church of Scotland, Danish Missions, Red Sea Mission Team and Sudan Interior Mission were actively involved in medical and social work until they were forced to evacuate the country.

Political instability and social unrest have been prevalent since independence was established in 1967. The economy is continually bolstered by foreign aid. Subsistence farming by half the people contrasts with industries and shipping services in Aden. The People's Democratic Republic of Yemen is located in an area described by economists as the "arc of instability." Major powers of the world actively compete for control of land bordering the Red Sea and Arabian Sea.

The PDRY includes three islands and the crucial port of Aden which may become excellent military facilities in the Gulf of Aden and the Indian Ocean. All ships which pass through the Red Sea pass the shores of the PDRY. Thus Aden remains "the eye of Arabia" to everyone.

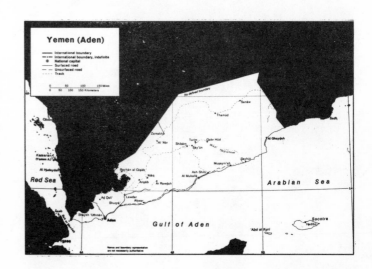

*This program is jointly carried out by the Strategy Working Group of the Lausanne Committee for World Evangelization and MARC, a ministry of World Vision International. For further information on the program, please write: MARC, 919 West Huntington Drive, Monrovia, CA 91016 U.S.A.*

# UNREACHED PEOPLES

Many distinct unreached people groups live in the PDRY. Nearly 1400 separate tribes are arranged in confederations called "zei." Chiefs "Immams" and Muslim holymen "Sayyids" provide strong leadership. The tribes vary according to locality and occupation. Four major classifications describe the tribes. Agriculturalists are located in fertile regions which are able to maintain permanent settlements. Pastoralists live in permanent settlements surrounded by grazing land where they raise sheep, cattle and goats. Semi-nomadic tribes remain settled as long as natural conditions permit but are often forced to journey to alternate locations by floods and droughts. They often survive by engaging in subsistence farming and livestock herding. Nomads, including the Bedouin, spend their entire lives traveling from oasis to oasis while herding their livestock. They are noted for their camel breeding and trading.

The tribes basically maintain Islamic law for both civil and religious matters. Sayyids serve as judges and enforcers of the Quran. They are traditionally arbitrators of disputes and mediators in differences among feuding tribes. The communist government in Aden has attempted to diminish the importance of tribal and religious hierarchies.

Cultural traditons have remained unchanged in the isolated regions. Most tribes were virtually self-sufficient through local trade until the 20th century. Cultural changes rendered by colonialism and communism left the people dependent on and controlled by others. Present government policies include the forced settlement of the portion of the population which is semi-nomadic or nomadic (10%). One of the top priorities of the government is the settlement of the 156,000 Bedouin nomads. However, the nomadic Bedouin do not adapt to the life of the agriculturalist easily. The government gathers the young Bedouin boys, the very strength and future of the Bedouin society, and forces them to attend school through the seventh grade. Tribal ties are weakened as the people are subjected to the regulations of centralized government. As a result of these efforts by the government, thousands of tribesman have joined the nearly 300,000 refugees who have settled in the Yemen Arab Republic. Some of the tribes of the northeast have been able to escape government encroachment and are isolated enough to avoid everyone. The Mahra tribes of the extreme eastern protectorate are apparently the descendants of the Himyarites. For centuries they were actively involved in trade. They were the middlemen in extensive trade with India, Africa and the Near East. Subsistence farming and camel breeding were significant segments of their lifestyle. Their language, Mahri, is unrelated to modern Arabic. They were contacted by Christian missionaries in the fourth century and several churches were established among them. Constant oppression by Muslims since the seventh century prevented any continuance or expansion of Christianity. Little is known about their syncratistic beliefs.

The inhabitants of Socotra Island differ from most mainland Arabs. They are descendents of Greek, Portuguese, African and Arab merchants and travelers who intermarried and have settled in the coastal towns. Indigenous islanders are nomadic herdsmen who live in the highlands of the interior. They are directly related to the al-Mahra tribes and speak a language very similar to Mahri. Nearly 12,000 inhabitants are divided equally among the two groups.

Africans were taken to al-Yaman for centuries as slaves. Smaller groups include the Hujurs in the western part and Sibyan in the Hadramat region. A group of Somalia (20,000) are located in and around Aden.

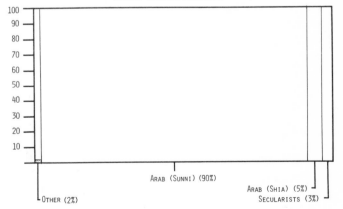

POPULATION COMPOSITION OF THE PEOPLE'S DEMOCRATIC REPUBLIC OF YEMEN
(SHADING INDICATES CHRISTIANS)

ARAB (SUNNI) (90%)
ARAB (SHIA) (5%)
SECULARISTS (3%)
OTHER (2%)

NOTE: THESE FIGURES ARE REPRESENTATIVE APPROXIMATIONS. THEY SHOULD BE SEEN AS INDICATORS OF MAGNITUDE, NOT PRECISE.

## NATIONAL CHURCHES

Churches, church services and church related activities are forbidden in the PDRY.. The few believers within the country must be extremely careful in any small group gatherings they hold. Persecution is certain for any Christians discovered attempting to congregate.


## FOREIGN MISSIONS


Church history documents describe the ministry of the apostle Bartholomew in Arabia. Himyarites from al-Yaman were among the first converts. They were evangelized by Bishop Theophilus who was sent in 350 A.D. to work among them. Tribal chiefs were converted to Christianity and churches were established in Aden, which at that time was a trade center. A navigator and geographer of the sixth century wrote about Christians, bishops, monks and martyrs among the Himyarites in al-Yaman.

### PROTESTANT

Ion Keith-Falconer established a mission station at Sheik Othman near the port of Aden in 1885. He was a Scottish nobleman and Cambridge graduate who committed himself to taking the gospel to the Muslims of Arabia. His efforts were halted when he was severely weakened by the harsh environment and died just two years after his arrival. The Church of Scotland continued the work he had started and maintained a hospital for eighty years. The missionaries of the Church of Scotland who continued the work were forced to evacuate the hospital in 1965. They had worked closely with nationals and other missionaries in establishing the Church of South Arabia in Aden. An ordained national pastor had assumed full responsibility for the church ministry just prior to the forced evacuation of expatriots. The Sudan Interior Mission entered Aden in 1945 to minister to the Somalis who had crossed over from the Horn of Africa. Many of the Somalis were despised by Muslim Arabs and readily accepted the help which missionaries offered. Several small groups were converted to Christianity.

The Red Sea Mission Team began work in 1951. Sixteen missionaries were working in three island cities by 1965 and only four of them were men. Mobile medical clinics consisted of one doctor, three nurses and several national workers riding to villages in donkey caravans. A transitional government invited the Red Sea Mission Team to return following a three year exile period. The government imposed no restrictions and welcomed the medical services offered. Only four nurses responded to the opportunity and worked in several clinics on different days. By 1972 the invitation was revoked and all workers were forced to leave.

A recording studio in Aden produced Arabic programs which were broadcast over Radio E.L.W.A. in Liberia. The station was closed and all ministry terminated because of terrorist attacks which accompanied the pre-independence movement. Contacts with Yemenis were maintained for a few years but expatriots with Sudan Interior never returned.

Danish missionaries began working in Arabia as early as 1901 and merged with the Danish Church Mission in 1946. They worked closely with the Church of Scotland and assisted in establishing the Evangelical Church of South Arabia in 1963. All missionaries were forced to evacuate when a group of Muslim terrorists set fire to the church and homes of the foreigners.

Workers from the Bible Churchmen's Society were able to visit a group of the Christians in the Aden province periodically. They provided evangelical literature and fellowship for the isolated Christians. Their ministry ceased in 1975 because their visits caused the government to increase the persecution of the Christians.

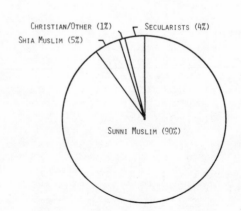

RELIGIOUS COMPOSITION OF THE
PEOPLE'S DEMOCRATIC REPUBLIC OF YEMEN

CHRISTIAN/OTHER (1%)    SECULARISTS (4%)
SHIA MUSLIM (5%)

SUNNI MUSLIM (90%)

## MAJOR CHRISTIAN ACTIVITIES

Christian activities of any kind are prohibited. Christians have not been permitted to enter PDRY in any capacity since 1972. Christians were not allowed to continue medical work which had been in established for nearly 100 years.

## NATION AND ITS PEOPLE

### ETHNIC COMPOSITION

Distinctions betweenthe city dwellers and rural cultivators, pastoralists and nomads are widespread and extensive. Most citizens of the PDRY are Arabs and ethnic differences are minor. Arabs of the northern region (Adnani) differ from the Arabs of the southern region (Qahtani). Historically, the Sayyids and tribes were Adnanis and the Quhtani dwelt primarily in coastal towns and cities. In contemporary terms, very little differentiation exists except among Bedouin nomads, the tribes of Mahra and the inhabitants of the highlands of Socotra.

Women in the cities have much more freedom and many more rights than those women in rural areas. Government regulations have been passed to restrict discrimination. In 1974 a law was passed in Aden which forbids polygamy. Women are required to be at least sixteen years old before marrying and couples may not be more than twenty years apart in age. Seclusion and veiling of women still continues in rural areas.

### POPULATION

Approximately 1,800,000 people live in the PDRY. The annual growth rate (3.3%) and the emigration rate have remained relatively high. Advancements in medicine and foreign aid have increased the life expectancy from 35 years in 1960 to 45 years old in 1978. Over 55% of the population is between the ages of 15 and 65.

Population density varies significantly according to geographic regions. Over 15% of the population is concentrated in the Aden region and another 18% live in the coastal settlements and towns. The rural population (57%) is scattered throughout arable regions with an average of 14 people per square kilometer. Semi-nomadic and nomadic tribes are dispersed throughout the wilderness regions with approximately six people per square kilometer.

### LANGUAGE AND LITERACY

Arabic has been the official language of the PDRY since 1967 and has been used and understood for centuries. English is also used extensively in Aden for trade and education. Indigenous languages include Mahri and the Socotrans variety of Himyatite.

Literacy also varies significantly. The Adenese are fairly well educated and have a literacy rate of 50%. The rural population has a much lower literacy rate of 10%. Women, nomadic and semi-nomadic people have as low a literacy rate as 5%.

### RELIGION

The indigenous Arabs follow the Shafi form of Sunni Islam. Other Arabs form a small minority which follow the Shia sect. Islam has been the state religion since 1970. Major doctrines taught by Sunni Muslims include a literalist interpretation of the Quran. They reject the association of anything with God. This includes the prophets, saints and the Quran. All these are important but not like God. Attendance at public prayer and adherence of the Five Pillars of Islam is mandatory. These include recitation of the creed, daily prayer, alms giving, fasting and pilgrimage.

### GEOGRAPHY AND CLIMATE

The PDRY is situated near the southern end of the Arabian peninsula along the Gulf of Aden and the Arabian Sea. The islands of Socotra, Perim and Kamaran are part of the nation state. Borders with the only neighboring countries, Yemen Arab Republic, Saudi Arabia and Oman are in some cases undefined. Much of the mainland is dry and rocky. The Arabian Peninsula plateau is mostly granite covered by sedimentary limestone and sand. The major important topographical area is the Wadi-Hadhramaut, which means "Death is Present." It is a fairly narrow valley running parallel to the coast about 160 to 240 kilometers (100 to 150 miles) inland. Most of the nations few fertile sections of the nation are located in the upper and middle parts of the Hadhramaut.

The climate is hot with a few monsoons yielding from 5 to 55 centimeters (2 to 22 inches) of rain each year. Aden receives an annual average of 12 centimeters (5 inches) of rain and the barren mountains 50 to 75 centimeters (20 to 30 inches). The deserts may receive 2 centimeters (1 inch) in five to ten years.

## HISTORY

The area known as the PDRY was once a part of Arabia Felix, meaning happy and prosperous Arabia. It turned out to be that for the traders and merchants who clamored for the frankincense, myrrh, spices, pearls and silks which they craved and found in al-Yaman. Aden was the eye of al-Yaman.

Entrepreneurs stopped in al-Yaman for years but never influenced the lives of the tribesmen. Islam gradually was adopted by the people as a result of the itinerant pilgrims of several prophets and holy men who were sent by Muhammad. By 630 A.D. over half of the tribes were converted to Islam and joined with others in prosyletizing their neighboring tribes. Al-Yaman became a theocratic state for 1300 years.

The divisions and schisms which developed within Islam from the seventh to twelfth centuries significantly affected the history of the region. A lengthy period of feuding among the tribes, chaos among ruling powers and factions within Islam left the area in a state of constant turmoil. By the time the Ottoman Turks conquered the area there was little hope for uniting the people. The Turks brutally imposed Sunni Muslim doctrines which infuriated the Shia tribes and caused them to move to the western highlands.

The PDRY has been influenced significantly by British colonialism. For 128 years the area was a British Protecterate and Aden was a British Crown Colony for part of that time. The city of Aden has always been affected by foreigners from Africa, Asia and the Near East. Aden developed rapidly and distinctions between urban and rural inhabitants increased consistently. The remainder of the protectorate was not influenced as much.

The people were granted independence in 1967 and the PDRY was formed. The British moved out rapidly and a period of turmoil followed. Some principles and systems established during the colonial era continued. Progress in the cities and lack of development in rural regions are still evident. Most policies were changed and many radical and reactionary ideologies implemented.

The people rebelled against foreign influence and control yet found themselves very dependent on and affected by government policies of the Soviet Union, Oman, Saudi Arabia, Yemen Arab Republic and the People's Republic of China.

## ECONOMY

The dual economy of industry in Aden and subsistence farming in the rural areas have both undergone radical changes in recent years. The shipping industry falteredwith the closing of the Suez Canal in 1967. The number of ships stopping for refueling, servicing, loading and unloading dropped from 6000 to 1300. Most of the British moved out that same year and thousands of educated Indians, Pakistanis and Arabs followed.

Agriculture and fishing recorded the only increases. The South Arabian Sea has one of the richest fishing banks in the world but equipment and processing facilities were nonexistent for the Yemenis. The Soviet Union moved in with funds and equipment to develop a modern fishing industry. Agriculture and fishing supports 75% of the population. The lack of useable water on the land is acute. There are no rivers running through the land except the flood runoff from the monsoons. With the reopening of the Suez Canal in 1975 and industrial development assistance accepted from other nations, the economy has revived. It is still one of the 29 least developed nations of the world. West Germany is developing a plan for sewage and water services. France provides medical supplies and equipment. The People's Republic of China has built hospitals and Hungary provides pharmaceutical supplies.

# CHURCH STATISTICS FOR PEOPLE'S DEMOCRATIC REPUBLIC OF YEMEN

Note: Statistics have been taken from different sources and are the most current data available. Definitions of "membership" vary among churches and may not always be comparable.

| Church or Mission Name | Communicants (Full Members) | Community (Estimate) |
| --- | --- | --- |
| PROTESTANT | | |
| ROMAN CATHOLIC | | |
| ORTHODOX | | |

## SELECTED BIBLIOGRAPHY

The sources listed below are to help the reader find additional information on this country and Christian ministries there. This list does not try to be comprehensive or complete.

DOCUMENTS

General

Encyclopedia Britannica, Chicago, Benton Publishers, 1977.

Kurian, George Thomas, Encyclopedia of the Third World, New York, Facts on File Publication, 1978.

Nyrop, Richard F., Area Handbook for the Yemens, Washington D.C., Government Printing Office, 1977.

Sweet, Louise E., The Central Middle East, New Haven, Human Relations File, 1971.

Wallace, John, The Middle East Yearbook, London, England, I.C. Magazines Ltd., 1978.

Christian

Hoke, Donald E., The Church in Asia, Chicago, Moody Press, 1975.

Johnstone, Patrick J., World Handbook for World Christians, South Pasadena, William Carey Library, 1976.

Kane, J. Herbert, A Global View of Missions, Grand Rapids, Michigan, Baker Book House, 1971.

Mansfield, Paul, The Arab World, New York, Thomas Y. Crowell Co., 1976.

## ACKNOWLEDGMENTS

The information in this profile was taken from many sources which were the best available to the editors at the time of preparation. However, the accuracy of the information cannot be guaranteed. Views expressed or implied in this publication are not necessarily those of World Vision. The editors have tried to present the ministries of various organizations in an objective manner, without undue bias or emphasis. Where we have failed, we apologize for erroneous impressions that may result and request that comments and corrections be sent to MARC, 919 West Huntington Drive, Monrovia, California, USA, 91016. We appreciate and acknowledge the comments and contributions of various organizations and individuals in the preparation of this publication.

# STATUS OF CHRISTIANITY COUNTRY PROFILE

# QATAR

**QATAR**
— International boundary
⊛ National capital
— Road

0  10  20  30  40  50
Miles

UNREACHED PEOPLES

SUMMARY

AREA - 10,360 square kilometers (4,000
    square miles)
POPULATION - 200,000
RELIGION - 86% Sunni Muslim, 11% Shia
    Muslim, 3% Christian

Until recent years the desert peninsula of
Qatar held little promise for its less
than 30,000 native inhabitants. Oil,
however, has revolutionized the lives of
the Qataris in the oil rich Gulf State.
Qatar's wealth, population and status in
international affairs has grown
explosively in the last two decades.

Qatar's native population is nearly
entirely Sunni Muslim of the strict Wahabi
sect. This explains the low level of
receptivity to Christianity

By 1979, the majority of the population in
Qatar was non-Qatari. Christianity is an
entirely expatriate phenomenon and
Christians do comprise a small percentage
of the population. Qatar is both
ethnically and religiously diverse.

The vast majority of Qatar's population
are Muslims and the majority of these are
part of the Sunni sect of Islam. Qatari
Arabs number 30,000 and account for 15% of
the total population. Arabs from other
countries (expatriates) number 70,000 and
are also predominantly Sunni Muslims.
These two groups are particularly
resistant to the Gospel.
All Arab groups combined form only 50% of
the total population of Qatar.

The second largest ethnic group is the
Pakistanis, who number 45,000 and comprise
27% of the total population. They also
are predominantly Muslims, but small
groups of Christians do exist among them.
The Pakistanis of Qatar are potentially
receptive to the Gospel though they are
virtually unreached at present. The few
Pakistani Christians are being encouraged
to reach their countrymen by utilizing
Islamic forms for communicating Christian
meanings. Approximately 25,000 Indians
reside in Qatar.

This program is jointly carried out by the Strategy Working Group of the Lausanne Committee for World Evangelization
and MARC, a ministry of World Vision International. For further information on the program, please write: MARC, 919
West Huntington Drive, Monrovia, CA 91016 U.S.A.

A number of Christian Indians gather for fellowship . The small groups of Christians appear to be ideally located and constituted to reach the unreached Indians of Qatar. The 25,000 Iranians are mostly Shia Muslims. Their highly developed religious traditions require a culturally sensitive approach for effective communication of the Gospel.

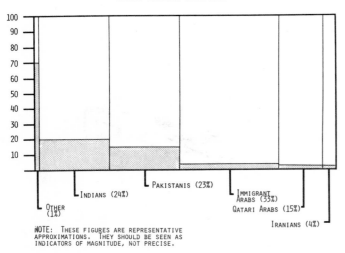

POPULATION COMPOSITION OF QATAR
(SHADING INDICATES CHRISTIANS)

OTHER (1%)
INDIANS (24%)
PAKISTANIS (23%)
IMMIGRANT ARABS (33%)
QATARI ARABS (15%)
IRANIANS (4%)

NOTE: THESE FIGURES ARE REPRESENTATIVE APPROXIMATIONS. THEY SHOULD BE SEEN AS INDICATORS OF MAGNITUDE, NOT PRECISE.

## CURRENT STATUS OF CHRISTIANITY

Qatar has had virtually no Christian history until the 20th century. Very little missions work has ever been attempted and Christianity is regarded as a phenomenon among and for strangers. Most Christians live in the major port city of Doha with just a few smaller groups residing in the ports of Zekrit and Umm Said as well as the oil center of Bukran. Visibility of Christians is most evident among Indian and Pakistani communities where immigrant Christians live and work among their own people. There are no recognized church buildings and only one resident clergyman. All Christian activities are conducted on an informal basis.

## NATIONAL CHURCHES

### PROTESTANT CHURCHES

One Anglican church of primarily European constituencey meets in the auditorium of the British school. A few Indian and Arab immigrants are members and regularly attend. The Archdeacon of the Anglican Archdiocese of Jerusalem who lives in Abu Dhabi, a city in the UAE, spends several

days each month ministering to the Anglicans in Qatar. Many Indian immigrants are members of the Mar Thoma Church but since they do not have any facilities of their own they often meet with the Anglicans. Social gatherings for the two groups are often held separately. Three tiny Indian Brethren fellowships meet in Doha as well as a small Indian Pentecostal group. About 25 immigrant Arab Evangelicals are scattered throughout Qatar. They do not have an organized congregation but often meet for fellowship and Bible study. All worship services and inter-church relations are maintained on an informal basis.

## CATHOLIC CHURCHES

Catholics are by far the largest Christian church affiliate in Qatar with nearly 2,500 members. A Capuchin Father is the only resident clergyman in the entire country. Catholic congregations meet in Doha and at three other centers in cities. Meetings usually take place in oil company buildings as well as informal settings. Services are held in English. The majority of church members are Indians with a number of British Catholics and Arabs from nations of the Mediterranean region. A few Orthodox Christians attend Catholic worship services where no churches or gatherings of Orthodox Christians exist. The government rejected a proposal by the Father to construct a church building.

## ORTHODOX CHURCHES

One small congregation of the Syrian Orthodox Church of Malabar meets informally in Qatar. Other Orthodox Christians worship with the Catholics.

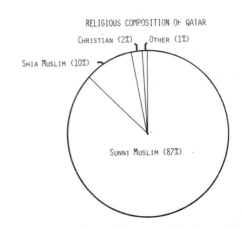

RELIGIOUS COMPOSITION OF QATAR

CHRISTIAN (2%)   OTHER (1%)
SHIA MUSLIM (10%)
SUNNI MUSLIM (87%)

## FOREIGN MISSIONS

### PROTESTANT MISSIONS

The Reformed Church in America (RCA) is the only Christian mission which has been actively involved on the Qatar Peninsula. Itinerant medical workers travelled through the area on a number of occasions from the 1920's to 1940's. Several close relationships were established with the local Amir (ruler), which led to an invitation for the RCA to establish a permanent medical clinic in 1948. The RCA was very short of personnel and workers were only sent to the clinic for a few months at a time. A medical missionary who was to have been sent as a permanent worker became seriously ill in 1951 and the mission was forced to turn the clinic over to the government and oil companies. Sentiment was expressed that an opportune moment for mission field development had been lost permanently. Other than itinerant medical work, no mission work has been done in Qatar.

### CATHOLIC MISSIONS

Catholic clergymen reside in Qatar only to minister to the needs of the expatriate population. There is no missions emphasis.

## MAJOR CHRISTIAN ACTIVITIES

### SOCIAL CONCERNS

Almost all Christian work in Qatar is focused on the nurture of the small Christian expatriate community.

### EVANGELISM

No active evangelistic program of any kind is existent among anyone other than "friendship evangelism" among expatriates. It is certain that any direct effort towards evangelism among the Arab population would be quickly suppressed. Friendship evangelism among oil workers and within immigrant communities is the only form presently used.

### BROADCASTING

Some broadcasts in Arabic are received in Qatar though no programs are specifically beamed in that direction.

### LITERATURE

At present there are no Christian bookstores in Qatar and the Scriptures are generally unavailable to anyone other than Christians.

## NATION AND ITS PEOPLE

### POPULATION

The latest estimate for the population of Qatar is 200,000. The annual growth rate is 8% and projections indicate a population of 500,000 by the year 2000. Only 30,000 are native Qataris and nearly 60% of the total population are not citizens. There are 70,000 non-Qatari Arabs who, like indigenous Arabs, are predominantly Sunni Muslims. Approximately 45,000 Pakistanis comprise the next largest ethnic group. Most Pakistanis are also Sunni Muslims but a significant amount are Christians. Many of the 25,000 Iranians are Shia Muslims. Indian immigrants number 25,000 and they too are Sunni Muslims. The number of Christians within the Indian population is proportionately higher than within any other of the many ethnic groups. Oil workers and diplomats from western nations number 3,000.

Most of the population of Qatar (75%) is centered in the capital, Doha. Two other ports , Zekrit and Umm Said, and the inland oil center of Dukhan, account for 24% of the remainder of the population. One of the unusual features of the population structure of Qatar is the fact that men outnumber women 3 to 1. The major explanation is the high number of workers residing in Qatar for strictly economic purposes. Most of them do not intend to settle there and are generally not content with social circumstances. Theories have been postulated that point to the possibilities of openness and receptivity towards Christianity on the part of expatriate communities in Qatar. There is a very small rural population in Qatar.

The ruling family is at the top of the social structure. The middle class is composed of merchants and expatriate workers. The lower class includes laborers in the cities and oil fields as well as the few nomadic Bedouin. Fast paced economic development has relieved many of the economic problems of the lower classes, many of whom send money to families living elsewhere. An extensive free educational and health care system is provided by the government. Housing is also becoming more readily available and with government subsidies, more affordable.

## LANGUAGE AND LITERACY

The official language of Qatar is Arabic. English is widely understood and used for business and educational purposes. Languages used by other ethnic groups include Farsi, Urdu, Malayam, Tamil, Baluchi and non-Gulf area dialects of Arabic. There are no accurate figures for the literacy rate, though it is now probably quite high since education is compulsory for all children of ages 6 through 16.

## RELIGION

Qatar is officially an Islamic state with 97% of the total population adherents of either Sunni or Shia Muslim doctrines. A majority (86%) of the immigrants and all of the indigenous Qataris are followers of the strict Wahabi sect of Sunni Islam. This particular sect originated in the 18th century in Arabia as a reform movement. Strong emphasis is placed upon the full and literal interpretation of the Quran for all legal and social matters. Many of the Iranian immigrants join with others to form an 11% Shia Muslim constituency. Nearly 3% of the total population is Christian but is represented only by those among the immigrant population.

## GEOGRAPHY AND CLIMATE

Qatar is located on a peninsula which is about 160 kilometers (100 miles) in length and between 56 and 80 kilometers (35-50 miles) in width. The terrain is barren and almost entirely flat with the highest point rising to only 100 meters (328 feet) in the Dukhan oil fields. Qatar is surrounded on three sides by the Arabian Gulf and borders Saudi Arabia and the United Arab Emirates to the south. Annual rainfall is between 2.5 to 22 centimeters (1-9 inches) Temperatures range from 48 degrees centigrade (117 degrees fahrenheit) in July to 6 degrees centigrade (40 degrees fahrenheit) in January. A shortage of useable ground water lead to the development and widespread usage of desalinization plants which now supply the majority of the water.

## HISTORY

Ruins found in Qatar date back to the third millienium B.C. No records of any major historical significance regarding the area have been discovered. In 1919

the British concluded an agreement with the Shaikh (ruler) of Qatar which was similar to those arranged with Kuwait and the South Arabia. It made provision for British control of international affairs along with protection by British forces. Exploration for oil began in the 1930's but was interrupted by World War II. Commercial oil production began in 1949 and Qatar has been involved in rapid development since that time.

The formation of the United Arab Emirates was a development strongly encouraged by Qatar. However, at the time the treaty with Britain ended, Qatar decided to not join the UAE and became a fully independant state instead. Affairs of state were delayed briefly in 1971 due to a bloodless coup which brought the regime of Sheikh Khalifa al-Thani to power. Development has proceeded unabated since that time.

## GOVERNMENT AND POLITICAL CONDITIONS

Qatar is a monarchy ruled hereditarily by the Al-Thani family. Affairs of state are administered through a council of 14 ministers. There is also a 30 member advisory council. The judicial system includes higher and lower courts with judgements based on the Shariat law from the Quran. Qatar's armed forces are quite small but modern. The government is heavily influenced by Saudi Arabia. Throughout the 1970's, Qatar has been quite stable.

## ECONOMY

Ninety-nine percent of Qatar's revenues are derived from oil and per capita income has risen to US$ 8,320. Qatar is self-sufficient in vegetables as a result of a growing agricultural system which utilizes modern irrigation techniques. Yearly production is now over 20,000 tons. New projects in poultry farming and livestock raising have begun. The fishing industry also does over US one million dollars worth of business annually. One large steel smelting plant has been constructed at a cost of US$ 350 million in a joint project with the Japanese. The Qatari riyal is equivalent to US$ .25 in 1979.

# CHURCH STATISTICS FOR QATAR

Note: Statistics have been taken from different sources and are the most current data avaiable. Definitions of "membership" vary among churches and may not always be comparable. Not all known churches have been included in this list.

| Church or Mission Name | Communicants (Full Members) | Community (Estimate) |
|---|---|---|
| PROTESTANT | | |
| Anglican | | 350 |
| Arab Evangelical | | 25 |
| Indian Brethren | | 45 |
| Indian Pentecostal | | 30 |
| Mar Thomite | | 150 |
| CATHOLIC | | |
| Combined Traditions | | 2,500 |
| Orthodox | | |
| Syrian Orthodox of Malabar | | 100 |

## SELECTED BIBLIOGRAPHY AND INFORMATION SOURCES

DOCUMENTS

General

Area Handbook for the Peripheral States of the Arabian Peninsula, Washington D.C.: Stanford Research Institute, 1971

Fisher, W.B., The Middle East and North Africa, London, England: Europa Publications Limited,1978

Wallace, John, The Middle East Yearbook, London, England: I.C. Magazines Limited, 1978

Weekes, Richard, Muslim Peoples: A World Ethnographic Survey, Westport: Greenwood Press, 1978

Christian

Dayton, Edward, Mission Handbook Monrovia: MARC, 1976

Horner, Norman, Present Day Christianity in the Gulf States, New Jersey: Occasional Bulletin,

## ACKNOWLEDGEMENTS

The information in this profile was taken from many resources which were the best available to the editors at the time of preparation. However, the accuracy of the information cannot be guaranteed. Views expressed or implied in this publication are not necessarily those of World Vision. The editors have tried to present the ministries of various organizations in an objective manner, without undue bias or emphasis. Where we have failed, we apologize for erroneous impressions that may result and request that comments and corrections be sent to MARC, 919 West Huntington Drive, Monrovia, California 91016, USA. We appreciate and acknowledge the comments and contributions of various organizations and individuals in the preparation of this publication.

# STATUS OF CHRISTIANITY COUNTRY PROFILE

# SAUDI ARABIA

## SUMMARY

AREA - 2,238,000 square kilometers
      (864,000 square miles)
POPULATION - 7.8 million
RELIGION - 90% Wahhabi Sunni, 9% Shia
      Muslim, 1% Christian and Other

Saudi Arabia holds the largest proven crude oil reserves in the world and ranks third among crude oil producers, making it the single most powerful member of the Oil Producing and Exporting Countries (OPEC). All oil revenues, US $62 million per day, accrue to the government, whose spending circulates the oil money through the economy. Probably no other government has a more direct and immediate control over the economic life of its citizens. Government spending focuses on improving living conditions, expanding education, and industrial development through a series of Five Year Plans.

Religion is the most important factor in Saudi culture. Saudi Arabia draws its national identity from the fundamentalist version of Islam preached late in the 18th century by Muhammad ibn Abd al-Wahhab. The present king and all his predecessors have been direct descendents of both Wahhab and the first Saud. The Quran is the nation's constitution and the Sharia

is the legal system. Authorities enforce the strictest and most puritanical form of Islam practiced anywhere in the world. Music, dance and cinema are banned and alcohol may not be imported. However, the affluent obtain all these products through the black market and use them in private.

Conservatives within the Saudi power structure are concerned that traditional Muslim mores will fail before the onslaught of western ideas. It is also questionable whether an absolute monarchy can withstand the ideas brought home by western-educated youth. Political parties and labor unions are banned and the press is censored. Television sets throughout the Kingdom receive Egyptian and Iraqi programs. The Saudis are gambling that they can open the door to the West just long enough to industrialize and educate and to make their economy self-sufficient. Political tensions and the social problems fostered by "too much too soon" strain Saudi society.

*This program is jointly carried out by the Strategy Working Group of the Lausanne Committee for World Evangelization and MARC, a ministry of World Vision International. For further information on the program, please write: MARC, 919 West Huntington Drive, Monrovia, CA 91016 U.S.A.*

All permanent residents of Saudi Arabia
are Muslims and apostasy is punishable by
death.  The public practice of other
religions is not tolerated although most
Muslim jurists have held that Christians
and Jews should receive a special
protected status within Islam as "Peoples
of the Book." The Saudis rationalize their
exclusiveness by emphasizing that they are
guardians of the two sacred sites of
Islam, Mecca and Medina, and that Arabia,
home of the Prophet and scene of his
ministry, is sacred in the eyes of Muslims
throughout the world.

In mid-1977, there were 1.5 million
foreigners working in Saudi Arabia.  An
estimated 15,000 Americans live within the
Eastern Province.  The Arabian American
Oil Company (ARAMCO) employs approximately
1,700 Americans, many of whom have brought
their families.  Yemenis and Sudanese fill
the menial jobs which Saudis avoid.  The
remainder of foreign workers are
Palestinians, Jordanians, Syrians,
Egyptians, Pakistanis, Iranians, and
Koreans.

Foreign dependents, most of whom do not
speak any Arabic, are isolated within
company or consular compounds, venturing
forth only when necessary.  Western
women's attire is openly resented by Saudi
conservatives and tends to restrict women
to their homes.  Wives are forbidden to
hold jobs outside the home and where this
law is ignored women are usually limited
to menial typing or clerical jobs.  They
are hidden or sent home when visitors or
government officials arrive.

ARAMCO has sought to cushion its families
by building three large compounds, located
in Ras Tanura, Abqaiq, and Dhahran.  These
little American towns in the desert,
barricaded behind a security fence furnish
them with grocery stores, movie theaters,
restaurants, baseball fields and swimming
pools which partially offset the "compound
claustrophobia" they experience.

The Saudis are very homogeneous ethnically
and linguistically and are primarily from
indigenous Arab tribes.  One major
distinction is made between nomadic tribes
and tribes settled in towns and
agricultural oases.  Shiite Muslims of the
Eastern Province, who suffer
discrimination and are forbidden certain
of their rites, form the only large
indigenous minority.  In the Hejaz there
is a mixture of Turks, nonpeninsular
Arabs, and non-Arab Muslims due to the
religious pilgrimages in the 18th and 19th
centuries.

A large but unstable resident Christian
community does exist within Saudi Arabia.
Due to Saudi restrictions, many of these
peple must do without the support of their
respective churches while living in a
foreign situation.

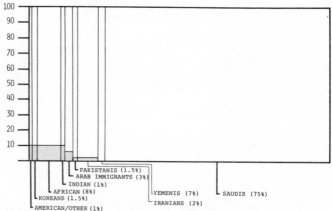

POPULATION COMPOSITION OF SAUDI ARABIA
(SHADING INDICATES CHRISTIANS)

PAKISTANIS (1.5%)
ARAB IMMIGRANTS (3%)
INDIAN (1%)
AFRICAN (8%)
KOREANS (1.5%)
AMERICAN/OTHER (1%)
YEMENIS (7%)
IRANIANS (2%)
SAUDIS (75%)

NOTE:  THESE FIGURES ARE REPRESENTATIVE
APPROXIMATIONS.  THEY SHOULD BE SEEN AS
INDICATORS OF MAGNITUDE, NOT PRECISE.

Only non-Saudis are permitted to practice Christianity and all church services are held within foreign living compounds. The largest congregations are in the East Province, primarily serving oil company employees and U.S. Military personnel in the Dhahran area. Entry visas are never given to clergymen and most ministers officially enter the Kingdom as teachers or social counselors. The Roman Catholic Vicariate Apostolic enjoys the concessions of a Vatican diplomatic passport. Crosses and clerical garb are not permitted nor may clergy legally conduct marriage ceremonies.

Religious work among oil company employees is hindered by the ARAMCO's Government Relations Department, which seeks to avoid unpleasant confrontations with the Saudi authorities. Periodically, clergymen appointed to Dhahran are denied permanent residence and must commute to oil camps from Bahrain.

## PROTESTANT CHURCHES

Interfaith services are held regularly at Ras Tanura, Abqaiq, and Dhahran. In the past they have been lead by a Presbyterian minister. There is also an Anglican Chaplain in Dhahran. Other services are being held within consulates in Jedda and Riyadh, and in private homes by visiting pastors, who are legally "unofficial."

## CATHOLIC CHURCHES

Catholics are served by the Vicariate Apostolic of Arabia based in Abu Dhabi. Catholics total nearly 13,000 throughout the entire Arabian pennisula. Mass is said regularly in the East Province in oil camp theaters. Other congregations are served by traveling clergy.

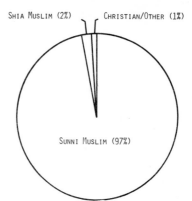

RELIGIOUS COMPOSITION OF SAUDI ARABIA

SHIA MUSLIM (2%)          CHRISTIAN/OTHER (1%)

SUNNI MUSLIM (97%)

# FOREIGN MISSIONS

The vast majority of Saudis have never been reached by Christian missions. Although Christian communities and mission institutions flourish in neighboring Bahrain and Kuwait, missions have seldom penetrated central Arabia, and even then only with short-term medical missions.

Saudi Arabia remained impenetrable to Christian mission work from the late 7th century until the 1840's, when the work was carried out entirely by itinerant missionaries, traveling with camel caravans and undergoing great hardships. Jesuit priests entered the peninsula in 1841 and eventually established a base in Aden. In 1888 the work was entrusted to the Minor Capuchin Brothers. Protestant missions saw a beginning as the Church of Scotland sent several independent pioneer workers to the area.

## PROTESTANT MISSIONS

Protestant mission work, especially in the Arabian Gulf area, can be said to have been started towards the end of the 19th century through the dedicated work of Samuel Zwemer. Zwemer and two fellow seminary students received a clear call to the field in Arabia and persevered, setting up their own independent American Arabian Mission. Today there are permanent American Missions in Kuwait, Bahrain, and Muscat which support hospitals, schools, and churches.

The American Mission tried from the very beginning to penetrate beyond the coastal states into the heart of Arabia, but with little success. Missions which received permission to temporarily work in Saudi Arabia were medical. This was before vast oil revenues enabled the Saudis to build their own facilities. Medical doctors of the American Mission labored a lifetime trying every contact and invitation, no matter what hardships were involved. King Ibn Saud frequently sent for medical service, beginning in 1917 and again in the 1918 influenza epidemic. He personally welcomed a special team from the Mason Memorial Hospital in 1944 which concentrated for six weeks on treating eye ailments. An offer to build a permanent hospital in Hofuf in 1956 was refused and another door had closed.

In 1976 there were four North American Protestant Ministries. The Bible Presbyterian Church listed three staff members, and the Presbyterian Church in America (Mission to the World) listed one. Earlier, the Church of Christ Worldwide Evangelization Crusade listed one worker in Arabia.

One mission which undoubtedly reached many Saudis was the American medical mission located in the Buraimi Oasis (once claimed by both Saudi Arabia and Abu Dhabi). The work began at the invitation of the Sheikh of Abu Dhabi. In 1966, 20 staff members treated over 28,000 patients.

## MAJOR CHRISTIAN ACTIVITIES

### EVANGELISM

Evangelistic work in Saudi Arabia is carried on through individual personal witness. Saudi Muslims are often very willing to discuss religious and theological differences, and are always intensely curious about the differences in lifestyle, clothing, food, and marriage customs which they see in foreign residents. Dialogue is the best tool available although there is always the risk that a third party could report one to the religious authorities for attempting to convert a Muslim. Foreigners who work directly for the Saudi government, particularly in the universities, are bluntly told that religious discussions will result in immediate deportation.

### BROADCASTING

There are daily evening broadcasts in Arabic from Cyprus via Trans World Radio. Middle East Lutheran Radio, broadcasting on the Cyprus Broadcasting Corporation (BBC) airs programs in Arabic. IBRA Radio has Christian programming on Radio Trans Europe. Adventist World Radio, the "Voice of Hope", is also carried on Radio Trans Europe. The BBC Eastern Mediterranean Relay has an Arabic service; it is unknown whether this includes any religious programming.

### LITERATURE and BIBLE DISTRIBUTION

The press in Saudi Arabia is heavily censored. The ARAMCO English newspaper, The Arabian Sun, avoids all controversial topics and seldom includes religious material other than articles about Muslim holiday. Saudi customs officials confiscate any Christian religious materials they happen to see. Materials shipped by sea or air freight are unlikely to escape confiscation unless they are part of an ARAMCO or consular shipment.

Materials in Arabic are available due to a number of Christian presses located in other countries. There are excellent Christian bookstores in Kuwait and Bahrain. The Worldwide Evangelization Crusade has published an Arabic bi-monthly entitled "Soon."

## SOCIAL CONCERN

Historically, missions in the area have been primarily medical, seeking to reach out to a primarily nomadic people still living under unhygienic medieval conditions. There is hope of someday providing schools as well as medical assistance. But the existence of government sponsored free education from kindergarten through university and well-equipped, no expense-spared hospitals indicate that pioneer days are past.

## NATION AND ITS PEOPLE

## POPULATION

In 1978, the population of Saudi Arabia was estimated at 7.8 million people. About 95% of the people live on 5% of the land. Population is concentrated in a few major cities and in three population belts: a western area from Taif south to Mecca and Asir, the central Nejd with its cluster of oases, and the eastern oil field region and the Qatif oasis. Perhaps as many as 50% of the people still turn at least occasionally to a nomadic life.

The average age of the population is one of the youngest in the Middle East. Almost half of the population is under 15. Better medical and sanitary facilities have increased the life expectancy from age 30 in rural areas (1963), to 45 for the total population in 1974. The annual birthrate is 2.75% and the death rate is 20 per 1,000. The Bedouin raise the mortality statistics because they are often out of reach of government health care. Infant mortality rate is often 60% among the Bedouins.

The population is becoming increasingly urban, as oil revenue generated jobs draw workers to the towns and cities, which are growing at a rate of 6%. The government, which views the Bedouin as a principle obstacle to the unity of the state, has several resettlement projects in operation. These new settlements are designed with the combined motives of encouraging the Bedouin to settle permanently and of exploiting areas with agricultural or water resource potential.

## COMPOSITION

As in other Middle East countries, Saudi culture divides into three groups, each of which fits into a particular ecological niche. Nomadic pastoralists exploit the marginally productive desert regions. Settled agriculturalists exploit the oases, while city dwellers provide commercial, religious, educational and artisan services.

The culture of Saudi Arabia shows a high degree of uniformity and the Saudi value system is founded on Islam, family, and tradition. Descent and family membership traditionally determine social status far more than personal wealth. The individual is expected to subordinate his personal interests to those of his family and to consider himself a member of a group whose importance outweighs his own.

Until after World War II, there was no middle class except for a few commercial families concentrated in port towns. Oil provided both the impetus and the opportunity for the development of a new middle class. Public employment grew during the 1950's from a base of a few hundred to 50,000 civilian employees and 35,000 military personnel. This number increased another 50% in the 1960's. Opportunities for educated young Saudi men are practically limitless.

The social milieu of a woman's family affects her circumstances to some extent. Segregation of the sexes is far more strict in the towns, where women are confined to the home and their social contacts limited to an exclusively feminine sphere.

## LANGUAGE AND LITERACY

Arabic is the language of Saudi Arabia, while English is stressed in all secondary schools. The government provides free education from kindergarten through university, sending many young men abroad for specialized studies. Schools for girls were not established until 1960 but are now available, elementary through college, in segregated curriculum. Plans for the next five years (1975-80) include increasing elementary student enrollment from 600,000 to 1 million. The current literacy rate is about 15%.

## RELIGION

Sunni Islam is the only recognized religion in Saudi Arabia. The strict teachings of Muhammad ibn Abd al-Wahhab are enforced. Wahhab took a literalist view of the Quran and taught that the

101

worst sin was "shirk," the association of anything with God. Innovations, practices not specifically sanctioned by the Prophet or his followers earlier than the 3rd century of Islam, were denounced. All special relationships with God were rejected, including Suffism, saints, and Shia imams, as were all ecstatic practices believed to foster such relationships. Taken literally, Wahhabism forbids smoking, shaving, strong language, and any adornment of places of prayer. Attendance at public prayer is required. This code is enforced by a religious police force. the "muttawwiun," who work under the Committee for Encouragement of Virtue and the Discouragement of Vice.

## GEOGRAPHY AND CLIMATE

The area of Saudi Arabia is 2,238,000 square kilometers (864,000 square miles). The country lies between the Persian Gulf and the Red Sea and shares borders with Jordan, Iraq, Kuwait, The United Arab Emirates, the Yemen Arab Republic and the People's Democratic Republic of Yemen.

The climate is hot desert, with no rivers or permanent bodies of water. Coastal cities are subject to high humidity. Asir province is somewhat different, with high volcanic mountains, 50.8 centimeters (20 inches) of rain per year, and the only natural forest in the country.

## HISTORY

The first known Arabian civilizations were coastal agricultural settlements in the East Province with ties to the al-Ubaid culture of Mesopotamia (5000 BC). The east coast of Arabia seems to have been part of the land of Dilmun which had its center on the island of Bahrain (4000-1800 BC). In classical times few outsiders penetrated the interior, although the spice trade to southern Arabia was of vital importance to the Egyptians and Romans.

The centers of the new Islamic Empire soon moved from Mecca to Syria and later Iraq. Arabia was not united into one nation until the conquests of Abk al-Aziz ibn Saud (1902-53), who utilized a military force of fanatic Wahhabi tribesmen, the Ikhawan. The current ruler, Khaled, is the son of Abd al-Aziz.

## GOVERNMENT

Saudi Arabia is an absolute monarchy with the king usually serving as Prime Minister. The current monarch, Khaled, is in poor health, and most of the duties of government fall to his successor-designate, Crown Prince Fahd.

The King, following democratic desert tradition, makes himself accessible to his people through the custom of frequent public court sessions.

The country is directly managed by a Council of Ministers, consisting mainly of Princes of the House of Saud, with extreme centralization in Riyadh. There are six major and 12 minor provincial units, administered by governors. Political parties are not permitted.

## ECONOMY

Saudi Arabia's only major product is crude oil, and the country holds 25% of the world's proven oil reserves. In 1977, Saudi Arabia exported 3.9 billion barrels of oil worth over US $35 billion. The government, through a series of Five Year Development Plans, is attempting to use this revenue to industrialize and to eventually relieve the economy from such an extreme dependence on oil.

In fiscal year 1975 oil contributed 87% of the GDP, agriculture less than 1%, construction 3%, and industry, commerce, and services the remainder. Saudi Arabia must import over 75% of its food.

CHURCH STATISTICS FOR SAUDI ARABIA

Note: Statistics have been taken from different sources and are the most current data available. Definitions of "membership" vary among churches and may not always be comparable.

| Church or Mission Name | Communicants (Full Members) | Community (Estimate) |
|---|---|---|
| PROTESTANT | | |
| ROMAN CATHOLIC | | |

SELECTED BIBLIOGRAPHY

The sources listed below are to help the reader find additional information on this country and Christian ministries there. This list does not try to be comprehensive or complete.

DOCUMENTS

General

Geddes, C.L., Analytical Guide to the Bibliographies on the Arabian Peninsula, Denver, Colorado: American Institute of Islamic Studies, 1974.

Nyrop, Richard F. et al, Area Handbook for Saudi Arabia, Washington: U. S. Government Printing Office, 1977.

Christian

Dayton, Edward R., Mission Handbook: North American Protestant Ministries Overseas, Monrovia, California: Missions Advanced Research and Communications Center, 1976.

Foy, Felican A. O. M., editor, Catholic Almanac 1978, Huntington, IN: Our Sunday Visitor Inc., 1977.

Goddard, Burton L., editor, The Encyclopedia of Modern Christian Missions, Camden: Thos. Nelson and Sons, 1967.

ACKNOWLEDGMENTS

The information in this profile was taken from many sources which were the best available to the editors at the time of preparation. However, the accuracy of the information cannot be guaranteed. Views expressed or implied in this publication are not necessarily those of World Vision. The editors have tried to present the ministries of various organizations in an objective manner, without undue bias or emphasis. Where we have failed, we apologize for erroneous impressions that may result and request that comments and corrections be sent to MARC, 919 West Huntington Drive, Monrovia, California, USA, 91016. We appreciate and acknowledge the comments and contributions of various organizations and individuals in the preparation of this publication.

# STATUS OF CHRISTIANITY COUNTRY PROFILE

# SYRIA

## SUMMARY

AREA - 180,000 square kilometers (72,300 square miles)
POPULATION - 7.6 million (mid-1976)
RELIGION - 73% Sunni Muslim, 17% Other Muslim, 10% Christian, 0.5% Other (Jews, Yazidis, Circassians)

Damascus has always been a paradise in tumult. It has been ruled by Egyptians, Aramaeans, Hebrews, Assyrians, Babylonians, Persians, Greeks, Nabataeans, Romans, Byzantines, Arabs, Mongols, Ottoman Turks, and French. It learned to live with them all, and with Armenians, Kurds, and Circassians.

Syria's 7,596,000 inhabitants form a varied and somewhat tolerant nation. The area has been Islamic for more than 1300 years, but "religious coexistence" is an important aspect of life in Syria's capital city. Damascus is the site of the traditional Garden of Eden, according to the Syrians; the oasis where Cain wandered with Abel before burying him; the location of Saul of Tarsus' conversion to Christ, and the city which contains the Umayyad Mosque, a holy place of Islam. With such a history, it is no wonder that Sunni, Shiah and other Muslims walk the same roads and shop the same bazaars as Orthodox, Catholic and Protestant Christians and even some Jews.

The 10% of Syria's people who are Christians face a challenging task in sharing God's truth with their Muslim and Jewish friends. Social ministries of the churches and missions -- education, medicine and relief -- proclaim compassion to people, most of whom have little receptivity to the Christian message. All ministries must be carefully conducted within the bounds of what the Muslim-oriented socialist government allows. There are, however, opportunities to strengthen the church in Syria. Doors are open and hearts seem ready for wider scripture distribution. Student camps, pastors' meetings, crusades and a Bible institute under the patronage of Arab pastors would be effective ways of sharing God's truth.

Will Syria's urban businessmen, nomadic herdsmen and farmers, shopkeepers and craftsmen, liberated women, refugees and blacksmiths have an opportunity to embrace the good news of Jesus?

*This program is jointly carried out by the Strategy Working Group of the Lausanne Committee for World Evangelization and MARC, a ministry of World Vision International. For further information on the program, please write: MARC, 919 West Huntington Drive, Monrovia, CA 91016 U.S.A.*

# UNREACHED PEOPLES

The major unreached peoples in Syria are followers of Islam. Sunni Muslims account for 73% of Syria's population and other Muslim groups, primarily Shiites, bring the total Muslim population to about 90%. Non-Muslim unreached people groups include Jews, Yazidis and Circassians, together only 0.5% of the total population.

Several ethnic groups make up the Sunni Muslim community. Arabs account for about half the population of the entire country. They are, as other Muslim groups, very unresponsive to Christianity. Although their literacy is high, Bible distribution among them is very sparse. About 8% of Syria's people are Bedouins; some of these cultivate crops or raise livestock. The rest of the Bedouins are nomadic tribes, including Ruwala, Hassana, Butainat, Abadah, Fadan Walad, Fadan Kharsah, Shammar al Zur and Shammar al Knarsah. Kurdish-speaking people comprise 6% of the country's population; they are mainly farmers, with a few urbanites and nomads. There is a higher percentage of Christians and Shiah Muslims among the Kurds than among the other Sunni Muslim groups; however, Sunni Islam still claims 95% of this group. Almost all Palestinian refugees (4% of the total population) are Sunni Muslims, as are the seminomadic herders and farmers called Turkomen (3%). All of these groups speak Arabic; the Kurds (Kurdish) and Turkomen (Turkish) are bi-lingual. Resistance to Christianity is high.

Shiah Islam is the religion for 17% of the people of Syria. The largest of the several Shiah Muslim groups is the Alawites (12% of the population), who form a sect of Shiah Islam. They are generally rural poor people, living as share-croppers or settled farmers. Some, however, serve as military officers. Four tribal groups are Alawites: Kalibyah; Khaiyatin; Haddadin, and Matawirah. Druzes, 3% of the population, are members of a Christo-pagan Shiah sect. The Ismailis, making up a Misari sect of Shiah Islam, are 1.5% of the population. Less than 1% of the people in Syria are Arab Shiah Muslims. As with the other Muslim groups, response to Christianity is negative.

Other unreached groups with very little interest in Christianity are the Yazidis, Jews and Circassians. Together they comprise only 0.5% of the total country population. The Yazidis, numbering 10,000, speak Kurdish and Arabic. The Jews (3-4000) speak Arabic and are

generally peddlers, shopkeepers or artisans. The tribally-organized Circassians (25,000) live mostly in villages and do farming, herding, masonry or blacksmithing.

About 10% of the population is Christian. Christians come from several ethnic groups, but are mostly Arab or Armenian. They are generally better educated, and live in urban areas.

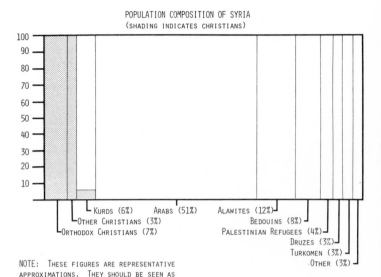

POPULATION COMPOSITION OF SYRIA
(SHADING INDICATES CHRISTIANS)

Kurds (6%)    Arabs (51%)    Alawites (12%)
Other Christians (3%)
Orthodox Christians (7%)    Bedouins (8%)
Palestinian Refugees (4%)
Druzes (3%)
Turkomen (3%)
Other (3%)

NOTE: These figures are representative approximations. They should be seen as indicators of magnitude, not precise.

## CURRENT STATUS OF CHRISTIANITY

During the days following the ascension of Jesus, as the church grew and spread, a man named Saul of Tarsus began a journey to persecute Christians in Damascus. On the way, he was dramatically confronted by the living Christ. Three days later, Saul was baptized in Damascus and began his Christian growth.

The area now known as Syria is rich with a history of Christianity dating back to before the conversion of the Apostle Paul. The cities of Antioch, where the disciples were first called Christians, and Damascus are representative of a movement that spread throughout Syria and beyond. By the fourth century, Christianity was fairly widespread in the country; 20 Syrian bishops attended the Council of Nicea in A.D. 325.

Despite Muslim control of Syria since the seventh century, Christianity has survived. There is a need for more training of priests in the Orthodox churches. Hindrances to the growth of the Protestant church include the lack of workers, need for more scripture distribution, small amount of mission activity, lack of Bible institutes and training centers, and political and social restrictions in the country. Among the general population, receptivity to the Gospel is little at best.


## NATIONAL CHURCHES


About 10% of Syria's people today are Christians, with the Orthodox and other eastern traditions involving about 7% of the population. The Catholic tradition embraces approximately 3% of the total population, while Protestants account for only about 0.5%.

### CATHOLIC

Of the Catholic churches in Syria, the Greek Catholic (Melkite) has the largest community. Most are Arabs. It is followed by the Armenian Catholic, Syrian Catholic and Maronite churches, all of which are about the same size. The Armenian rite church is composed primarily of Armenians, and the Syrian and Maronite churches primarily Arab people. About 45 priests, some European, serve the Latin-rite Catholic Church in Syria; its mostly Arab community is half the size of the Armenian, Syrian and Maronite rites. Smaller still is the Chaldean church, which also ministers primarily to Arabs. The Greek Catholic (Melkite) Church operated 31 schools prior to 1967, and the Latin-rite Catholics may still operate a seminary, dispensary, a few hospitals and schools, and student ministries.

### PROTESTANT AND ANGLICAN

Protestant Christians in Syria are led by about 40 ordained and 40 lay ministers. The National Evangelical Synod of Syria and Lebanon has perhaps the largest community, composed mostly of Arabs. The Armenian Evangelical Church, ministering to Armenians primarily, is half the size of the Synod. Less than half the size of the Armenian church is the mostly Arab National Evangelical Christian Alliance Church. Other churches represented in Syria include the Church of the Nazarene, mostly Arab; the Seventh-day Adventist Church, mostly Arab with some expatriates; the Christian Aid Mission, and the Baptist church. The National Evangelical Synod of Syria and Lebanon supports a hospital and elementary and secondary schools, and the Church of the Nazarene, a school.

### ORTHODOX

From the start, the Syrian church was eastern in orientation. The first major split from the Orthodox Church occured in 431 at the Council at Ephesus, when the Assyrian Church of the East (East Syrian Church) was born. Historically called Nestorians, the people belonging to this church now dislike that term. The Oriental (Non-Chalcedonian) Orthodox Churches broke away from the Eastern (Byzantine) Orthodox Church in 451, at the Council of Chalcedon.

The largest percentage of Syria's Christian population belongs to the Orthodox churches, the Greek being the largest. Most of its congregations are Arab. The Armenian Orthodox Church, almost two-thirds the size of the Greek, is composed mostly of Armenians. The basically Arab Syrian Orthodox Church is a little over one-third the size of the Greek-rite church. Orthodox churches operate a few schools and monasteries. Greek Orthodox priests tend to be open to having their congregations attend evangelical meetings.

The Assyrian Church of the East, a non-Orthodox, eastern church, has a community in Syria one-sixth the size of the Greek church.

### CHRISTIAN COUNCILS

Member churches of the Middle East Council of Churches in Beirut, Lebanon, include the National Evangelical Synod of Syria and Lebanon, Armenian Evangelical Churches, the Episcopal Church and Syrian, Greek and Armenian Orthodox Churches.

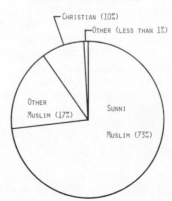

RELIGIOUS COMPOSITION OF SYRIA

Christian (10%)

Other (less than 1%)

Other Muslim (17%)

Sunni Muslim (73%)

## FOREIGN MISSIONS

Ten U.S. Protestant mission agencies, with undetermined numbers of personnel, and a Franciscan Catholic order, with 25 European and Syrian missionaries, are active in Syria. Medical and educational ministries seem to be the major foci.

## CATHOLIC

Syria affiliated from the start with an eastern form of worship, using Greek or Syriac liturgy. The official split between the Greek East and the Latin West came in 1054, with the Syrians being among those who did not recognize the authority of Rome. In the 16th, 17th and 18th centuries, certain groups broke away from the Orthodox churches to reunite with Rome. They retained their eastern rites, but recognized the Pope. Called Uniate Churches, they have a well-developed indigenous structure, with national leadership.

The Latin-rite (Roman) church has had small representation in Syria throughout the centuries. In the thirteenth century, the city of Aleppo became a Crusader center; today it is the residence of the Apostolic Vicar. Almost half the Latin-rite Catholics reside here.

The Roman Catholic community is served by European and Syrian priests; 25 are Franciscans and about 20 are Jesuits. Many more sisters work throughout the country.

## PROTESTANT

Ten mission agencies from the United States minister in Syria. Among those working there longest are the Armenian Missionary Association, which has a clinic; the Church of the Nazarene, which operates or supports schools, and the United Presbyterian Church in the USA. Others include Child Evangelism Fellowship, Christian Aid Mission, Jesus to the Communist World, Livingstone Memorial Mission, Lutheran World Federation (USA), Lutheran World Relief and World Wide Missions. The total number of personnel from these agencies is not known. Ministries of some mission agencies, notably the Reformed Presbyterian Church in North America and the Christian and Missionary Alliance, were turned over to the indigenous church, the National Evangelical Synod of Syria and Lebanon, in the 1960's.

## ORTHODOX

Because of Syria's historical affiliation with Eastern Orthodoxy, the church has developed Syrian leadership. Expatriate Orthodox mission efforts have basically been unknown.

About 7% of the population is Greek Orthodox, Oriental Orthodox, or connected with the Assyrian Church of the East. The latter, though not Orthodox, is eastern in tradition.

## MAJOR CHRISTIAN ACTIVITIES

## EVANGELISM

The Christian Alliance Church in Damascus in involved in sharing the good news and communicating God's truth to about 15,000 Arabs, middle and low class people, and students. Christ Church in Aleppo is working with 10,000 Arabs and Armenians Because of governmental restriction, most of this type of ministry should be conducted under the patronage of Arab pastors. Student camps, pastors' meetings, a Bible institute and crusades are all needed to share this truth with Muslim friends.

## BROADCASTING

Although there are no Christian sending or receiving stations in Syria, Arabic broadcasts can be heard in the country. These include programs from Trans World Radio in Monaco and Cyprus, ELWA in Liberia, and Far East Broadcasting Association. There is a need for more follow-up and more programs, but it is difficult to accomplish this when Syria is very closed to non-Muslim, non-Communist literature or broadcasting and when mail is censored.

## LITERATURE

There is no known Christian publishing house in Syria. Reliance on Christians in Beirut, Lebanon, for literature was almost completely stopped during the civil war in Lebanon from late 1975 to 1977. Christian literature in the Arabic and Armenian languages would have great potential to reach the masses. Story books would also be helpful, along with high quality essays, to reach the literate or highly educated portion of the population.

## BIBLE TRANSLATION AND DISTRIBUTION

Translations of the entire Bible are available in Arabic, French, Armenian and Syriac. About 44% of Arabic speakers are literate. A Kurdish New Testament was translated in 1872, and Scriptures are being translated into the Circassian language. The nearest Bible Society office is located in Beirut, Lebanon. Recent United Bible Society scripture distribution figures are:

|            | 1976    | 1975   |
|------------|---------|--------|
| Bibles     | 982     | 581    |
| Testaments | 2,019   | 1,153  |
| Portions   | 50,239  | 3,671  |
| Selections | 64,342  | 46,266 |
| Total      | 117,582 | 51,671 |

Although there is good scripture distribution activity in Aleppo, the country generally needs much more. People are hungry for God's word and doors are open for this type of ministry. Scriptures in Arabic and Armenian have potential for helping the most people.

## EDUCATION (THEOLOGICAL AND CHRISTIAN)

Theological education in Syria appears to be limited to the one Latin-rite Catholic seminary and a few Orthodox monasteries. Training centers for sharing the good news and a Bible institute are greatly needed. The Greek Catholic (Melkite) Church operated 31 schools prior to 1967, and the Latin-rite Catholics probably still operate some schools and student ministries. The National Evangelical Synod of Syria and Lebanon supports elementary and secondary schools, and the Church of the Nazarene, a school. The Orthodox churches also operate a few schools.

## SOCIAL CONCERN

Much church and mission activity consists of educational or medical ministries. There are a few Catholic hospitals and a Latin-rite Catholic dispensary. The National Evangelical Synod of Syria and Lebanon, in cooperation with the United Presbyterian Church in the U.S.A., operates four elementary and five secondary schools, with a combined enrollment of over 3500, and a 30-bed hospital in Nebek, which assists over 1000 in-patients and 7200 out-patients annually. One additional clinic is operated by the Armenian Missionary Association. Lutheran World Relief continues to provide ongoing refugee assistance in Syria.

## POPULATION

Syria's mid-1976 population of 7,596,000, including Palestinian refugees, is growing by 3.3% per year. Half of all Syrians lived in urban areas in 1976, and 80% live in the narrow western part of the country. Damascus, the capital city, and its suburbs housed over 1,334,000 persons in 1973; its population doubled between 1959 and 1973. Other major cities in order of size are Aleppo, with 646,000 persons in 1973, Homs, Hama, Latakia and Deir-ez-Zor. About 51% of Syria's people are male, and 49% are female. Half the total population is under 15.4 years.

## COMPOSITION

Arabs account for half the population; most are Sunni Muslims. Adherents of the Alawite sect of Shiah Islam comprise 12%, Bedouins 8%, Orthodox and East Syrian Christians 7%, and Kurdish Sunni Muslims 6%. Palestinian refugees, also Sunni Muslims, make up another 4% of Syria's people. Groups which are each 3% of the population are Turkomen (predominantly Sunni Muslims), Druzes (Christo-pagan sect of Shiah Islam), and Catholic and Protestant Christians. The Ismailis, a Misari sect of Shiah Islam, comprise 1.5%, and the Yazidis, Jews and Circassians combined make up another 0.5%.

Socio-economically, Syria's people fall into three broad categories--urban dwellers, villagers and tribal peoples. Half the population is concentrated in cities. Industrialists and former landowners comprise the primarily Sunni Muslim old elite. These people, along with the religious leaders and teachers, make up the upper class. The middle class urban groups include the military, many of whom are Alawites, the bureaucracy, traders, artisans, professionals and clerks. Small merchants, both Christian and Muslim, and migrant workers are considered urban lower class. In villages live many medicine men and women, farmers, small storekeepers, herders, tenants and sharecroppers. Landowners usually live in nearby cities. Bedouins--nomads, farmers and herders--are the predominant tribal peoples.

## LITERACY AND LANGUAGES

About 41% of Syria's people are literate. Among Arabs literacy reaches 70%, while among the Bedouins it is only 5%. Arabic is the official language, but Kurdish and Armenian are also spoken in the country.

French is widely understood and English is used in larger cities, probably because both are taught widely as second languages in schools.

## RELIGION

The predominant religion, Sunni Islam, embraces about 73% of the population. Other Muslims, including Shiah Muslims, comprise an additional 17%. About 10% are Christians--Orthodox, Catholic and Protestant combined. The Greek, Armenian and Syrian Orthodox churches, along with the Assyrian Church of the East, embrace over 7% of the total population. Three percent belong to one of the six Catholic traditions. Protestants account for only about 0.5% of the population. There is an upward growth trend in the Protestant evangelical denominations, but the Muslim and Jewish communities remain about the same.

## GEOGRAPHY AND CLIMATE

The Middle Eastern nation of Syria shares its borders with the Mediterranean Sea and Lebanon on the west, Turkey on the north, Iraq on the east, and Jordan on the south. About 45% of the land is arable, and of that 70% is cultivated. The western portion and Mediterranean coast, where 80% of the people live, is suitable for farming because it receives 25-100 centimeters (10-40 inches) of rain yearly. The climate ranges from cold weather with frost and snow to over 43 degrees centigrade (110 degrees Fahrenheit). Syria's resources include petroleum and natural gas deposits, plus a variety of metals and minerals.

## HISTORY

Syria, a center of ancient civilization, was occupied by many peoples before the time of Christ and later by the Greeks, Romans, Nabataeans, Byzantines, and even portions by Crusaders. Damascus was the provincial capital of the Mameluke Empire from 1260 to 1516. Then the area came under the rule of the Ottoman Turks in 1517; they remained in control, except for a brief occupation by Egypt from 1832-40, for the next 400 years. The French occupied Syria during most of the time between 1920 and 1946, when it received independence. Unstable politics, including a coup in 1954, led to the unsuccessful merger of Egypt and Syria. In 1961 Syria reestablished itself as an independent state, the Syrian Arab Republic. The government changed several times in the 1960's. A bloodless coup in 1970 brought Lt.-Gen. Hafiz al-Assad to power; he was elected President the next year and continues to lead the country in relative stability. Syria entered hostilities with Egypt against Israel in 1973. Since 1975 President Assad's government has been trying to help resolve the civil war in Lebanon.

## GOVERNMENT AND POLITICAL CONDITIONS

Syria is a republic with an elected President and a Council of Ministers. A 173-member People's Council was appointed in 1971. The new permanent Constitution approved in 1973 differs little from the provisional one in effect since 1964. It no longer states that Islam is the religion of the State, but Islamic law is the major legislative source and the Chief of State must be a Muslim. Syria's judicial system is a combination of Ottoman, French and Islamic laws.

The Ba'ath Party of power, founded by a Syrian Christian, proclaims "Unity, Freedom, and Socialism". It advocates state ownership of the means of industrial production, redistribution of agricultural land, and establishment of a Socialist revolution in all the Arab world. Assad's leadership tends to be pragmatic and stable.

The Syrian Army is key to changes of government. The Ba'ath Party has been successful in building support from the leftist-oriented army.

## ECONOMY

Agriculture, forestry, hunting and fishing occupied about 51% of Syria's people in 1973. Manufacturing and mining accounted for 11%; trade, catering, hotels for 9%, and transport and communications for 4%. Petroleum production, refining and transit charges provided 15% of the GNP in 1975. Major exports for 1975, in decreasing value, were crude petroleum and related products, cotton, other textiles, preserved foods, beverages and tobacco, and vegetables and fruit. Principal imports for 1975 were primarily base metals and manufactures, vehicles, and preserved foods, beverages and tobacco. In 1975 Syria's imports amounted to almost twice the monetary value of the nation's exports.

In March 1977 3.70 Syrian pounds were equivalent to one U.S. dollar. Syria's GNP for 1975, in January 1977 prices, was US $5 billion. Per capita GNP for 1974 was US $560, with a growth rate of 4.2% between 1965 and 1974.

# CHURCH MEMBERSHIP STATISTICS FOR SYRIA

Note: Statistics have been taken from different sources and are the most current data available. Definitions of "membership" vary among churches and may not always be comparable.

| Church or Mission Name | Communicants (Full Members) | Community (Estimate) |
|---|---|---|
| **PROTESTANT** | | |
| Armenian Evangelical Church | | 5,000 |
| Baptist church | | |
| Christian Aid Mission | | |
| Church of the Nazarene | 132 | |
| National Evangelical Christian Alliance Church | 200 | 2,000 |
| National Evangelical Synod of Syria and Lebanon | 1,675 | 10,000 |
| Seventh-day Adventist Church | 210 | |
| | | |
| **CATHOLIC** | | |
| Armenian Catholic Church | | 22,000 |
| Chaldean Catholic Church | | 6,000 |
| Greek (Melkite) Catholic Church | | 64,000 |
| Latin-rite Catholic Church | | 10,000 |
| Maronite Catholic Church | | 19,000 |
| Syrian Catholic Church | | 20,000 |
| | | |
| **ORTHODOX** | | |
| | | |
| Armenian Orthodox Church | | 122,000 |
| Greek Orthodox Church | | 200,000 |
| Syrian Orthodox Church | | 80,000 |
| | | |
| **ASSYRIAN** | | |
| | | |
| Assyrian Church of the East | | 30,000 |

# SELECTED BIBLIOGRAPHY AND INFORMATION SOURCES

The sources listed below are to help the reader find additional information on this country and Christian ministries there. This list does not try to be comprehensive or complete.

## DOCUMENTS

### General

Azzi, Robert, "Damascus, Syria's Uneasy Eden", National Geographic, April 1974.
Area Handbook for Syria, Washington, DC: The American University, 1971.
Background Notes, Washington, DC: U.S. State Department, 1977.
Foreign Money Quotation List, Los Angeles: Deak and Co., March 9, 1977.
Kloss, H. and G.D. McConnell, Linguistic Composition of the Nations of the World, volume 1, Quebec: University of Laval Press, 1974.
Sewell, John W., U.S. and World Development: Agenda 1977, New York: Praeger, 1977.
The Middle East and North Africa 1976-77, London: Europa, 1976.
United Nations Population and Vital Statistics Report, New York, April 1, 1977.

### Christian

Dayton, Edward R., editor, Mission Handbook: North American Protestant Ministries Overseas, Monrovia, CA: MARC, 1976.
Foy, Felician A., editor, Catholic Almanac, 1977, Huntington, IN: Our Sunday Visitor, Inc., 1976.
Grimes, Barbara F., editor, Ethnologue, Huntington Beach: Wycliffe Bible Translators, Inc., 1974.
Horner, Norman, Rediscovering Christianity Where It Began, Beirut: Heidelberg Press, 1974.
International Christian Broadcasters, World Directory of Religious Radio and Television Broadcasting, South Pasadena: William Carey Library, 1973.
United Bible Societies Directory, 1975.

## ORGANIZATIONS

Bible Society in Lebanon, P.O. Box 747, Beirut, Lebanon
Near East Council of Churches, Beirut, Lebanon

## ACKNOWLEDGEMENTS

The information in this profile was taken from many sources which were the best available to the editors at the time of preparation. However, the accuracy of the information cannot be guaranteed. Views expressed or implied in this publication are not necessarily those of World Vision. The editors have tried to present the ministries of various organizations in an objective manner, without undue bias or emphasis. Where we have failed, we apologize for erroneous impressions that may result and request that comments and corrections be sent to MARC, 919 West Huntington Drive, Monrovia, California, USA 91016. We appreciate and acknowledge the comments and contributions of various organizations and individuals in the preparation of this publication.

# STATUS OF CHRISTIANITY COUNTRY PROFILE

# TURKEY

## SUMMARY

AREA - 785,710 square kilometers (302,169 square miles)
POPULATION - 40.2 million (mid-1976)
RELIGION - 99% Muslim; Jews and Christians

Though they occupy nearly the same territory, Turkey today contrasts sharply with Asia Minor of biblical times. By the fourth century after Christ, the area was completely evangelized by Christians; present-day Turkey has a Christian population of less than 1%. Turkish presence in the area of the Anatolian Plateau began during the ninth century, and Islam, the religion brought by the Turks, dominates public and private life, in spite of the efforts of recent leaders to secularize the country.

Of the 0.4% of the population that is Christian, about 87% are Orthodox, 11% are Catholic and 2% are Protestant. Christianity mostly claims people from ethnic minorities, such as Armenians and Greeks; converted Turks are extremely rare. Muslims (99% of the population) affiliate with one of three sects: Sunni, Shiah and Yazidi.

Most of the people in the country are ethnically Turkish. About 7% are Kurds, a tribal group with cultural and religious characteristics somewhat different from Turks. Other ethnic minority groups include Arabs, numbering 300,000, and Jews, whose 30,000 population is decreasing. Three Caucasian Muslim groups in the country are Circassians (70,000), Georgians (50,000) and Lazis (30,000).

Although no resident foreign missionaries are allowed in Turkey today, ministries continue quietly through Christians who work secular jobs and witness on an individual basis. Eighteen mission agencies minister in some way in Turkey, including organizations that broadcast from outside the country. A great hindrance to the spread of the gospel in the country is the hostility of Muslims to Christianity; converted Muslims face ostracism and special hardships from family and friends. Major ministries center on broadcasting, distribution of Scriptures and other Christian literature, and education.

Turkey's present constitution was drafted in 1961 and provides for a parliamentary democracy. Recent years have seen violence related to political events; marshall law has been used at times in an attempt to keep order. The Constitution permits religious freedom, although in reality there are severe restraints on religions other than Islam.

Although the welfare of Turkey's people improves slowly, the country continues to be financially dependent on international agencies. Rapid inflation and imbalance in trade payments challenge Turkey in its attempt to become a financially independent, industrialized society.

The challenges facing the Church in Turkey are great; political, cultural and ethnic identification creates a barrier against Christianity that promises to be difficult to overcome in the future.

This program is jointly carried out by the Strategy Working Group of the Lausanne Committee for World Evangelization and MARC, a ministry of World Vision International. For further information on the program, please write: MARC, 919 West Huntington Drive, Monrovia, CA 91016 U.S.A.

# UNREACHED PEOPLES

Virtually all of Turkey's population is unreached. The unreached ethnolinguistic groups are Turks, Kurds, Arabs, Caucasians, and Jews. These can be broken down into still smaller subgroups.

All but a handful of the Turks are Muslims. They can be broken down into the following major groups: rural agricultural people, industrial workers, construction workers, returned migrant workers, and university graduates. For most of them, but particularly in the eyes of the villagers, the mosque is a sacred institution.

About 7% of the population, or 3,000,000 people, are Kurdish. They are mainly tribal, agricultural Muslims who live in mountainous areas and claim an ethnic loyalty that crosses political boundaries. There are several subtribes and dialects within the Kurdish people, including the Doudjiks, Kizibakhs, Karmanjis and Zazas. There are also three major religious subgroups: Sunni, Alevi (Shiah) and Yazidi. The popularity and influence of dervish orders, which are outlawed in Turkey, among the Kurds indicates a cultural temperament different from that of the Turks.

Although there are only about 30,000 Jews in Turkey, and emigration is causing a further dwindling of their numbers, there is great diversity among them. Most live in Istanbul and Izmir as owners of small shops and businesses. Homogeneous subgroups include Sephardic Jews, who came originally from Spain in 1492 and speak Spanish; Ashkenazi Jews, and Istanbul Jews. Two groups are considered heretical by the Jews because of their affiliation with Islam; they are the Donme and Karaites.

There are approximately 300,000 Arabs in modern Turkey, most of whom are concentrated along the Syrian border in the province of Hatay. Arabic is their mother tongue and they are generally tribal in their social organization. Originally brought in as laborers, they now work in agriculture, small shops, and small businesses.

Three Caucasian Muslim peoples are found in Turkey: Circassians, Georgians, and Lazis. Each is a distinct group both in language and location. The approximately 70,000 Circassians occupy the Adapazari region and are the owners of small farms or work as farm laborers. The 50,000 Georgians, including the subgroup of Abkaz

farmers, dwell in northeast Turkey, in Coruh, and some in the northwest. The 30,000 Lazis dwell in Rize, also in the northeast; they are ethnically Greek.

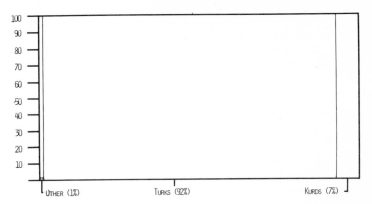

POPULATION COMPOSITION OF TURKEY
(SHADING INDICATES CHRISTIANS)

NOTE: These figures are representative approximations. They should be seen as indications of magnitude, not precise.

## CURRENT STATUS OF CHRISTIANITY

Once the home of many thriving churches planted by the Apostle Paul, Turkey is today one of the most impregnable strongholds of Islam in the world. Steeled against Christianity since the days of the Crusades, and generally misinformed concerning the teachings of the gospel, the Turkish people equate their ethnic identity with adherence to Islam. Out of a population of 40.2 million only 0.4% are Christians; and the vast majority of these are of ethnic groups other than Turkish. The number of converted Turks who have demonstrated a solid commitment to Christ is less than 50. Of the Christians in Turkey, 2% are Protestant, 11% are Catholic, 20% are Greek Orthodox and 67% are Oriental Orthodox. Although the Orthodox churches are the predominant Christian bodies, their long history of severe persecution from Muslims has discouraged present-day attempts to evangelize.

Since Turkey became a Republic under Kemal Ataturk in 1923, it has been a secular state. Despite the clear tolerance of other religions indicated in the 19th and 20th articles of the Constitution, there has been a high degree of state pressure directed against Christian evangelism. Evangelization is made even more difficult by religious, linguistic, cultural, and temperamental factors inherent in the people themselves.

FOREIGN MISSIONS

Asia Minor, which covered approximately
the same area as modern Turkey, was
thoroughly evangelized by the fourth
century. However, with the gradual
spiritual decay precipitated by heresies,
lukewarmness, and a waning interest in
evangelism, the fires of these once great
churches began to flicker. When the
Islamic Turks began their invasion of the
land in the ninth century, they found a
dead and degenerate Christianity which
they were quick to obliterate. Since the
fall of Constantinople in AD 1453,
Christianity in Turkey has been all but
eradicated. It mostly exists among
minority groups.

In 1820 the American Board of
Commissioners for Foreign Missions sent
two missionaries to Turkey. In 1831 they
sent one more. Mission work centered on
education and scripture translation.
Throughout years of effort, these workers
found only the Armenians to be receptive.

Initially hoping to work through a revived
Armenian Gregorian Church, missions in
Turkey soon discovered that this would not
be possible; in 1846 evangelicals within
the Armenian Church were excommunicated.
In 1847 the first evangelical church was
formed in modern Turkey.

The Armenian Evangelical Church grew
rapidly. In 1865 there were 152 foreign
missionaries working with 800 Armenian
workers in 111 churches with 12,000 full
members. Schools, colleges, and
theological seminaries were established.

This promising movement of Armenians to an
evangelical faith was brought to an
immediate end by a severe persecution of
all Armenians in the late 19th century.
The resultant migration from Turkey has
left only three Armenian Evangelical
churches in Turkey, and all of these are
in Istanbul. Only 0.4% of the population
is Christian today.

No official "missionaries" are allowed in
Turkey today. However, concerned
Christians have taken secular jobs and in
the normal course of life, share the
message and power of the gospel in their
own lives.

A total of 18 missionary organizations are
known to have ministries directed toward
the Turks. This includes Catholics and
Seventh-day Adventists, plus radio
broadcasting from outside Turkey.
Approximately 81 North American and
European personnel are involved, of which

31 focus their efforts particularly on
evangelism.

The United Church of Christ Board for
World Ministries, the descendant of the
first mission in Turkey, today sponsors
several schools and a hospital. It is the
largest mission, with 44 North American
personnel in 1975, a decline from the 63
workers they had in Turkey in 1972. They
stay in the country as teachers or
professionals in secular positions.
Operation Mobilization is the second
largest mission in Turkey, with 15 career
missionaries and about 25 short-term
workers a year. The mission is engaged in
literature distribution; workers are
reported to have been arrested and
deported at times. The United Bible
Societies are engaged in Bible translation
and literature distribution work. The
Southern Baptist Church has two career
missionaries working in the Galatian
Baptist Church in Ankara. World Wide
Missions is supporting a national
preacher.

The Seventh-day Adventists have one church
with a community of 141 which is staffed
by three nationals.

The Roman Catholic missionary presence has
declined from four to three in the last
three years.

Estimates put the actual number of Turks
who are practicing Christians from 25 to
75, a number terribly minute in proportion
to the population of Turkey. There are
several house fellowships meeting
regularly in Istanbul, Ankara, Izmir, and
the Adana area. Others are scattered in
the rest of the country with little or no
opportunity for fellowship.

Language and culture are obvious
hindrances to western missionary
endeavors. The intense identification of
ethnic group with religious conviction,
and the threat of ostracism from one's
family make conversion to Christianity a
very difficult decision for a Turk.
Ostracism from one's family removes one
from the possibility of marriage and
economic security.

Islam, in practice the national faith of
Turkey, is the greatest obstacle to
Christianity in Turkey. Though Kemal
Ataturk attempted to secularize Turkey, it
continues as a leading source of Muslim
pilgrims to Mecca. Nationality and
religion are so fused that it is believed
that every "true" Turk is a Muslim.

# NATIONAL CHURCHES

## PROTESTANT CHURCHES

Most of the Protestant churches were founded in the 19th century. Protestantism is but a tiny minority within the Christian population of Turkey. Total Protestants number only about 3,000, or less than 2% of all the Christians in Turkey. They are almost completely from ethnic minorities. Most are Europeans, and others are primarily Armenians and Greeks; there are a few Arab, Kurdish and Assyrian Christians. Most Protestant churches are located in Istanbul. The largest groups are the German Lutherans, Armenian Evangelicals, Anglicans, and Pentecostals. The Southern Baptists started a church in 1966.

There is an encouraging report that several independent evangelical fellowships have sprung up among the Turks and other ethnic groups. Small groups of believers meet in the major cities. There are only a handful of these loose bodies of converted Muslims, and they usually meet in secret.

## CATHOLIC CHURCHES

Most of the 20,800 Catholics in Turkey affiliate with the Uniate churches; those churches that reunited with Rome during the centuries of the ecumenical councils. Armenian Catholics comprise the largest Uniate body. Chaldean and Syrian Catholic churches generally use Syriac liturgies, while the Melkites prefer Arabic. These three churches are smaller than the Armenian church. The Greek Catholic churches use Greek and Turkish rites.

When combined with those using the Latin rite, Catholics of all kinds make up 11% of all the Christians in Turkey.

## ORTHODOX CHURCHES

Orthodoxy is the predominant form of Christianity in Turkey; there are approximately 162,000 Orthodox believers. More specifically, adherents of Oriental (non-Chalcedonian) Orthodox Churches comprise 67% of the Christians in Turkey, while Greek Orthodox Christians make up 20% of the total Christian population. The Oriental bodies in the country are the Armenian Orthodox Church, numbering 65,000, and the Syrian Orthodox Church, which totals 60,000.

All these Christian bodies have a long history in the Near East. All descend from churches which had their beginings in apostolic times. The Oriental Orthodox churches rejected Nestorian doctrine, but then also rejected the Christology of the Council at Chalcedon (AD 451).

The Syrian Church descends from an early body of Syriac-speaking Nestorians, and Syriac remains the liturgical language.

The Greek Orthodox Church, which embraced the Council at Chalcedon in the fifth century, claims most of the very small minority of Greeks in Turkey. It includes the Patriarchate of Constantinople (35,000) and the Patriarchate of Antioch (2000).

Armenians and Greeks, who are both historically Orthodox, are concentrated in the city of Istanbul. There are few Christians in Turkey who reside outside of this major city. The Syrian Orthodox Christians, however, are located in the southeastern region of Turkey called Mardin.

## GROWTH

Of the churches that have reported their statistics, all are declining in membership. This decline parallels minority population statistics; minority groups such as the Armenians, who have historically suffered severely under the Turks, are emigrating from Turkey. Emigration of Christians probably explains the generally slower growth of the cities with a heavy Christian population, in comparison with the faster growth of other cities. Ethnocentrism and lack of missionary evangelistic outreach help discourage membership growth.

## COOPERATIVE AGENCIES

Two churches, the Greek Evangelical and the German Protestant, are affiliated with an international council of their respective ecclesiastical traditions.

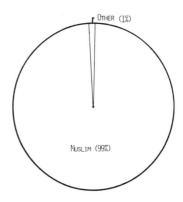

RELIGIOUS COMPOSITION

Other (1%)

Muslim (99%)

# MAJOR CHRISTIAN ACTIVITIES

The following descriptions are intended to make readers aware of the potential for various types of ministries. Not all church agencies are specifically mentioned.

## EVANGELISM

Many types of Christian witness are present in Turkey, and although none are greatly successful, some are more fruitful than others. Tract distribution with a Bible correspondence course offer has been somewhat effective. In 1977 one school received 50 letters a month requesting courses. Though most do not complete these courses, those that demonstrate genuine interest are visited personally. About 2000 have written for a course since 1965.

Another method has been to take secular work in Turkey, and then engage in personal or friendship evangelism. Fellow college students and friends meet in coffee shops. Others are invited to dinner where they hear and see the Christian life.

The most effective witnesses in Turkey are converted Turks. Western missionaries can be effective, but Armenian and Greek missionaries are an anathema to the Turks.

Some agencies are attempting to reach Turkey through the many Turkish migrant workers in Europe. These Turks are much more open to evangelism, though still very resistant and conservative. Religious freedom in Germany has caused more to hear the gospel; thus, more are converted.

## BROADCASTING

Two-thirds of Turkey's population lives in villages and they, along with many urban dwellers, depend on radio as their primary source of news. Most Turks own a radio. In 1978 Trans World Radio was broadcasting six short-wave programs a week to Turkey, and one medium-wave program per week to Turkish-speakers in Europe. The Far Eastern Broadcasting Association is broadcasting to Turkish-speakers in northwest Iran. IBRA radio broadcasts two Turkish programs a week by short-wave. All of these groups broadcast from outside of Turkey.

## BIBLE TRANSLATION AND DISTRIBUTION

Bible translation and distribution has been tedious in Turkey. A project to modernize the antiquated Turkish translation was begun in 1965, but the work has progressed slowly; the Gospel of Mark was completed in 1976 and published in 1978. Revision of other Gospels is in progress.

The Bible Society is based in Istanbul where it has a bookshop and a colporteur whose job it is to keep secular bookshops supplied with Bibles and New Testaments. There is one other Christian bookshop in Turkey, located in Tarsus. The other bookstore in Istanbul closed in 1971. About 1000 to 1500 Bibles are sold each year. Distribution of Bible portions has increased from 15,000-20,000 in 1970 to 27,000 in 1974. Given the population growth rate of 1,000,000 each year, this distribution is reaching a smaller proportion of the population each year.

## EDUCATION

The United Church of Christ Board for World Ministries operates a girl's secondary school at Izmir, a girl's school at Istanbul, and a boy's school at Tarsus. A lack of funds and teachers forced the closing of a boy's school at Talas in the late 1960's. In 1963 the four schools had a total of 1400 pupils. No religious training is permitted in these schools by the government. The former Robert College, founded in Istanbul as a Christian college, was taken over by the government and renamed; it is no longer allowed to give religious instruction. The situation has deteriorated since Wilbur Smith said in 1963, "Without a doubt Christian education in Turkey is today at the lowest ebb that it has been for over a century."

## SOCIAL CONCERN

Little Christian outreach was possible to the victims of the 1976 earthquake which killed thousands of Turks and left many thousands more homeless. Among other groups, World Vision and World Wide Missions tried to send money for relief but were unsuccessful. The Turkish government restricted outside aid through Turkish Christians.

In medical ministries, the United Church of Christ has one hospital in Gaziantep.

# NATION AND ITS PEOPLE

## POPULATION

With a population of 40.2 million in mid-1976 and an annual growth rate of 2.6%, Turkey is expected to have a population of about 71.3 million persons in the year AD 2000.

The population density is about 48 people per square kilometer (125 per square mile) with 42% of the people living on 50% of the land. The fertile coast lands and European Turkey are the most densely populated, while the southeastern portion is the most sparsely populated. There are approximately 35,000 villages. The annual urban growth rate has been 6% indicating rapid urbanization. In 1970 it was estimated that 38.7% of the population lived in cities and that 12% of the population lived in cities over 100,000 persons.

Istanbul, with 3,860,000 people, is the largest city. Ankara 2,570,000), the capital city, Adana (1,000,000), and Izmir (1,660,000) are other major cities.

## COMPOSITION

The predominant ethnic group is the Turks who make up 92% of the population. The Kurds, a people with a strong national identity, comprise 7% (about 3 million) of the population. The remaining 1% consists of several distinct ethnic groups: Arabs (0.3 million), Causasian peoples (Circassians, with 70,000, Georgians, with 55,000, Lazis, with 30,000), Greeks (70,000), Armenians (69,000), Jews (30,000), and the Donme. The non-Muslim, non-Turkish ethnic groups (Greeks, Armenians, Jews) are often treated as a single group by the Turks, and do themselves, on occasions, associate across ethnic barriers.

## LITERACY AND LANGUAGES

About 55% of the adult population of Turkey is literate. The Turkish government has made a determined effort to educate its people. More than 90% of primary aged children attend school for some part of the year. In 1975 there were 5,400,000 children in primary school. During the same year there were about 1.5 million in secondary schools and 219,000 in higher education.

There is a plethora of languages spoken in Turkey, but Turkish is the mother-tongue of at least 90% of the population. Kurdish, a language akin to Persian, is spoken by about 7.1% and Arabic by 1.2%. Greek, Circassian, Armenian, Georgian, Ladino, Yiddish, and Lazi are spoken by very small minorities.

## RELIGION

Islam claims over 99% of Turkey's population. The Turks, Kurds, Arabs, and Caucasians are almost completely Muslim. The Sunni sect is the predominant Islamic group. The very small religious sect of the Domne is a synthesis of Islam and Judaism, and is considered heretical by both faiths. The non-Muslim population consists of Jews and Greek and Armenian Christians. Proselytizing by non-Muslims is legally permitted, but in practice very difficult.

## GEOGRAPHY AND CLIMATE

The land of Turkey forms a great land bridge between Europe and Asia. In its European sector, west of the Sea of Marmara, it borders Greece and Bulgaria. The Black Sea forms most of its northern boundary, with the USSR and Iran touching its eastern boundary. To the south are Iraq, Syria, and the Mediterranean Sea.

The total land area is about 735,710 square kilometers (302,169 square miles), somewhat smaller than the states of Texas and Louisiana combined. The country consists of two basic topographical units, the high Anatolian Plateau and the lower, more fertile, coastal regions. Western Anatolia is fertile and wheat is the principal crop. Eastern Anatolia is much more mountainous and infertile.

The average rainfall in Anatolia is over 30 centimeters (12 inches) per year, with a minimum of 20 centimeters (8 inches) a year. In central Anatolia there is a heavy rainfall in December and then again in late April and early June—a time known in Ankara as "the forty afternoons", since a thunderstorm is expected daily at about 4:00 pm.

## HISTORY

The Anatolian Plateau has been the home of many great nations, from the biblical Hittites of the second millennium BC, to the "Greeks" of Paul's missionary journeys. The Turkish occupation, which began with their migration from Central Asia in the ninth century AD, has been relatively brief. In 1071 the Oguz tribe conquered most of Anatolia and began the Seljuk dynasty. A mid-13th century invasion of Moguls set the Turkish occupation back until fresh migrations under Osman brought the plateau under Turkish control once again. The conquest

of Constantinople in 1453 began the
600-year reign of the Ottoman Empire.  In
the 16th century this empire was at the
zenith of its power, ruling from Moscow to
Vienna, Ethiopia to the Indian Ocean.
Defeat along with the Germans in World War
I brought an end to the empire.

A Greek invasion in 1919 caused a war of
independence which, under Kemal Ataturk,
was won in 1922.  In 1923 Turkey was
declared a republic, and Kemal Ataturk,
its first president, began a program of
reform and westernization.  Free elections
were held in 1950, at which time the
Democratic Party took power.  Economic
problems and internal tensions led to a
military coup in 1960.  In 1961 the
present Constitution was drafted.

## GOVERNMENT AND POLITICAL CONDITIONS

The Republic of Turkey is a parliamentary
democracy with executive, legislative, and
judicial branches.  The executive branch
consists of a powerful president, who is
elected by the combined legislature to a
seven-year term, and a prime minister,
selected by the president to be the head
of the government.  The legislature,
called the Grand National Assembly,
consists of the National Assembly, with
450 members, and the Senate, with 184
members.  The judicial branch consists of
a Court of Causation and the
administrative Council of State.

Although there are a multitude of
political parties in Turkey, the
Republican People's Party, Justice Party,
Democratic Party, and National Salvation
Party are the major political units.  A
coalition of the Justice and National
Salvation parties gained power in April
1975 and have continued in power to this
date.  Anyone over 21 years old may vote.

## ECONOMY

Turkey's Gross National Product was $35.9
billion dollars in 1975;  the annual
growth rate is 7%.  The per capita income
in the same year was $893 and its growth
rate is about 6% per year.  This increase
falls far short of the soaring inflation
which has been as high as 20% in recent
years.

Agriculture is Turkey's primary industry,
involving 64.1% of the labor force.
Turkey continues to be highly subsidized
by international monetary agencies and by
individual nations.  A severe deficit in
balance of payments and a soaring rate of
inflation make her attempts at
industrialization more difficult.

# CHURCH MEMBERSHIP STATISTICS FOR TURKEY

Note:  Statistics have been taken from different sources and are the most current data available.  Definitions of "membership" vary among churches and may not always be comparable.

| Church or Mission Name | Communicants (Full Members) | Community (Estimate) |
|---|---|---|
| **PROTESTANT AND ANGLICAN** | | |
| Anglican Church | | 300 |
| Armenian Evangelical Church | | 800 |
| Armenian Protestant Church | 220 | 300 |
| German Protestant Church | 400 | 900 |
| Greek Evangelical Church | | 200 |
| Pentecostal Church | | 300 |
| Seventh-day Adventist Church | | 200 |
| Southern Baptist Church | 59 | 80 |
| **CATHOLIC** | | |
| Armenian Catholic Church | | 10,000 |
| Chaldean Catholic Church | | 1,500 |
| Greek Catholic Church | | 800 |
| Maronite Church | | 800 |
| Melkite Church | | 400 |
| Roman Catholic Church | | 7,000 |
| Syrian Catholic Church | | 300 |
| **ORTHODOX** | | |
| Armenian Orthodox Church | | 65,000 |
| Greek Orthodox Church | | 35,000 |
| Patriarchate of Antioch | | 2,000 |
| Syrian Orthodox Church | | 60,000 |

# SELECTED BIBLIOGRAPHY AND INFORMATION SOURCES

The sources listed below are to help the reader find additional information on this country and Christian ministries there. This list does not try to be comprehensive or complete.

## DOCUMENTS

### General

"Background Notes", Washington DC: Superintendent of Documents, 1976.

Bliss, Beatrice, The Turk, San Francisco: Georgetown Press, 1976.

Garnett, Lucy M.J., "Albanian Women", The Women of Turkey, Vol. 2, London: David McNutt, 1891.

Nyrop, Richard F. et al, ed., Area Handbook for the Republic of Turkey, Washington, DC: American University Press, 1973.

Peters, Richard, The Story of the Turks: From Empire to Democracy, New York: C. S. Publishing Co., Inc., 1959.

Yasa, Ibraim, Hasanogian: Socio-economic Structure of a Turkish Village, Ankara: Public Administration Institute for Turkey and the Middle East, 1957.

### Christian

Horner, Norman A., Rediscovering Christianity Where it Began, Beirut: Heidelberg Press, 1974.

Smith, Wilbur, "The Gospel and the Turk", Decision, 1963.

## ACKNOWLEDGMENTS

The information in this profile was taken from many sources which were the best available to the editors at the time of preparation. However, the accuracy of the information cannot be guaranteed. Views expressed or implied in this publication are not necessarily those of World Vision. The editors have tried to present the ministries of the various organizations in an objective manner, without undue bias or emphasis. Where we have failed, we apologize for erroneous impressions that may result and request that comments and corrections be sent to MARC, 919 West Huntington Drive, Monrovia, California, USA 91016. We appreciate and acknowledge the comments and contributions of various organizations and individuals in the preparation of this publication.

# STATUS OF CHRISTIANITY COUNTRY PROFILE

# UNITED ARAB EMIRATES

## SUMMARY

AREA - 85,000 square kilometers (33,000 square miles)
POPULATION - 300,000
RELIGION - 92% Sunni Muslim; 2% Shia Muslim; 6% Christian, Hindu and other

The United Arab Emirates (UAE) lie on the southeastern seaboard of Arabia. The area was known as the Pirate Coast up until the twentieth century. In recent decades the area has been called the Trucial States, the Trucial Shaikdoms and Trucial Oman. The seven nation states of Abu Dhabi, Dubai, Sharjah, Ras El Khaymah, Ajaman, Um El Quain and Fujayrah now form the United Arab Emirates. The confederation was established following the British withdrawal from the Gulf colonies and protectorates. A provisional constitution was established in 1971 which provided for a Supreme Council of Rulers, headed by the ruler (Shaik) of Abu Dhabi, a Federal Council of Ministers a Federal National Council and a Supreme court. The provisional constitution was extended for five years after the rulers failed to agree on a permanent constitution although it was only intended to operate from 1971 to 1976.

Building a modern society on the sand is a formidable task even with a billion dollars a year from oil revenues and a small population. The UAE have one of the highest per capita incomes in the world. The government regulates the expenditure of money by providing housing, medical care and employment for all citizens. A modern industrial society is emerging. Historic problems of scarcity of water and usable agricultural land still plague the UAE, but measures being taken by several cooperating nations are beginning to resolve some of the problems.

Extremely rapid development since 1968 has resulted in the quadrupling of the population. Workers and executives, sweepers and educators, highly trained and untrained foreigners entered the UAE from around the world. Most of the population (58%) is concentrated in the cities of Abu Dhabi and Dubai. Approximately 75% of the total population are foreign laborers, many of whom do not intend to stay long.

The federation exists primarily because Sheikh Zayed of Abu Dhabi offers strong leadership and makes provision for 98% of the funds needed for the federal budget.

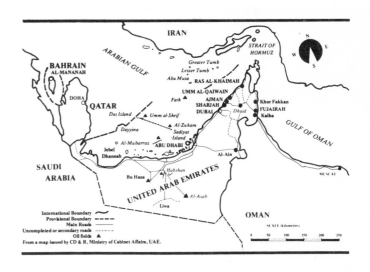

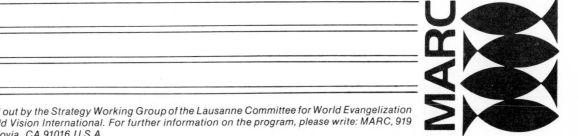

*This program is jointly carried out by the Strategy Working Group of the Lausanne Committee for World Evangelization and MARC, a ministry of World Vision International. For further information on the program, please write: MARC, 919 West Huntington Drive, Monrovia, CA 91016 U.S.A.*

## UNREACHED PEOPLES

Iranians are numerous in Abu Dhabi, Dubai and Sharjah where they constitute 25% of the total population. They consist of three distinct sub-groups. The southern Iranians are the largest and oldest immigrant group. Generally, they come from the coastal regions, speak Arabic as well as Farsi and in many instances have been settled for several generations. Some of the wealthier Gulf merchants are among this group. The Baluch come from southeastern Iran and Pakistan. They speak their native Baluch language, are generally among the lower strata of the work force and are the lowest paid immigrant laborers. Blue eyed and fair skinned immigrants from northern and central Iran primarily speak Farsi. Many of them are merchants who immigrated after the discovery of oil. The Iranian merchant community is one of the most active in all of the Emirates. Nearly all Iranians are Shia Muslims exept for the predominantly Sunni Baluch. It is considered prestigious by the Iranians, particularly the Arabic speaking southerners, to prove that they are descendents of Arabs who migrated to Iran from the Gulf region. As immigrants to the UAE, they are simply returning to their homeland. The celebration of Shia Muslim festivals is a common occurrence and they are not restricted. According to long-time residents who are Sunni Muslims the Shia are politically and spiritually "clean."

Pakistani immigrants are also quite diverse. The three major groups include the Pushto-speaking Pathans from the Northwest Frontier Province, the Urdu and Punjabi-speaking immigrants from Sind and the Baluch from Baluchistan and the Makran coast. The Baluch are actually part of the same people group as the Baluch from Iran. The Pathans and the Boluchs exist in large numbers in Dubai and Abu Dhabi. They comprise significant portions of the unskilled labor force. Despite their numbers, neither group has exerted any influence in government affairs. The Punjabs are the smallest group but are almost exclusively merchants, professionals and skilled workers of the middle class. Many of the intellectuals tend to be active in politics.

The Indians are a highly visible people group even though they constitute only 6% of the population. Unlike the Iranians and Pakistanis, the majority of Indians are merchants, professionals, artisans and skilled workers. English speaking Indian clerks and accountants are especially

numerous. In view of limited economic opportunities in India, the immigrants consider employment in the UAE a means of supporting families in India. Some are also engaged in activities connected with the smuggling trade. The smuggler's route lies principally between the ports of Dubai, Ras Al Khaymah and Khawr Fakkan in the UAE and along the west coast of India. Some small groups of low status, uneducated immigrant Indian laborers have immigrated including the Keralans.

Immigrant Arabs constitute 6% of the population and the number is constantly growing. The largest group are the Palestinians who are generally skilled technicians and "white collar" workers. They are the most disliked and often suspected of involvement in radical political movements. Contrary to their image, however, most Palestinians are actually concerned primarily with insuring economic gains.

Almost without exception, the Arabs from the Fertile Crescent countries and Egypt are employed in skilled jobs. The Jordanians, who are respected and trusted, are found in security forces in Abu Dhabi and as legal advisors throughout the lower gulf. They often work with Sudanese Arabs, a much smaller group who are regarded as particularly efficient in municipal affairs. The Egyptians tend to be involved in civil service jobs as administrative assistants in government ministries and teachers. Lebanon and Syria, like Egypt, Jordan and Iraq, have been the sources of doctors, lawyers, nurses, teachers, and administrators.

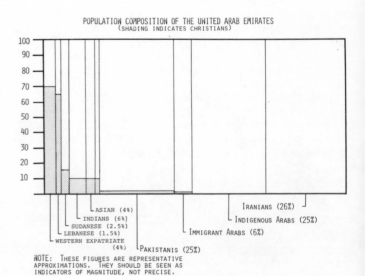

POPULATION COMPOSITION OF THE UNITED ARAB EMIRATES
(SHADING INDICATES CHRISTIANS)

ASIAN (4%)
INDIANS (6%)
SUDANESE (2.5%)
LEBANESE (1.5%)
WESTERN EXPATRIATE (4%)
PAKISTANIS (25%)
IMMIGRANT ARABS (6%)
IRANIANS (26%)
INDIGENOUS ARABS (25%)

NOTE: THESE FIGURES ARE REPRESENTATIVE APPROXIMATIONS. THEY SHOULD BE SEEN AS INDICATORS OF MAGNITUDE, NOT PRECISE.

# CURRENT STATUS OF CHRISTIANITY

The Christian Church has always enjoyed the kind treatment of the rulers, government and people of the UAE. They have supported Christian churches, places of worship, hospitals, clinics and schools. Over 50,000 Christians (6.2%) reside in UAE; including 20,000 Catholics, 18,000 Evangelicals and 12,000 Orthodox.

Families are generally strongly opposed to individuals converting to Christianity. A slight degree of tolerance on the part of others allows those who truly desire to change religions to do so. Arabs of the UAE have been expressing increased receptivity.

## NATIONAL CHURCHES

### PROTESTANT CHURCHES

Two Anglican churches have been built in the UAE, with one in Abu Dhabi and one in Dubai. The church in Dubai is actually more interdenominational than Anglican. At least one independent evangelical church is located in each of the cities of Abu Dhabi, Dubai, and Sharjah. The Evangelical Community Church located in Abu Dhabi, has a growing congregation including nearly 50 children. The Independent Community Church of Dubai has 100 adults with a Sunday school of 200 children. A new Pentecostal group is also meeting in Dubai. The Sharjah Independent Church has a very small congregation.

An Indian fellowship meets each Friday in Al Ain and three Indian churches presently exist in Abu Dhabi alone. A Brethern group meets in The Evangelical Alliance Mission (TEAM) facilities. and a Pentecostal group, and Mar Thomite group have house-churches. Though no specific data is avaiable it is likely that similar groups are meeting in Dubai and Sharjah.

Small groups of Pakistani believers meet together in Al Ain, Abu Dhabi, Dubai, and Sharjah and TEAM has fellowship meetings for Arabic speaking people in Al Ain.

It is one of the few church ministries among local Arabs. The fellowship consists of Arab believers associated with the mission hospital and is directed by a Lebanese Arab and his family. A fellowship of expatriate Arabs have called its own pastor, a Syrian, who has much experience in the ministry. The group has several Muslim converts and the pastor travels to Dubai each week to minister to Arab expatriots.

### CATHOLIC CHURCHES

Three churches have been built in Al Ain, Abu Dhabi and Dubai for the 20,000 Roman Catholics. Two schools are connected with the Cathederal Center in Abu Dhabi. An apostolic delegate oversees the entire Vicariate Apostolic of Arabia, of which the UAE is a part. There are proportionately more Catholics in the UAE than in any other Arab nation except Lebanon.

### ORTHODOX

A Syrian Orthodox church with 200 members is centered in Abuda Dhabi and a smaller gathering is reported in Dubai.

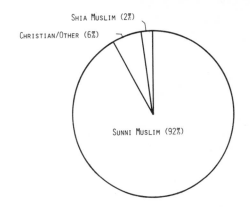

RELIGIOUS COMPOSITION OF THE UNITED ARAB EMIRATES

SHIA MUSLIM (2%)
CHRISTIAN/OTHER (6%)
SUNNI MUSLIM (92%)

# FOREIGN MISSIONS

## PROTESTANT MISSIONS

The Evangelical Alliance Mission (TEAM), is the largest missionary organization working in the UAE. They are actively working in two strategic areas in Al Ain and Abu Dhabi. Their ministry has been continually growing since original efforts in 1960. They operate and maintain a clinic and hospital in Al Ain. Although the government provides excellent modern hospital facilities, the demands for Oasis Hospital Services still continue. In 1977 the forty bed hospital cared for approximately 62,000 out-patients and 2,300 in-patients. Christian Arabs from Jordan and Lebanon as well as nurses and paramedics from India share with TEAM missionaries in the hospital ministry. Out-patient clinics provide a means for introduction to the Gospel through literature distribution and personal testimonies. For in-patients, a reading room and bookstore are available. An intercom system in each room provides music, Scripture reading and sermons on cassette tapes when desired. The Christian Center in Abu Dhabi includes a three bedroom house with a guest unit, a four unit apartment complex, a house converted into a chapel which holds over a hundred people comfortably, three additional rooms for Christian education and permission to build further facilities on surrounding vacant lots. Fellowship meetings are held in English, Arabic and several Indian languages at the Center. TEAM is also the only group planting churches among the Arab expatriots.

World Evangelization Crusade (WEC) abandoned its work in Dubai due to lack of personnel. WEC still maintains a medical clinic and related ministry in Fujayrah with four western women. The Bible Presbyterians also have four western women ministering through a small medical clinic at Sharjah. The work of the Reformed Presbyterians at Ra`s Al Khaymah was terminated in 1973 after more than fifteen years of operation. A married couple had operated a small clinic quite successfully, but their property was confiscated and were forced to discontinue the ministry completely. The Middle Eastern Christian Council operates a bookstore in Abu Dhabi. The Family Bookstore has a Lebanese manager and a young Danish woman working in that particular ministry.

## CATHOLIC MISSIONS

Catholic missionaries operate two schools at the Cathederal Center of Abu Dhabi. One school has lessons taught in both Arabic and English. Enrollment for the 1976-1977 school year was 800 pupils. The other school is staffed by nuns from India who teach the classes in Hindi, Urdu and Arabic. More than 300 Indian and Pakastani children attended classes in the 1976-1977 school year. As immigration continues, expectations for large increases in enrollment are high.

## MAJOR CHRISTIAN ACTIVITIES

### EVANGELISM

Evangelistic work in the UAE is done largely through the ministry of medical missions. The medical work allows opportunities for devotions, afternoon women`s and men`s Bible studies, weekly fellowship meetings and strong patient follow-up.

### BROADCASTING

Two international radio stations with programs in Arabic, and other languages, can be easily heard in the UAE. Radio Voice of the Gospel from Addis Ababa, Ethiopia and Far Eatern Broadcasting Association in the Seychelles Islands, are frequently listened to by immigrants and residents.

### LITERATURE

TEAM operates a literature and cassette ministry in conjunction with its hospital ministry. Literature in Arabic, Urdu, Farsi, Somali, and English is available through the hospital bookstore. The Middle East Christian Council manages a bookstore at the Christian Center in Abu Dhabi and literature in all languages is available. Bibles are readily available and immigrants in particular make use of the Christian materials.

### EDUCATION

No theological or accredited biblical training exists in the UAE. Several correspondence courses are available in a variety of languages. Personal discipling is carried on at the Christian Center as well as in homes.

## SOCIAL CONCERN

The only Christian involvement in social areas has been that of hospital and clinical ministries. Presently, missionaries are only allowed to enter the UAE under the sponsorship of medical facilities. They have been encouraged and even funded by and with full cooperation of the rulers and people. Over 50,000 Christians reside in UAE.

## NATION AND ITS PEOPLE

## POPULATION

The early 1979 estimate for total population was 800,000 including over 600,000 (75%) immigrant laborers and workers. A majority the population live in the cities of Abu Dhabi and Dubai and other coastal towns. About half of the population is of non-Arab origin.

## ETHNIC COMPOSITION

The coastal settlers, particularly in Abu Dhabi and Dubai, are traditionally seafarers. They range from the Gulf waters to as far as the Indian subcontinent. In the back country, the Bedouin, 90% of which are illiterate and unskilled, are mostly herdsmen and part-time oasis farmers. They retain their basic cultural patterns as they move from oasis to oasis with their sheep, goats, and camels. The upper end of the scale is defined as "le petit bourgeoisie." Clerks, government workers, businessmen, skilled laborers and students are primarily from foreign countries. They are characterized by possessions, including cars, refrigerators and home air-conditioning.

Those in the skilled and semi-skilled labor forces are less affluent. Even the lowest paid indigenous workers are well off in comparison to most Middle Easterners. The small number of students educated in foreign countries form a small "intelligentsia" class which is quite articulate and often involved in politics. Traditionally members of the ruling class (Shaykks) and their families have wielded a great deal of power.

Foreign experts and skilled technicians together with the newly educated and recently urbanized citizens form the nucleus of a growing middle class.

## LANGUAGE AND LITERACY

Arabic is the official language of the UAE. Approximately 50% of the total population is fluent in Arabic and a large segment of the non-Arab population is conversant in it. Farsi, Urdu, and English are other major languages spoken. Because of the diversification of the thousands of immigrants, several other languages and dialects are spoken. Literacy among the nationals is 15% to 25%. Immigrant professionals undoubtedly have a much higher literacy rate.

## RELIGION

The Sunni form of Islam is the national religion of the UAE. Nearly 92% of the total population adhere to its principles, which include a literalist interpretation of the Quran. They reject the association of anything with God. This includes the prophets, saints and even the Quran, all of which are important but not like God. Another 2% of the population, mostly immigrants, adhere to the Shia Muslim doctrines which propose that the prophets were models of godliness and teachers of correct behavior. They were also believed to be the authoritative interpreters of the Quran. Nearly 6% of the total population adheres to some form of Christianity.

## GEOGRAPHY AND CLIMATE

The area of the UAE is 85,000 square kilometers (33,000 square miles). Five ecological regions are distinct and affect the lives of the people. A low desert including a large salt flat, the narrow coastal plain, the hot sandy coast plateau, the sandy and flat mountains and the barren, flat high desert pose major challenges for life and development. Temperatures range from 4.4 degrees to 54.4 degrees centigrade (40-130 degrees Fahrenheit), depending on the proximity to the sea breezes and seasonal differences. Average rainfall is 10 centimeters (4 inches) though variations occur. Some desert areas receive virtually no rain while coastal villages may receive frequent showers.

## HISTORY

For centuries, the remote areas along the Persian Gulf were a haven for pirates, enterprising pearl fisherman and nomadic Bedouin. In 1853, the Sheiks (rulers) signed an agreement making their territories British Protectorates. They pledged themselves and their lands to a permanent maritime truce, thus the adoption of the name Trucial States. As late as 1960, when the oil money had just begun to flow in, Abu Dhabi was described as a little village of palm thatch huts and mud villas overlooked by a fort and a British political agency. With modern technology implemented and development surging, the lives and lands of the people of the UAE are rapidly changing.

## ECONOMY

The oil revolution has brought several foreign banks rushing to the desert. Shortly after oil prices quadrupled in 1973, there were only fourteen banks and six local moneychanging institutions. By 1978 over fifty-five banks existed with more than 350 branches. Some overspeculation occurred but no serious consequences ensued. Inflation has been a major problem but as oil prices are increased and better management principles are applied the economy is stabilized. It is very expensive to live in the UAE especially if any western conveniences are desired. Some three bedroom apartments rent for US$ 2,000 per month with an average electric bill of US$ 700 in the summer months.

Within a year after the federation was established, a substantial foreign aid program was developed. The Abu Dhabi Fund for Arab Economic Devlopment has dispursed nearly 25% of the gross national income in the form of grants and soft loans. Nations throughout the Middle East have been significantly aided by UAE relief and development funds. One of the most elaborate and effective welfare systems in the world benefits all citizens of the UAE. Free housing, education and medical care are available from the government. Water and electrical bills are waved and even food purchases are subsidized. The government is willing to give money to supplement Bedouin nomads who desire to continue ancient cultural patterns.

CHURCH STATISTICS FOR UNITED ARAB EMIRATES

Note: Statistics have been taken from different sources and are the most current data available. Definitions of "membership" vary among churches and may not always be comparable. Not all known churches have been included in this list.

| Church or Mission Name | Communicants (Full Members) | Community (Estimate) |
|---|---|---|
| PROTESTANT | | |
| Indian | | |
| Brethren | 60 | 140 |
| Pentecostal | 60 | 140 |
| Mar Thomite | 200 | 300 |
| Pakistani | 20 | 80 |
| Independent Evangelical Community | 150 | 6,000 |
| Anglican | 800 | 3,000 |
| CATHOLIC | | |
| Roman | 15,000 | 4,000 |
| Other | | 1,000 |
| ORTHODOX | | |
| Syrian | | 200 |
| Other | | 100 |

# SELECTED BIBLIOGRAPHY

The sources listed below are to help the reader find additional information on this country and Christian ministries there.  This list does not try to be comprehensive or complete.

## DOCUMENTS

### General

Anthony, John Duke, Arab States of the Lower Gulf People, Politics and Petroleum,

Fenelon,K.G., The Trucial States,A Brief Economic Survey, Beirut, Lebaon:  Khayais,
     1969

Kurian,George Thomas, Encyclopedia of the Third World, New York:  Facts on File, 1978

Mann, Clarence C., Abu Dhabi:  Birth of an Oil Shaikdom, Beirut, Lebanon:  Khayais,
     1969

Tiffin, John, Abu Dhabi, New York:  CBS, 1977

Two Glorious Years in the History of the Emirate of Abu Dhabi, Beirut, Lebanon:  Beirut
     Printing Press, 1969

Wallace, John, The Middle East Yearbook London, England:  IC MAgazines Ltd., 1978

Whelan, John, Meed Special Report :  Meed Publishers, 1977

### Christian

Crawley, Winston, Know Your Baptist Missionaries, Richmond:  Department of
     Communications, 1978

Foy, Felician A.,1978 Catholic Almanac Huntington:  Our Sunday Visitor, Inc., 1977

Kane, J.  Herbert,A Global View Of Christian Missions Grand Rapids:  Baker Book House,
     1971

Queen Of Sheba's Land,Beirut, Lebanon:  Nowfel Publishers

## ORGANIZATIONS

Red Sea Mission Team, P.O. Box 990, Kerrville, TX 78028
Southern Baptist Foreign Mission Board, P.O.  Box 6597, Richmond,  VA 23230

## ACKNOWLEDGEMENTS

The information in this profile was taken from many sources which were the best available to the editors at the time of preparation.  However, the accuracy of the information cannot be guaranteed.  Views expressed or implied in this publication are not necessarily those of World Vision.  The editors have tried to present the ministries of various organizations in an objective manner, without undue bias or emphasis.  Where we have failed we apologize for erroneous impressions that may result and request that comments and corrections be sent to MARC, 919 West Huntington Drive, Monrovia, California, USA, 91016. We appreciate and acknowledge the comments and contributions of various organizations and individuals in the preparation of this publication.

# STATUS OF CHRISTIANITY COUNTRY PROFILE

# YEMEN ARAB REPUBLIC

SUMMARY

AREA - 195,000 square kilometers (75,290 square miles)
POPULATION - 5,721,000
RELIGION - 50% Sunni Muslim, 49% Shia Muslim, 1% Christian and other

"I am against my uncle's son and my uncle's son and I are against the stranger." Ancient Arab proverb

Yemen Arab Republic, Yemen Sanaa, North Yemen; as many different names as there have been recent ruling powers in southwest Arabia. The people of the Yemen Arab Republic, the Yemenis, are potentially a self-sufficient people. Historically, they have chosen to remain isolated from other nations and have not been educated. They view the problems of isolation and education as major challenges for the twentieth century. The Yemen Arab Republic is one of the poorest nations in the world. It does not bother most Yemenis to be poor and they claim that they would rather be left alone by other nations. The educated populace realizes the impact which the Yemen Arab Republic can make by participating in international politics involving all the nations of the Middle East. Extensive changes have occured in the last five years as the

Yemenis work hard to usher the Yemen Arab Republic into the modern world. Repercussions of rapid change plague the government and people.

Reactionary religious groups and feuding tribes have caused division within the nation and have been involved in conflicts with other nations. Strife is especially acute with the People's Democratic Republic of Yemen with which the Yemen Arab Republic was once united. Several attempts to reunite the countries have ended in violence.

The Yemen Arab Republc is not left alone by other nations because the Yemenis possess what others want. Some of the richest soil in the Middle East is found in the highlands of the Yemen Arab Republic. It is cultivated easily and could produce high yields with some basic technological improvements. Another important resource is the people. The Yemen Arab Republic has one of the highest population densities in the Middle East. These people pose a major threat to the interests of other Arab nations and world powers seeking to control the Middle East.

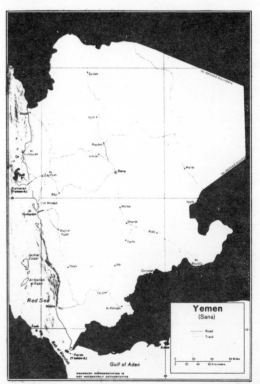

Yemen (Sana)

*This program is jointly carried out by the Strategy Working Group of the Lausanne Committee for World Evangelization and MARC, a ministry of World Vision International. For further information on the program, please write: MARC, 919 West Huntington Drive, Monrovia, CA 91016 U.S.A.*

# UNREACHED PEOPLES

Islam is the state religion of the Yemen Arab Republic. It dictates religious doctrines and governs every element of culture for the Yemenis people. Two main branches of Islam, Sunni and Shia, are represented by two large and distinctively different people groups.

The Zaidis (Zaydiis), a group of over 400 tribes who live in the mountainous northern region, adhere to the doctrines of the Shia sect. They maintain strict monotheism with the expressed conviction that no historical or contemporary figure or object, including the Quran, approaches the status of or is in any way similar to God himself. The Zayids compromise 40% of the population and are very powerful in all areas of national and international affairs.

The tribes are aligned in four major groups. The Ashid and Bakil tribes in the northern highlands follow the strong leadership of Abdullah-al Ahmar, who identifies with and is supported by Saudi Arabia. The central tribes of Akk and Madhhij are more independent and collaborate with either the northern tribes backed by Saudi Arabia or the coastal settlers backed by Egypt and the Soviet Union. The Ismailis tribe is a unique people group with a population of approximately 50,000. They value and adhere to occult Muslim teachings rather than the traditional written doctrines of Islam. Leadership is provided for the Ismailis by a "dia," which is similar to a pharoah. Each "dia" is part of the Makrami family with a detailed geneology recording the ancestory of Ismail, the seventh ruler of South Arabia and "dia" of the seventh century. Secret revelations as ancient as the cult itself are discussed only among the family of the "dia." No accurate information regarding the sect is presently available.

The inhabitants of the coastal and southern regions of the Yemen Arab Republic are part of the Sunni Muslim sect and are the largest group (50%) within the population. Historically, they have been a more settled community. For centuries they have been dominated by the Zaidis. Recently, with backing of the People's Democratic Republic of Yemen and the Soviet Union, they have been fighting for supremacy.

Yemeni society is also divided into a caste system similar to that of India. Each group has a particular status and task. The Sayyids are unarmed and perform the duties of holy men. The mashaykh, or qadi class, are descendants of the prophet Hud and preserve an ancient network of clans and lineages. They carry on responsibilities as judges in both religious and civil matters. The artisans and craftsmen form guild groups which are highly organized and differentiated according to the nature of each particular craft.

Akhadm refers to those of negroid descent brought from Somalia and Ethiopia as slaves, a practice which continued until 1962 when slavery was officially terminated. Restrictions and social prohibitions still exist and discrimination against the Akhadm is common. The people in the Akhadm class perform the despised duties of sweepers and are compared with the untouchables of India. Their lifestyles reflect the customs and cultures of their relatives in Africa, which include animism and syncretism. They are a downtrodden and despised group of people. They are the most open and receptive to Christianity of all the people groups and a few have converted to Christianity. The untouchable Akhadm are the only group with any Christian community other than foreign diplomats, hospital staffs and industrial development personnel.

The Yemenis were virtually unreached by Christians for 1300 years although they were located in an area which was once a part of the ancient Biblical kingdom of the Queen of Sheba. Islam revolutionized the cultural, political and social perspectives of the people and continues to affect every aspect of life for the Yemenis.

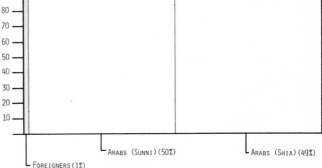

POPULATION COMPOSITION OF THE YEMEN ARAB REPUBLIC
(SHADING INDICATES CHRISTIANS)

ARABS (SUNNI) (50%)  ARABS (SHIA) (49%)  FOREIGNERS (1%)

NOTE: THESE FIGURES ARE REPRESENTATIVE APPROXIMATIONS. THEY SHOULD BE SEEN AS INDICATORS OF MAGNITUDE, NOT PRECISE.

Christianity has had very little influence upon the Yemenis since it´s practice is forbidden.  It is associated with capitalistic and imperialistic foreigners. The government welcomes any aid which missionary organizations or any other agencies offer as long as they understand that prosyletization is not permissible. The government of the Yemen Arab Republic commends the work of various Christian organizations for their work in hospitals, clinics and schools throughout the nation.

## NATIONAL CHURCHES

National churches in the Yemen Arab Republic exist only in the form of small group gatherings in the homes of missionaries.  National workers, patients and expatriots can meet at the hospitals for informal discussions and sharing. Actual church services are forbidden among the Yemenis.

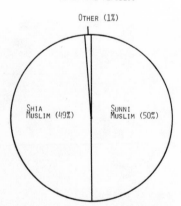

RELIGIOUS COMPOSITION OF THE
YEMEN ARAB REPUBLIC

OTHER (1%)

SHIA MUSLIM (49%)     SUNNI MUSLIM (50%)

## PROTESTANT MISSIONS

The Minister of Health for North Yemen requested the Southern Baptist Foreign Mission Board to open and provide staff for a medical clinic in December of 1963. Dr. James Young, a missionary doctor, had visited the Minister of Health in Sanaa and offered to help establish such a facility.  He was given complete responsibility and opened a small clinic in Taiz in 1964 with his wife and one other nurse.  Four years later a 60 bed Baptist Hospital opened in Jibla and over 1400 inpatients and 24,000 outpatients were treated by seven missionary workers and seven national assistants.  Facilities were expanded to 70 beds and a medical school was opened in 1973 to train Yemeni students.  Over 27 Southern Baptist missionaries now work in the hospital and school.  They are committed to meeting the physical needs of the people and providing progressive medical facilities. Over 69 national workers assist the foreign medical staff in the clinics and hospitals.

MAP International, an affiliate of Missionary Services Inc., makes shipments of medicines and hospital supplies donated to missionary doctors.  The average shipment to the Yemen Arab Republic for a six month period is 34,000 pounds of medicines and supplies worth over US$ 159,000.

The Red Sea Mission Team is a cooperative effort of 21 British, American and Australian missionaries working in nine clinics.  They were allowed to enter the Yemen Arab Republic in 1970 with a mission station in Sanaa, a clinic in Uarim and a clinic in Tihama.  Mobile clinics journey to the highland tribes in donkey caravans. The Red Sea Mission Teams specialize in providing primary schools and clinics through which literature is distributed. They are committed to serving the Muslims of Arabia and cooperate with New Zealanders working with the World Wide Evangelistic Crusade.

The Swedish Pentecostals have been well accepted in Taiz where they operate a trade school.  The government is pleased with the technical training being offered within the Yemen Arab Republic and has allowed some religious instruction.

## CATHOLIC MISSIONS

For the first time in 1400 years, Catholic priests and lay persons were invited in 1973 to work in the Yemen Arab Republic as staff in the government hospital. They were specifically prohibited from engaging in proselytization. Twelve missionaries from the United States and several volunteers from India were sent to serve the Yemenis. The volunteers from Calcutta, India were followers of Mother Teresa. Catholic relief services offer community development assistance with food-for-work projects, construction of schools, clinics, dams, wells, resevoirs, vocational training centers, prison rehabilitation, forestry projects, agricultural projects, leprosy work and medical training facilities.

## MAJOR CHRISTIAN ACTIVITIES

Christian activities are restricted to the services of medical personnel and school teachers. Christian broadcasts are forbidden in the Yemen Arab Republic. Two shortwave broadcasts in Arabic aired from outside the country can be clearly received. One is the Radio Voice of the Gospel from Ethiopia and the other is the Far East Broadcasting Association in Victoria, Seychelles Islands. The missionaries in the Yemen Arab Republic work with radio stations by informing others of the programs being broadcast. The only literature distribution allowed is among patients of the hospitals who ask for it. Though the Bible is readily available in Arabic, sales and distribution are forbidden.

## POPULATION

The official population figure for the Yemen Arab Republic is 6,500,000 but it must be noted that over 1,225,000 Yemenis work in Saudi Arabia, Kuwait, Indonesia and Singapore. Nearly half of the adult population works overseas where higher wages can be earned. Young men do this to enable them to pay the brideprice which is still required of men in their culture. With a growth rate of 2.9% per year, the population continues to rise and the density remains relatively high at 33 persons per square kilometer (86 per square mile). Much of the land is cultivated or is barren highlands which means that the actual density of the populated land is much higher. Only 15% of the total population live in cities or large towns. The other 85% have settled in small villages and farming communities throughout the highlands and coastal plains.

## COMPOSITION

Nearly 80% of the families involved in farming work as sharecroppers. They are forced to pay a large part of their harvest in return for the use of land owned by a few wealthy overlords. There are very few nomadic tribes in the northern highlands. Life expectancy for the Yemenis is 45 years. A high mortality rate of 46% for children under 15 years old means the birth rate must remain exceptionally high.

Five major tribal groups inhabit the northern highlands and are expressively independent. They recognize the authority of Saudi Arabia. Their own leadership comes from Muslim holy men and military generals. The Zaidis have entered contemporary international politics with ancient traditions and independent spirits.

The more complacent Sunni Muslim tribes have settled along the coastal regions of the Red Sea. Although they are the largest group (50%), they have not tended to actively assert themselves in politics. Many farmers are content to work in the fields during the morning and spend the afternoon chewing "qat," a mildly narcotic plant.

Continuing civil strife and ancient traditions have caused a low priority to be given to education. The Kuttab, the traditional Muslim schools, were held responsible for education. Their primary emphasis was the memorization of the Quran. An optional secular grade school system was introduced in 1971 but only 15% of the eligible students attended. Girls represented only 12% of the student population by 1973. All secondary school teachers in secular institutions were foreigners. Since most Yemeni college students graduated from institutions outside the Yemen Arab Republic, it is not surprising that 50% never return to their homeland. The need for educators continues and foreigners are requested to fill primary, secondary, university and vocational training positions. A university was opened to train Yemeni students within the country in 1978.

## LANGUAGE AND LITERACY

The only language spoken by all Yemenis is Arabic. A few tribes and African descendents speak ancient dialects but also know and predominantly use Arabic. The small percentage of the population which is educated or involved in business and trade also use English. The literacy rate for the Yemenis is one of the lowest in the world at 15% for men and 5% for women.

## GEOGRAPHY AND CLIMATE

Yemen Arab Republic is isolated at the southwestern corner of the Arabian Peninsula. The People's Democratic Republic of Yemen borders on the south and southwest. Like so many other issues, boundaries with Saudi Arabia are undefined. The coastline is 450 kilometers (281 miles), with the coastal plain region, the Tihama, extending inland from the Red Sea 50 to 100 kilometers (31-62 miles). The arid coastal region receives only 13 centimeters (5 inches) of rainfall each year. Precipitation is much more abundant during the two separate rainy seasons, March to May and July to September. As much as 87 centimeters (35 inches) of rain falls during those two seasons.

Agricultural productivity is proportionate to the manpower available to plant and harvest. Ancient hand farming on terraces is still common and much land is still not used for anything even resembling mechanized farming. The climate is generally temperate with cool dry winters and warm summers. Major problems result from droughts which occasionally occur because no measures are taken to store water in reservoirs.

## HISTORY

The area once known as the Yemen Arab Republic was once a part of Arabia Felix meaning happy and prosperous Arabia. It indeed was for the traders and merchants as they clammered for the frankincense, myrrh, spices, pearls and silks which they found in al-Yaman. Entrepreneurs stopped in al-Yaman for years but never influenced the lives of the native tribesmen. Islam was adopted gradually by the people as a result of the itinerant pilgrims of several prophets and holy men sent by Muhammad. Over half of the tribes were converted to Islam by 630 AD and joined with others in prosyletizing their neighboring tribes. Al-Yaman became a theocratic state for 1300 years.

The divisions and schisms which developed within Islam from the seventh to twelfth centuries significantly affected the history of the region. A lengthy period of feuding among the tribes, chaos among ruling powers and factions within Islam left the area in a state of constant turmoil. By the time the Ottoman Turks conquered that area, there was little hope for uniting the people. The Turks brutally imposed Sunni Muslim doctrines which infuriated the Shia tribes. Zaidis resistance movements resulted in the overthrow of direct Turkish control in all matters other than foreign affairs. Zaidis Imams, who functioned as chiefs, established themselves as absolute monarchs and ruled for 400 years. The British controlled several ports in the area for 100 years but never affected the rule of the Imams, who maintained strict isolationist policies until 1958.

Fifteen coups have been reported and instability has been accepted as the status quo. Saif-al Islam Ahmad reigned in a period of turmoil following the assassination of his father Imam Yahya in 1948. The initial steps which he took towards establishing contact with other nations in a confederation with Egypt failed. He died just 14 years later and his son was ousted in a coup three weeks after taking office. Imam Badr escaped death and fled to the highlands where he organized the tribes as the royalist army. A civil war ensued as the republicans aided by Egypt were confronted with the experienced guerrilla type warfare of the royalist army. A constitution was ratified in 1970 and elections finally occured the next year. Another coup overthrew the elected government in 1974 and Ibrahim al-Hamadi obtained presidency but was assassinated just three years later. His successor, President Ghashmi was assassinated one year later in an explosion of a bomb placed in the briefcase of a visiting emissary from the People's Democratic Republic of Yemen. The two had been making arrangements for Ghashmi's visit to South Yemen when the explosion occured.

Amidst the instability there is widespread cooperation by other nations with the government in providing aid and council in matters of development. The People's Republic of China and West Germany cooperate in building and repairing roads. The Soviet Union and Denmark send top agronomists to help modernize agriculture in the fertile and potentially productive highlands. Czechoslavakia supplies jeeps and the United States supplies airplanes. Saudi Arabia has furnished funds for government activities and social concerns. The Yemen Arab Republic has so far been able to solicit funds from many different sources without undue restrictions or qualifications. They are involved in very complicated economic and political development plans.

## ECONOMY

Over 90% of the resident economically active population is engaged in farming, using 43% of the land. Agricultural products, including sorghum, millet, barley, cotton, corn, and qat represent 90% of the total value of exports. Deficit spending is made possible through the grants and loans from Kuwait, Saudi Arabia, the United Arab Emirates and other nations. In addition, the United Nations classifies the Yemen Arab Republic as one of the least developed nations of the world and thus provides funds and materials.Extensive natural resources are not available and economic development is not as rapid as in other nations of the Middle East. Approximately 80% of the personal income of the Yemenis comes from family members working outside the country.

CHURCH STATISTICS FOR YEMEN ARAB REPUBLIC

Note: Statistics have been taken from several different sources and are the most current data available. Definitions of "membership" vary among churches and may not always be comparable.

| Church or Mission Name | Communicants (Full Members) | Community (Estimate) |
| --- | --- | --- |
| PROTESTANT | | |
| CATHOLIC | | |
| ORTHODOX | | |

## SELECTED BIBLIOGRAPHY AND INFORMATION SOURCES

The sources listed below are to help the reader find additional information on this country and Christian ministries there. This list does not try to be comprehensive or complete.

DOCUMENTS

General

American Council of Voluntary Agencies For Foreign Service, Yemen, New York: Technical Assistance Information Clearing House, 1976

Field, Michael, Middle East Annual Review, Essex, England:Middle East Review Co. Ltd., 1977

Kurian, George Thomas, Encyclopedia of the Third World, New York: Facts On File, Inc., 1978

Nyrop, Richard F., Area Handbook For the Yemens, Washington D.C.: U.S. Government Printing Office, 1977

The Middle East, London, England: Magazines Ltd., 1977-1978

Christian

Crawley, Winston, Know Your Baptist Missionaries, Richmond: Department of Communications, 1978

Foy, Felician A., editor, 1978 Catholic Almanac, Indiana: Our Sunday Visitor, 1977

Kane, J. Herbert, A Global View Of Christian Missions Grand Rapids: Baker Book House, 1971

Queen Of Sheba's Land, Beirut, Lebanon: Nowfel Publishers

ORGANIZATIONS

Red Sea Mission Team, P.O. Box 990, Kerrville, TX. 78028

Southern Baptist Foreign Mission Board ,P.O. Box 6597, Richmond, VA. 23230.

## ACKNOWLEDGEMENTS

The information in this profile was taken from many sources which were the best available to the editors at the time of preparation. However, the accuracy of the information cannot be guaranteed. Views expressed or implied in this publication are not necessarily those of World Vision. The editors have tried to present the ministries of various organizations in an objective manner, without undue bias or emphasis. Where we have failed we apologize for erroneous impressions that may result and request that comments and corrections be sent to MARC, 919 West Huntington Drive, Monrovia, California, USA, 91016. We appreciate and acknowledge the comments and contributions of various organizations and individuals in the preparation of this publication.

# III
# UNREACHED PEOPLES

# UNREACHED PEOPLES

Within each country there are distinct groups of people. These groups must be viewed in the context of the country's history and way of life, for they are certainly part of a larger whole. But each group is unique too, and must be seen in a separate sense. We must look at countries and at people groups.

## WHAT IS A "PEOPLE GROUP"?

A people group is a part of a society that has some basic characteristics in common that cause it to feel a sense of oneness yet set it apart from other groups.

The unifying characteristic may be language, religion, economic status, occupation, ethnic origin, geographic location or social position.

For example, a distinct group based on ethnic, language and geographic characteristics might be the Quechua of Bolivia; while a sociological group might be the urban university students of France.

It is important to see that groups may share a common way of life and sense of oneness because of social, occupational, or economic characteristics, as well as language or ethnic origin.

## WHO ARE "UNREACHED" AND "UNEVANGELIZED" PEOPLE?

Christians have different definitions of the terms "unreached" or "unevangelized". For our purposes we can describe an unreached or unevangelized people as a people who has not received or responded to the gospel. This unresponsiveness may be due to lack of opportunity, to lack of understanding, or because the people have not received enough information about the gospel message in its own language and through the eyes of its own culture so that it can truly respond to Christ.

We consider a people "unreached" when less than 20 percent of the members of the group are practicing Christians, that is are active members of the Christian community.

By "Christian" we mean adherents (church members, families and followers) of the historic Christian communions: Protestant, Anglican, Orthodox, Roman Catholic and such independent groups as may claim the Bible as the basis of faith and Jesus Christ as Lord and Savior.

## HOW CAN THESE UNREACHED PEOPLES BE EVANGELIZED?

To evangelize these unreached peoples we must first find out who they are. We must discover where they live and learn as much about their culture as possible. We should also know about the current Christian witness, the availability of scripture in the local language, and the receptivity of the group to the gospel.

With this information a culturally appropriate approach can be developed to reach a particular people group - an approach based on a realistic assessment of the group's culture and their needs. (See Planning Strategies for Evangelism, by Edward R. Dayton for more details on developing an approach.)

WHAT NEEDS TO BE DONE?

To gather, store, and analyze this type of information is a tremendous job, but a necessary one if the Church today is going to fulfill the Great Commission.

To aid the Church in ths task, World Vision's Missions Advanced Research and Communication Center (MARC) maintains a computerized compilation of information on people groups from all over the world. This data is continually updated and expanded, and is published annually in a series entitled UNREACHED PEOPLES. Most of this information is supplied by individuals who send in MARC's survey questionnaires.

These questionnaire respondants provide the basic data that is needed to begin planning a way to reach peoples who have yet to know Jesus Christ. With this information, God's people can not only plan and act with greater efficiency, but they can also pray with greater insight.

The purpose of a world wide data gathering effort is to give Christians everywhere the information they need to think about their own situation and to seek to understand God's strategy for the people to whom God has called them.

As the Holy Spirit reveals new understandings of both the obstacles and the opportunities we face, we will be able to ask the right questions as to what God would have us do to reach the unreached.

THE NEXT STEP...

On the following pages there is a brief description of the peoples of the Middle East, followed by a listing of the people groups from this area for which there is some information in the MARC data files. (See the most recent volume of UNREACHED PEOPLES for a complete list of MARC's unreached peoples data). There is also a survey questionnaire to provide more information about these groups. Since people groups are continually changing, it is important to update and revise the material that has been collected. The questionnaire can also be used to provide new information on other groups from around the world.

This information on specific peoples, combined with country profiles, is an excellent place to begin the planning needed to reach the unreached. With this foundation laid, God's strategy for reaching a particular people can be discovered.

Living in an area that links three continents, the peoples of the
Middle East present an amazing variety of cultures, languages, and
ethnic backgrounds.  There is no single Middle East culture.  Rather,
many different cultures exist and each represents a unique way of
life.

There are three major groupings of peoples within the Middle East;
nomads, cultivators, and urban dwellers.  The nomads represent less
than 5% of the total population of this region.  Their numbers are
declining rapidly since there is no place for them in today's nation
states.  They are primarily stockbreedere, and move seasonally with
their herds.

Cultivators comprise the majority (50%-75%) of the people.  They are
sedentary rural villagers who live in mud-brick homes similar to their
ancestors.  Although they mainly practice subsistence agriculture,
more cash cropping is being done because of land reclamation and
irrigation schemes.  They are only recently experiencing some
improvement in their living conditions after centuries of poverty.

A growing number of individuals are urban dwellers.  They are
economically and politically dominant since the cities are
traditionally centers of trade and religious activities.  The citizens
are grouped by ethnic or religious ties, each occupying a particular
area within the city.  They receive most of the benefits of
modernization, which widens the gap between urban and rural peoples.

Several factors contribute to the diversity among the people groups of
the Middle East.  First, the harsh terrain and vast distances of this
region have created geographical, and thus cultural isolation of many
groups.  Second, a variety of languages and dialects have supported
this diversity.  Individuals' speech patterns identify the people that
they have come from.  Third, the various expressions of religious
beliefs differ from group to group.  Although Islam is the dominant
faith throughout this region, it takes many forms, reflecting the
particular culture of the people who practice it.  All of these
elements have kept the different cultures of the Middle East
relatively distinct and provide the background against which any
evangelism must be done.

The Middle East is now in a time of tremendous change and this is
profoundly affecting the cultural patterns of the people.  Individuals
are migrating to the urban centers where they are exposed to different
ways of life.  Political unrest has created an entire sub-culture of
refugees who are cut off from their past and have no where to live.
Virtually all groups are experiencing culture change as the countries
they live in attempt to modernize .  Old traditions are being altered
as new demands are placed on the cultures.

In the midst of these changes there is now a new openness to the
gospel.  By learning more about the people groups of this area, we can
be more effective messengers of God's love to the peoples of the
Middle East.

| COUNTRY | NAME OF PEOPLE GROUP | POPULATION |
| --- | --- | --- |
| BAHRAIN | Bahrainis | 218,800 |
| | Immigrant Arabs | 36,000 |
| | Indians | 8,000 |
| | Pakistanis | 5,500 |
| CYPRUS | Turkish Cypriots | 11,500 |
| IRAN | Afshars * | 290,000 |
| | Agajanis * | 1,000 |
| | Ahl-i-Haggin * # | 500,000 |
| | Arab Jabbari * | 13,000 |
| | Arab-Shaibani * | 16,000 |
| | Arabs of Khuzestan * | 520,000 |
| | Armenians * | 280,000 |
| | Assyrians * | 105,000 |
| | Azerbaijani Turks * | 6,000,000 |
| | Baharlu * | 7,500 |
| | Bakhtiaris * | 590,000 |
| | Baluchi * | 700,000 |
| | Barbaris * | |
| | Bayats * | |
| | Bovir-Ahmadi * | 110,000 |
| | Galeshis * | 2,000 |
| | Georgians * | 2,000 |
| | Gilakis * | 1,950,000 |
| | Goudari * | 2,000 |
| | Gypsies * | 30,000 |
| | Hezareh * | |
| | Inallu * | 5,000 |
| | Jamshidis * | 1,000 |
| | Kazakhs * | 3,000 |
| | Kurds * | 2,000,000 |
| | Lors * | 1,890,000 |
| | Mamasani * | 1,100,000 |
| | Mazandaranis * | 1,600,000 |
| | Moqaddam * | 1,000 |
| | Nafar * | 3,500 |
| | Palanis * | |
| | Pashatuns * | 100 |
| | Pishagchi * | 1,000 |
| | Qadikolanis * | |
| | Qajars * | 3,000 |
| | Qara`i * | 2,000 |
| | Qaragoziu * | 2,000 |
| | Qashaqa`i * | 180,000 |
| | Sasanis * | 1,000 |
| | Shahsavans * | 65,000 |
| | Tajik * | 5,000 |
| | Talish * | 20,000 |
| | Tats * | 2,000 |
| | Teimuri * | 10,000 |
| | Teimurtash * | 7,000 |
| | Turkomans * | 550,000 |
| | Zargaris * | |

| COUNTRY | NAME OF PEOPLE GROUP | POPULATION |
|---|---|---|
| IRAQ | Arabs | 8,555,000 |
| | Kurds | 1,900,000 |
| | Lurs | 167,000 |
| | Persians | 222,000 |
| | Turkomans | 228,000 |
| ISRAEL | Arabs * | 500,000 |
| | Druze *# | 33,000 |
| | Jewish Immigrants | |
| | American *@ | 25,797 |
| | Argentinian *@ | 17,686 |
| | Australian *@ | 1,260 |
| | Brazilian *@ | 4,000 |
| | Mexican * | 1,000 |
| | Oriental | 910,000 |
| | Uruguan * | 2,700 |
| | Sabras | 1,280,000 |
| JORDAN | Muslims of Jordan * | 1,000,000 |
| | Palestinian Refugees * | 1,000,000 |
| KUWAIT | Baluchs | 5,000 |
| | Indians | 56,000 |
| | Kurds | 147,000 |
| | Kuwaitis | 531,000 |
| | Pakistanis | 55,000 |
| LEBANON | Arabs | 1,440,000 |
| | Druze | 120,000 |
| OMAN | Baluchs | 50,000 |
| | Indians | 12,000 |
| | Omanis Arabs | 700,000 |
| | Pakistanis | 10,000 |
| QATAR | Immigrant Arabs | 70,000 |
| | Indians | 25,000 |
| | Pakistanis | 45,000 |
| | Qatari Arabs | 30,000 |
| SAUDI ARABIA | Asians | 240,000 |
| | Immigrant Arabs | 180,000 |
| | Iranians | 120,000 |
| | Saudis | 4,500,000 |
| | Yemenis | 420,000 |
| SYRIA | Alawites *# | 600,000 |
| | Arabs | 3,800,000 |
| | Bedoiun | 608,000 |
| | Druze | 223,000 |
| | Palestinian Refugees | 304,000 |
| | Turkomen | 223,000 |
| | Yazidis | 10,000 |
| TURKEY | Arabs | 300,000 |
| | Circassians | 70,000 |
| | Georgians | 50,000 |
| | Kurds *# | 3,000,000 |
| | Lazis | 30,000 |
| | Turks | 36,800,000 |

| COUNTRY | NAME OF PEOPLE GROUP | POPULATION |
| --- | --- | --- |
| UNITED ARAB EMIRATES | Immigrant Arabs | 48,000 |
| | Indians | 48,000 |
| | Indigenous Arabs @ | 200,000 |
| | Iranians | 208,000 |
| | Pakistanis | 200,000 |
| YEMEN ARAB REPUBLIC | Ismailis | 50,000 |
| | Yemenis *# | 5,600,000 |
| PEOPLE`S DEMOCRATIC REPUBLIC OF YEMEN | Bedoiun | 156,000 |
| | Socotrans | 12,000 |
| | Zei Tribesmen | 90,000 |

NOTE:
   * Additional information available
   @ Prayer folder available
   # Expanded description in UNREACHED PEOPLE 79

# REACHING THE UNREACHED

Part of a program being carried out jointly by the Strategy Working Group of the Lausanne Committee for World Evangelization and MARC, the Missions Advanced Research and Communication Center, which is a ministry of World Vision International.

*919 West Huntington Drive, Monrovia, California, USA*

There are over 3 billion people in the world who do not know Jesus Christ as Lord and Savior. Large numbers of these people are not being reached by the gospel because they are hidden among larger populations or because the gospel message has not been expressed in ways that they can understand and respond to.

They are unreached people.

It has been estimated that there are at least 15,000 major unreached people groups, the vast majority of which have not been identified as to where they are and how they can be reached. This is a task for Christ's Church throughout the world. This is *your* task.

In order to understand and locate these unreached people the Strategy Working Group of the Lausanne Committee for World Evangelization has been working with the Missions Advanced Research and Communication Center (MARC). The early results of this research were presented at the Lausanne Congress on World Evangelization in 1974. Since then this worldwide effort has continued.

The on-going results are published annually in a directory entitled *Unreached Peoples*. As new information comes in from around the world, basic data about each group is listed and some 80 to 100 groups are described in detail. Information on each group is available for your use from MARC.

By publishing whatever information is available, the *Unreached Peoples* directory acts as a bridge between those who are discovering new unreached people, and those whom God has chosen to seek them out with the good news. Your contribution is important!

This questionnaire has been designed to make that task as simple as possible. We ask that you supply whatever information you can, trusting that the Lord of the Harvest has others who will supply what is missing.

Thank you for being a part of this grand vision that *every* person in the world may have an opportunity to know Jesus Christ.

52479A

# FINDING THE UNREACHED: YOU CAN HELP!

### You can help locate unreached people groups

You are part of a worldwide network of concerned Christians. There are millions upon millions of people in the world who have had little or no contact with the gospel of Jesus Christ. Because of this, we are asking you to help the Church locate and identify these peoples so it can reach them.

Within each country there are distinct and unique groups of people who may be unreached. This questionnaire is designed to help you describe such groups so that Christians everywhere may pray and consider how these groups might be reached with the gospel. This information will be continuously compiled and made available to the Church and her mission agencies. It appears each year in an annual directory, *Unreached Peoples,* produced by David C. Cook.

There are many different groups of people in the world. How varied they are! Consequently, this questionnaire may not always ask the best questions for understanding a particular people. The questions have been asked in a way that will give comparative information to as large a number of Christians as possible. Where you feel another form of question would better suit your situation, please feel free to comment.

### What is a "people group"?

A people group is a part of a society that has some basic characteristics in common that cause it to feel a sense of oneness, and set it apart from other groups. It may be unified by language, religion, economic status, occupation, ethnic origin, geographic location, or social position. For example, a distinct group based on ethnic, language and geographic characteristics might be the Quechua of Bolivia; a sociological group might be the urban university and college students of Colombia, or the urban industrial workers of France. It is important to see that groups may share a common way of life and sense of oneness because of social, occupational or economic characteristics, as well as because of language or ethnic origin. Therefore, whenever possible, *describe the smallest number of persons who make up a distinct group;* that is, don't say that all persons in a region or province are a group, rather describe the specific subgroups within that region or province.

### Who are the "unreached and unevangelized people"?

Christians have different definitions of the terms "unreached" or "unevangelized." For the purposes of this worldwide effort, we describe an unreached or unevangelized people as a people who has not received or responded to the gospel. This unresponsiveness may be due to lack of opportunity, to lack of understanding, or because the people has not received enough information about the gospel message in its own language through the eyes of its own culture so that it can truly respond to Christ.

We consider a people "unreached" when less than 20 percent of the members of the group are *practicing* Christians, that is, are active members of the Christian community. By "Christian" we mean adherents (church members, families and followers) of the historic Christian communions; Protestant, Anglican, Roman Catholic, Orthodox and such independent groups as may claim the Bible as the basis of faith and Jesus Christ as Lord and Savior. A group less than 20 percent Christian may yet need Christians from outside the group to help with the evangelism task.

### How you can provide information

The attached questionnaire has two parts. If you only have information for the first part, send that in now.

Please fill in one questionnaire for *each* people group with which you are familiar. Do not put several groups on one questionnaire. (If you need more questionnaires, ask for extra copies or photocopy this one, or typewrite the questions you are answering on a separate sheet of paper.) We realize that one person may not have all the answers to these questions. Just answer what you can. PLEASE DO NOT WAIT UNTIL YOU HAVE ALL THE INFORMATION REQUESTED ON THIS QUESTIONNAIRE. SEND WHAT YOU HAVE. Other people may provide information that you do not have. Thank you for your help!

When you have completed this questionnaire, please return it to:

Unreached Peoples Program Director
c/o MARC, 919 W. Huntington Drive, Monrovia, CA 91016 U.S.A.

# SURVEY QUESTIONNAIRE FOR UNEVANGELIZED AND UNREACHED PEOPLES

Do you see a group of people who are unreached or unevangelized? Identify them! As the Lord spoke to Ezekiel of old, so He speaks to us today. "Son of man, What do you see"?

Answers to the questions on these two pages will provide the minimum information needed to list this people group in the *Unreached Peoples* annual.

After you have read the directions, type or print your answers so they can be easily read. It is unlikely that you will have all the information requested. Do the best you can. What information you are lacking others may supply. If your information is a best guess or estimate, merely place an "E" after it. Send in what you have as soon as possible. Please ignore the small numbers next to the answers. They help others prepare your answers for the *Unreached Peoples* annual.

*"For this reason I bow my knees before the Father, from whom every family in heaven and on earth is named . . ."*
*Ephesians 3:14-15 (RSV)*

1. Name of the group or people: _____

2. Alternate name(s) or spelling: _____

3. Country where located: _____

4. Approximate size of the group in this country: _____

5. Vernacular or common language: _____

6. Lingua franca or trade language: _____

7. Name of religious groups found among this people:

| | % who are adherents of this religion | % who practice this religion |
|---|---|---|
| **CHRISTIAN GROUPS:** | | |
| Protestant | _____ % | _____ % |
| Roman Catholic | _____ % | _____ % |
| Eastern Orthodox | _____ % | _____ % |
| Other Christian: _____ (name) | _____ % | _____ % |
| **NON-CHRISTIAN GROUPS OR SECULARISM:** | | |
| _____ | _____ % | _____ % |
| _____ | _____ % | _____ % |
| _____ | _____ % | _____ % |
| _____ | _____ % | _____ % |
| TOTAL FOR ALL GROUPS: | 100 % | |

*"Brethren, My heart's desire and prayer to God for them is that they may be saved."*
*Romans 10:1 (RSV)*

8. In your opinion, what is the attitude of this people toward Christianity?

(01)☐ Strongly favorable    (02)☐ Somewhat favorable    (03)☐ Indifferent    (04)☐ Somewhat opposed    (05)☐ Strongly opposed

TURN THIS SHEET OVER FOR PAGE 2

1

52479B

9. Questionnaire completed by:

Name: _____ Date: _____

Organization: _____

Address: _____

_____

10. Who else might be able to provide information about this people?

| Name | Organization (if any) | Address |
|------|----------------------|---------|

_____

_____

_____

11. If you are aware of any publications describing this people, please give title and author.

_____

12. What other information do you have that could help others to understand this people better? What do you feel would help in evangelizing them?    *(Use additional sheet if necessary.)*

*"And how are they to believe in him of whom they have never heard? And how are they to hear without a preacher?"*
*Romans 10:14 (RSV)*

13. Are you also sending in pages 3 and 4? ☐ Yes  ☐ No

---

Please send whatever information you have immediately. Do not wait until you have every answer.

Mail to:

Unreached Peoples Program Director
c/o MARC, 919 W. Huntington Drive, Monrovia, CA 91016 USA

If you have any more information about this people group, please complete the following two pages as best you can. If not, please send in pages one and two now. If you can obtain more information later, send it in as soon as possible.

## PEOPLE DISTINCTIVES—What makes them different? Why are they a people group?

14. A number of different things contribute to create a distinctive people or group, one that in some way shares a common way of life, *sees* itself as a particular group having an affinity toward one another, and differs to some extent from other groups or peoples. What would you say makes the people you are describing distinctive? Check the appropriate box of as many of the following descriptions as *are important* in making this people distinctive. Use the following scale: "High" importance, "Medium" importance, "Low" importance. For example, if you thought that the fact that they had a common political loyalty was of medium importance in unifying and making a group distinctive, you would place an "X" in the middle box under "Medium".

Importance

High Medium Low

(01)☐ ☐ ☐ Same language
(02)☐ ☐ ☐ Common political loyalty
(03)☐ ☐ ☐ Similar occupation
(04)☐ ☐ ☐ Racial or ethnic similarity
(05)☐ ☐ ☐ Shared religious customs
(06)☐ ☐ ☐ Common kinship ties
(07)☐ ☐ ☐ Strong sense of unity
(08)☐ ☐ ☐ Similar education level
(09)☐ ☐ ☐ Other(s) _____
(please write in)

Importance

High Medium Low

(10)☐ ☐ ☐ Common residential area
(11)☐ ☐ ☐ Similar social class or caste
(12)☐ ☐ ☐ Similar economic status
(13)☐ ☐ ☐ Shared hobby or special interest
(14)☐ ☐ ☐ Discrimination from other groups
(15)☐ ☐ ☐ Unique health situation
(16)☐ ☐ ☐ Distinctive legal status
(17)☐ ☐ ☐ Similar age
(18)☐ ☐ ☐ Common significant problems

15. How rapidly would you say the lifestyle of this people is changing? (check one)

(01)☐ Very Slow Change    (02)☐ Slow Change    (03)☐ Moderate Change    (04)☐ Rapid Change    (05)☐ Very Rapid Change

*"And to him was given dominion and glory and kingdom, that all peoples, nations, and languages should serve him." Daniel 7:14 (RSV)*

## PEOPLE LANGUAGES—What do they speak?

Please list the various languages used by the members of this people:

| LANGUAGE TYPE | Primary name(s) of their language(s) | Approximate % who *speak* this language | Approximate % of people over 15 years of age who *read* this language |
|---|---|---|---|
| 16. Vernacular or common language: | _____ | _____ % | _____ % |
| 17. Lingua franca or trade language: | _____ | _____ % | _____ % |
| 18. Language used for instruction in schools: | _____ | _____ % | _____ % |
| 19. Language suitable for presentation of the gospel: | _____ | _____ % | _____ % |

20. If there is Christian witness at present, what language(s) is being used? _____

21. Place an "x" in the boxes that indicate the status of Scripture translation *in the language you consider most suitable for communicating the gospel* (question 19):

| | CURRENT STATUS | | | AVAILABLE | | |
|---|---|---|---|---|---|---|
| | Not available | In process | Completed | In oral form | In print | On cassette or records |
| (POR) New Testament portions | ☐ | ☐ | ☐ | ☐ | ☐ | ☐ |
| (NT) Complete New Testament | ☐ | ☐ | ☐ | ☐ | ☐ | ☐ |
| (OT) Complete Old Testament | ☐ | ☐ | ☐ | ☐ | ☐ | ☐ |

22. Of the <u>Christians</u> present among this people, what percent *over 15 years of age can* and *do read any language?*
_____ %

52479C

## CHRISTIAN WITNESS TO THIS PEOPLE—Who is trying to reach them?

23. If there are Christian churches or missions (national or foreign) now active *within the area or region where this people is concentrated,* please give the following information:

    (If there are none, check here: ☐)

| CHURCH OR MISSION Name of church, denomination | YEAR Year work began in this area | MEMBERS Approximate number of full members from this people | ADHERENTS Approximate number of adherents (community including children) | WORKERS Approximate numbers of trained pastors and evangelists from this people |
|---|---|---|---|---|
| _____ | _____ | _____ | _____ | _____ |
| _____ | _____ | _____ | _____ | _____ |
| _____ | _____ | _____ | _____ | _____ |

24. What is the growth rate of the total Christian community among this people group?

    (01)☐ Rapid growth     (02)☐ Slow growth     (03)☐ Stable     (04)☐ Slow decline     (05)☐ Rapid decline

25. In your opinion, what is the attitude of this people to religious change of any kind?

    (01)☐ Very open     (02)☐ Somewhat open     (03)☐ Indifferent     (04)☐ Somewhat closed     (05)☐ Very closed

26. In your opinion, what is the attitude of this people toward Christianity?

    (01)☐ Strongly favorable     (02)☐ Somewhat favorable     (03)☐ Indifferent     (04)☐ Somewhat opposed     (05)☐ Strongly opposed

27. Most people move through a series of more or less well-defined stages in their attitude toward Christianity. Parts of a people group will be further along than other parts. Here are ten categories that attempt to show this progression. However, locating people in some of these categories can be difficult, so to make things simpler some categories are combined in the questions that follow.

    In your estimation, what percentage of this people can be described as those who: (These percentages are exclusive. Do not include people more than once. Your total should add up to 100%.)

Have no awareness of Christianity . . . . . . . . . . . . . . . . . . . . . . . . . . . . . . . . . . . . . . . . . . _____ %

Have awareness of the existence of Christianity . . . . . . . . . . . . . . . . . . . . . . . . . . . . . . . . _____ %

Have some knowledge of the gospel . . . . . . . . . . . . . . . . . . . . . . . . . . . . . . . . . . . . . . . . _____ %

Understand the message of the gospel . . . . . . . . . . . . . . . . . . . . . . . . . . . . . . . . . . . . . . _____ %

See the personal implications of the gospel . . . . . . . . . . . . . . . . . . . . . . . . . . . . . . . . . . . ⎫

Recognize a personal need that the gospel can meet . . . . . . . . . . . . . . . . . . . . . . . . . . . . ⎬ _____ %

Are being challenged to receive Christ . . . . . . . . . . . . . . . . . . . . . . . . . . . . . . . . . . . . . . ⎭

Have decided for Christ, but are not incorporated into a fellowship (may be evaluating their decision) . . . . . . . . . . . . . . . . . . . . . . . . . . . . . . . . . . . . . . _____ %

Are incorporated into a fellowship of Christians . . . . . . . . . . . . . . . . . . . . . . . . . . . . . . . _____ %

Are active propagators of the gospel . . . . . . . . . . . . . . . . . . . . . . . . . . . . . . . . . . . . . . . _____ %

**TOTAL**     100 %

28. On the whole, how accurate is the information you have given us?

    (V)☐ Very accurate     (F)☐ Fairly accurate     (E)☐ Good estimate     (G)☐ Mainly guesses

29. Are you willing to have your name publically associated with this information?

    ☐ No     ☐ Yes     ☐ Yes, with qualifications: _____